COINS AND MEDALS

COINS AND MEDALS

THEIR PLACE IN HISTORY AND ART

BY THE AUTHORS OF
THE BRITISH MUSEUM OFFICIAL CATALOGUES

EDITED BY
STANLEY LANE-POOLE

SECOND EDITION

WITH NUMEROUS ILLUSTRATIONS

GYAN

Published by

Gyan Publishing House
5, Ansari Road
Daryaganj, New Delhi-110002
Phone: 011-47034999, 9811692060
E-mail: books@gyanbooks.com

Distribution Network
gyanbooks.com
India, USA, Canada, UK, Australia, France

ISBN : 978-81-212-6364-1 (PB)
First Published, 1892

2nd Impression 2022

Printed at: Gyan Press, Delhi.

COINS AND MEDALS
Author: *Edited by*:- STANLEY LANE-POOLE

COINS AND MEDALS

Their Place in History and Art

BY THE AUTHORS OF

THE BRITISH MUSEUM OFFICIAL CATALOGUES

EDITED BY

STANLEY LANE-POOLE

SECOND EDITION

WITH NUMEROUS ILLUSTRATIONS

1892.

PREFACE.

THE preſent work is intended to furniſh an anſwer to a queſtion that is often and properly aſked about any ſtudy of which the uſe and advantages are not immediately obvious. In the following chapters we have attempted to ſhow what coins can teach us; what is their value as documents of hiſtory and monuments of art; and what relations they bear to other branches of hiſtorical, artiſtic, and archæological reſearch. The book will be found of ſervice to the antiquary and the collector of coins; but it is primarily intended for the general ſtudent who wiſhes to know what he may expect to learn from any particular branch of numiſmatics.

The writers are or have been all Officers in the Department of Coins and Medals in the Britiſh Muſeum, except Profeſſor Terrien de la Couperie and myſelf, who, however, have been entruſted with the taſk of preparing the Chineſe and Mohammadan

Catalogues for the Department. A ſeries of eſſays which appeared in the *Antiquary* in 1883 forms the nucleus of the volume; but theſe have been reviſed and enlarged, while additional chapters and illuſtrations have been incorporated. A few misprints have been corrected in this ſecond edition, which is otherwiſe a reprint of the firſt.

In the abſence of any general guide to the ſtudy of coins, of a popular character, in our language, it is hoped that the preſent work may prove of value to many who have been accuſtomed to regard the ſcience of numiſmatics as little better than a diſtraction.

STANLEY LANE-POOLE.

ATHENÆUM CLUB,
June, 1892.

CONTENTS.

LIST OF ILLUSTRATIONS.

COINS AND MEDALS.

CHAPTER I.

THE STUDY OF COINS.

OF all antiquities coins are the ſmalleſt, yet, as a claſs, the moſt authoritative in record, and the wideſt in range. No hiſtory is ſo unbroken as that which they tell; no geography ſo complete; no art ſo continuous in ſequence, nor ſo broad in extent; no mythology ſo ample and ſo various. Unknown kings, and loſt towns, forgotten divinities, and new ſchools of art, have here their authentic record. Individual character is illuſtrated, and the tendencies of races defined.

To be a good Greek numiſmatiſt one muſt be an archaeologiſt; and it is a ſignificant fact, that the only archaeological book of the laſt century which ſtill holds its own is the *Doctrina Numorum Veterum* of Eckhel, now near its centenary. To be a great general numiſmatiſt is beyond the powers of one man. Some may know Greek and Latin enough, with ſuch maſtery of Engliſh, French, German, and Italian as the modern commentaries demand, to begin the ſtudy of Greek and Roman money. Thoſe who would enter the vaſt field of Oriental numiſmatics muſt be fortified with Arabic, Hebrew, Sanſkrit, and Perſian, beſides adding Spaniſh and Ruſſian to the other European languages ſtill neceſſary for their work. Even they muſt pauſe beneath the Himalayas, nor dare to croſs the Golden Cherſoneſe, unleſs they are prepared to maſter the uncouth languages and intricate characters of the further Eaſt. So vaſt a ſubject, and one needing ſuch high training, has between Eckhel's time and ours attracted few great ſtudents. Coins have been uſed as helps by archaeologiſts; but the great numiſmatiſt, who could maſter the richeſt provinces of the Eaſt or the Weſt, or even both, and dignify his ſcience as no longer ſervile but maſterly, is of our contemporaries. Such was De Saulcy, who has but lately left us to lament how much remained untold by a mind ſignally fruitful in giving forth its manifold treaſures. He has had his rivals, and he has his followers, ſome, like François Lenormant, who have already followed him, others, like Mommſen, ſtill living to maintain the high poſition recovered for numiſmatics.

Greek Coins. Thanks to their attractive beauty, and the ſkill of Eckhel, Greek coins have been beſt examined, and moſt carefully deſcribed; yet much remains unknown and unrecorded. Beſides the treaſures we are conſtantly digging out of well-known collections, every year brings to light from under the earth coins of new kings or cities, coins with freſh types of divinities and repreſentations of famous ſtatues. Moſt of theſe works, whether familiar or new in type, have the charm which the great gift of the Hellenic race, artiſtic power ruled by meaſure and form, threw over all that it handled. Thus Greek coins are the grammar of Greek art. In them we may trace its gradual growth, the ſtern grandeur of the laſt days of archaiſm, and the ſudden outburſt of full ſplendour, more marked in coins, however, by the influence of the contemporaries and followers of Pheidias than by that of the great ſculptor himſelf. While the original ſculpture of this age, in marble and bronze, might be contained within the walls of a ſingle muſeum, the coin-types may be counted by thouſands. No reſtorer has touched them, nor are they late copies, like the Latin tranſlations of Greek originals which confuſe the judge of ſtatues. Small indeed they are; yet large in treatment, and beautiful in material, whether it be rich gold, or the ſofter-toned electrum, or cold ſilver, or bronze glorified by the unconſcious colouring of the earth in which the coins have lain for centuries. Sometimes we can ſee the copy of a ſtatue,—no ſervile reproduction, but with ſuch proof of free work in varieties of attitude as ſhows that the artiſt, ſtrong in his power, was working from memory. Such is the Herakles of Croton, recalling a kindred ſtatue to the ſo-called Theſeus of the Parthenon. Bolder maſters took a theme like the winged goddeſs of Terina, and varied it with an originality which ſhowed they were worthy peers of the ſculptors and painters. Croton is a town with ſome place in hiſtory; but who, ſave a numiſmatiſt, has any thought for Terina, famous only for the ſurvival of her exquiſite coinage?

Schools of Art. While the ſequence of ſtyles is thus recorded, the ſtudy of coins unexpectedly reveals the exiſtence of local ſchools; ſhows in the marked manneriſm of the Italians, and ſtill more of the Sicilians, that they worked under the influence of gem-engravers; while the ſtrong central ſchool of Greece was ruled by ſculpture; the gentler and more ſympathetic rival of Weſtern Aſia Minor obeyed the taſte of painters; and the iſolated Cretans, leading a ſimpler and leſs cultured life, expreſſed their feeling in a free naturaliſm. The larger ſchools again had their diviſions, marking ſuch local differences as thoſe with which the ſtudy of mediæval Italian art has made us acquainted.

Portraits. With the age of Alexander all art is centralized in royal capitals, and provincial feeling diſappears. The great ſtyles can ſtill be traced in the money of the kings, the lofty naturaliſm of Lyſippus, the dramatic force of the Pergamene maſters, the theatrical tendency of their ſucceſſors. This we ſee in royal portraits; while the decline and the commercial tendency of art is witneſſed by the heraldic quality of the leſs important types.

The eye, dazzled with the beauty of Greek

money, is apt to take little heed of the knowledge lying beyond the province of art which is held within the narrow circle of a coin. Yet the mythological intereſt is only ſecond to the artiſtic; and when the artiſt had loſt his ſkill he produced thoſe neglected pieces of inferior work, the Greek money of the Imperial age, which preſerve the forms of famous temples, of great ſtatues, and even of pictures otherwiſe finally loſt to us.

The artiſts who engraved the Greek Imperial money, called to Rome, worked there for alien maſters. Mere copyiſts they were; yet more exact in portraiture, and better hiſtorians than their great predeceſſors. Too weak to be original, they were more faithful in rendering the preſent. To them we owe the marked lineaments of the earlier ſeries of Emperors, the cold Auguſtus; the coarſe Vitellius; Trajan, the ſimple ſoldier; Hadrian, the polite man of the world; and the philoſophic Antoninus and Aurelius, with their wayward and luxurious wives. Theſe engravers have left us a record of the art produced at Rome, and the art that was ſtored at Rome from the ſpoils of Greece, great buildings and famous ſtatues, with here and there a ſubject foreſhadowing in a new turn of ſtyle, of Roman birth, the future ſplendour of the Renaiſſance. But for hiſtory theſe men worked beſt, telling the ſtory of the firſt two centuries and a half of the Empire with a fulneſs that has entitled their money to be called an Imperial Gazette. Thus while Hadrian was viſiting the diſtant provinces, the Roman people,

Roman Coins.

when they went to market, ſaw in the new ſeſtertii, the magnificent bronze currency, the portrayal of the movements of the diſtant Emperor.

The Middle Ages.

The tranſition from Roman to mediaeval money is not ſudden. The one decays, and the other riſes from its ruins, owing as much and as little to it as the architecture of the Middle Ages owed to that of the Empire—as much in form, as little in ſpirit. Here hiſtory divides with art the claim to our attention. At firſt the intereſt is centred in the gradual introduction of Roman money among the barbarian conquerors of the Empire; but by degrees the growth of art attracts us, and we watch the ſame proceſs that marked the hiſtory of Greek coinage—the ſame ſucceſſion of ſtyles, the ſame peculiarities of local ſchools. But the art of the Middle Ages in the coins never riſes beyond the limits of decoration; and it is not till the claſſical Renaiſſance that we diſcover a worthy rivalry of the ancient maſters. The beginning of medals is of the time, if not due to the genius, of Petrarch; and the earlieſt works are of his friends the Lords of Carrara; but it was not till the middle of the fifteenth century that the great medallic art of Italy had its true origin. Piſano of Verona, who glories in the name of painter, was at once the founder of the art, and by far its greateſt maſter. His works are larger in ſize than the coins of antiquity and the Roman medallions, and are caſt, not ſtruck, in fine bronze. Deſpite an inferiority to Greek money in the ſenſe of beauty, the beſt Italian medals have a dignity of

Italian Medals.

portraiture, and a felicity of compoſition, that places them in only the ſecond rank, below the Greek works indeed, yet above the Roman. For if the Italian medalliſt had not the ſame ſenſe of beauty, he had the power of idealizing portraiture, not with the view of elevating the phyſical ſo much as the moral qualities. Piſano, notably, repreſented a man with all the poſſibilities of excellence that lay within his compaſs; and thus he is the greateſt of thoſe medalliſts who worked in portraits.

Modern Coinage

Modern coins of the European ſtates and their colonies are the loweſt in intereſt, and the medals of their great perſonages the leaſt lively in portraiture. But they have an hiſtoric value that entitles them to a place in all repreſentative collections, as at leaſt uſeful illuſtrations of the contemporary annals, and the readieſt means of bringing before the eye the chief figures of the times. A cloſer ſtudy reveals new and curious facts, and the character of the king or the tendencies of the ſtate receive an unexpected illuſtration.

Oriental Coins.

Oriental money, of larger range and more individuality than European, is worthy of more attention than it has received. The great branch of Mohammedan coinage is invaluable for a period of hiſtory when written records are often wanting or little to be truſted. Its decorative art has a charm in the fineſt work of the Shahs of Perſia and the Indian Emperors, but rarely is it more than a delicate rendering of an ornamental writing. The inſcriptions give the coins their true value, the dates and mints fixing the extent of a king's dominion, or recording the fact that he actually exercised the royal prerogative of coining. These legends have a bearing on the differences of race and faith, and even of literature and manners. The western Arabs coined their money with elaborate religious formulas, the heretical Khalifs of the race of 'Aly used mystical inscriptions, the Persians, the Indian Emperors and the Afghans inscribed poetic couplets, hard to decipher, from the occasional disregard of the order of words, and difficult to interpret, from the high-flown phrases in which royalty turned the language well-called the Italian of the East. Despite the general absence of figures, the result of the law of the Koran, there are some notable exceptions, as in the Turkoman coinage of the age of the Crusades, and the famous zodiacal coins of Jehángír and his still stranger Bacchanalian money, on which we see the emperor seated, holding the forbidden wine-cup in his hand.

Yet earlier in origin than the Mohammedan coinage, the native money of India has, like it, survived to our time. Beginning with the interesting Indian coins of the Greek princes, the so-called Bactrian money, and the contemporary rude punch-marked square pieces of native origin, it passes into the gold currency of the Guptas with interesting mythological subjects, Greek, Roman, and Indian, including a representation of Buddha, and closes with the Sanskritic money of our own time. Beyond India, China and the neighbouring lands have their money as unlike that of the reſt of the world as all elſe in the Far Eaſt, valuable alone ſor hiſtory, and for it moſt valuable; and curious for the occaſional departure from the forms which we aſſociate with the idea of coined money.

CHAPTER II.

GREEK COINS.

Bullion Money.

MANY centuries before the invention of the art of coining, gold and silver in the East, and bronze in the West, in bullion form, had already supplanted barter, the most primitive of all methods of buying and selling, when among pastoral peoples the ox and the sheep were the ordinary mediums of exchange. The very word *pecunia* is an evidence of this practice in Italy at a period which is probably recent in comparison with the time when values were estimated in cattle in Greece and the East.

The Invention of Coinage.

"So far as we have any knowledge," says Herodotus,[1] "the Lydians were the first nation to introduce the use of gold and silver coin." This statement of the father of history must not, however, be accepted as finally settling the vexed question as to who were the inventors of coined money, for Strabo,[2] Aelian,[3] and the Parian Chronicle, all agree in adopting the more commonly received tradition, that Pheidon, King of

[1] i. 94. [2] viii. 6. [3] *Var. Hist.*, xii. 10.

Argos, firſt ſtruck ſilver coins in the iſland of Aegina. Theſe two apparently contradictory aſſertions modern reſearch tends to reconcile with one another. The one embodies the Aſiatic, the other the European tradition; and the truth of the matter is that gold was firſt coined by the Lydians, in Aſia Minor, in the ſeventh century before our era; and that ſilver was firſt ſtruck in European Greece about the ſame time.

The earlieſt coins are ſimply bullets of metal, oval or bean-ſhaped, bearing on one ſide the ſignet of the ſtate or of the community reſponſible for the purity of the metal and the exactneſs of the weight. Coins were at firſt ſtamped on one ſide only, the reverſe ſhowing merely the impreſs of the ſquare-headed ſpike or anvil on which, after being weighed, the bullet of hot metal was placed with a pair of tongs and there held while a ſecond workman adjuſted upon it the engraved die. This done, a third man with a heavy hammer would come down upon it with all his might, and the coin would be produced, bearing on its face or *obverſe* the ſeal of the iſſuer, and on the reverſe only the mark of the anvil ſpike, an *incuſe* ſquare. This ſimple proceſs was after a time improved upon by adding a ſecond engraved die beneath the metal bullet, ſo that a ſingle blow of the ſledge-hammer would provide the coin with a *type*, as it is called, in relief, on both ſides. The preſence of the unengraved incuſe ſquare may therefore be accepted as an indication of high antiquity, and nearly all Greek

Earliest and Later Methods of Coining.

coins which are later than the age of the Perſian wars bear a type on both ſides.

Scientific Value of Greek Coins.

The chief ſcientific value of Greek coins lies in the fact that they are original documents, to which the experienced numiſmatiſt is generally able to aſſign an exact place in hiſtory. The ſeries of the coins of any one of the cities of Greece thus forms a continuous comment upon the hiſtory of the town, a comment which either confirms or refutes the teſtimony which has been handed down to us by ancient writers, or, where ſuch teſtimony is altogether wanting, ſupplies valuable evidence as to the material condition, the political changes, or the religious ideas of an interval of time which, but for ſuch evidence, would have been a blank in the chart of the world's hiſtory.

Perhaps the moſt attractive ſide of this enticing ſtudy lies in the elucidation of the meaning of the objects repreſented on coins, in other words, in the explanation of their types.

The hiſtory of the growth, bloom, and decay of Greek art may alſo be traced more completely on a ſeries of coins which extends over a period of cloſe upon a thouſand years than on any other claſs of ancient monuments.

Types.

Greek coin-types may be divided into two diſtinct claſſes: (*a*) Mythological or religious repreſentations, and (*b*) portraits of hiſtorical perſons.

Religious Aspect.

From the earlieſt times down to the age of Alexander the Great the types of Greek coins are almoſt excluſively religious. However ſtrange this may ſeem at firſt, it is not difficult to explain. It muſt be borne in mind that when the enterpriſing and commercial Lydians firſt lighted upon the happy idea of ſtamping metal for general circulation, a guarantee of juſt weight and purity of metal would be the one condition required. Without ſome really truſtworthy warrant, what merchant would accept this new form of money for ſuch and ſuch a weight without placing it in the ſcales and weighing it according to ancient practice? In an age of univerſal religious belief, when the gods lived, as it were, among men, and when every tranſaction was ratified by ſolemn oath, as witneſs innumerable inſcriptions from all parts of the Greek world, what more binding guarantee could be found than the invocation of one or other of thoſe divinities moſt honoured and moſt dreaded in the diſtrict in which the coin was intended to circulate?

Temple Coinage.

There is even good reaſon to think[1] that the earlieſt coins were actually ſtruck within the precincts of the temples, and under the direct auſpices of the prieſts; for in times of general inſecurity by ſea and land, the temples alone remained ſacred and inviolate. Into the temple treaſuries offerings of the precious metals poured from all parts. The prieſtly colleges owned lands and houſes, and were in the habit of letting them on leaſe, ſo that rents, tithes, and offerings would all go to fill the treaſure-houſe of the god. This accumulated maſs of wealth was not left to lie idle in the

[1] Prof. E. Curtius, *Numismatic Chron.*, 1870, p. 92.

ſacred cheſt, but was frequently lent out at intereſt in furtherance of any undertaking, ſuch as the ſending out of a colony, or the opening and working of a mine; anything, in fact, which might commend itſelf to the ſound judgment of the prieſts: and ſo it may well have been that the temple funds would be put into circulation in the form of coin marked with ſome ſacred ſymbol by which all men might know that it was the property of Zeus, or Apollo, or Artemis, or Aphrodite, as the caſe might be. Thus coins iſſued from a temple of Zeus would bear, as a ſymbol, a thunderbolt or an eagle; the money of Apollo would be marked with a tripod or a lyre; that of Artemis with a ſtag or a wild boar; that of Aphrodite with a dove or a tortoiſe—a creature held ſacred to the goddeſs of Love, in ſome of whoſe temples even the wooden footſtools were made in the form of tortoiſes.

State Coinage.

In this manner the origin of the ſtamps on current coin may be explained. But throughout the Greek world the civic powers almoſt everywhere ſtepped in at an early date, and took over to themſelves the right of iſſuing the coin of the ſtate. Neverthele ſs, care was always taken to preſerve the only ſolid guarantee which commanded univerſal reſpect, and the name of the god continued to be invoked on the coin as the patron of the city. No mere king or tyrant, however abſolute his rule, ever preſumed to place his own effigy on the current coin, for ſuch a proceeding would, from old aſſociations, have been regarded as little ſhort of ſacrilege. In ſome rare caſes, indeed, the right of coinage would even ſeem to have been retained by the prieſts down to a comparatively late period; for coins exiſt, dating from the fourth century B.C., which were iſſued from the famous temple of the Didymean Apollo, near Miletus, having on the obverſe the head of Apollo laureate and with flowing hair; and on the reverſe the lion, the ſymbol of the ſun-god, and the inſcription ΕΓ ΔΙΔΥΜΩΝ ΙΕΡΗ, "ſacred money of Didyma."

We will now ſelect a few of the almoſt innumerable examples of ancient coin-types in illuſtration of the religious ſignification of the ſymbols which appear upon them.

First in importance comes the plentiful coinage **Aegina.** of the iſland of Aegina, iſſued according to tradition by Pheidon, King of Argos, probably in the ſanctuary of Aphrodite, in Aegina, the firſt European mint. Theſe coins bear the ſymbol of the goddeſs, a tortoiſe or turtle; and they were ſoon adopted far and wide, not only throughout Peloponneſus, but in moſt of the iſland ſtates, as the one generally recogniſed circulating medium. When Pheidon firſt iſſued this new money, he is ſaid to have dedicated and hung up in the temple of Hera, at Argos, ſpecimens of the old cumbrous bronze and iron bars which had ſerved the purpoſe of money before his time.

Paſſing from Aegina to Athens, we have now **Athens.** before us the very ancient coins which Solon ſtruck when he inaugurated that great financial reform which went by the name of the Seifachtheia, a meafure of relief for the whole population of Attica, then overburdened by a weight of debt. By the new law then enacted (circ. B.C. 590), it was decreed that every man who owed one hundred Aeginetic drachms, the only coin then current, fhould be held exempt on the payment of one hundred of the new Attic drachms, which were ftruck of a confiderably lighter weight than the old Aeginetic coins.

The type which Solon chofe for the new Athenian coinage was, like all the types of early Greek money, purely religious. On the obverfe we fee the head of Athena, the protecting goddefs of the city; and on the reverfe her facred owl and olive-branch. Thefe coins were popularly called *owls*, γλαῦκες, or *maidens*, κόραι, πάρθενοι. Ariftophanes, who not unfrequently alludes to coins, mentions thefe famous owls in the following lines, where he promifes his judges that if only they will give his play their fuffrages, the owls of Laurium fhall never fail them :

> Firft, for more than anything each judge has this at heart,
> Never fhall the Laureotic Owls from you depart,
> But fhall in your houfes dwell, and in your purfes too
> Neftle clofe, and hatch a brood of little coins for you.[1]

Delphi. Paffing now into Central Greece, let us paufe for a moment at Delphi, the religious metropolis of the Dorian race. Delphi was effentially a temple-ftate, independent of the Phocian territory

[1] *Birds*, 1106 (Kennedy).

in the midſt of which it was ſituated. It was, moreover, the principal ſeat of the ſacred Amphictyonic Council. Here were held the great Pythian Feſtivals, to which all who could afford it flocked from every part of the Hellenic world. The town of Delphi, which grew up at the foot of the temple of Apollo, on the ſouthern ſlope of Parnaſſus, was in early times a member of the Phocian Convention; but as the temple increaſed in wealth and preſtige, the Delphians claimed to be recogniſed as an independent community; a claim which the Phocians always ſtrenuouſly reſiſted, but which the people of Delphi ſucceeded at length in eſtabliſhing. The town, however, as ſuch, never roſe to any political importance apart from the temple, upon which it was always *de facto* a mere dependency.

As might be expected, the coins iſſued at Delphi are peculiarly temple coins; and were probably ſtruck only on certain ſpecial occaſions, ſuch as the great Pythian Feſtivals, and the meetings, called Πυλαία, of the Amphictyonic Council, when many ſtrangers were ſtaying in the town, and when money would conſequently be in requeſt in larger quantities than uſual. At ſuch times markets or fairs were held, called πυλατίδες ἀγοραί, for the ſale of all kinds of articles connected with the ceremonies and obſervances of the temple; and at theſe markets a coinage iſſued by the prieſthood, which all alike might accept without fear of fraud, would be a great convenience.

The uſual type of this Delphian temple money

was a ram's head; the ram, κάρνος, being the emblem of Apollo, καρνεῖος, the god of flocks and herds. There is alſo another emblem, which, although it is uſually only an acceſſory ſymbol, and not a principal type, muſt not be paſſed over in ſilence, the dolphin (δελφίς). Here we have an alluſion to another phaſe of the cultus of Apollo, who, as we read in the Homeric hymn to Apollo,[1] once took the form of a dolphin when he guided the Cretan ſhip to Criſſa, whence, after commanding the crew to burn their ſhip and erect an altar to him as Apollo Delphinios, he led them up to Delphi, and appointed them to be the firſt prieſts of his temple.

On another coin ſtruck at Delphi we ſee the Pythian god ſeated on the ſacred Omphalos, with his lyre and tripod beſide him, and a laurel-branch over his ſhoulders; while around is the inſcription ΑΜΦΙΚΤΙΟΝΩΝ, proving the coin to have been iſſued with the ſanction of the Amphictyonic Council.

Boeotia. In the coinage of the neighbouring territory of Boeotia, the moſt ſtriking characteriſtic is that it is a ſo-called *Federal Currency*; that is to ſay, that the various Boeotian cities poſſeſſed from firſt to laſt ſufficient coheſion to be able to agree upon a common type, which might ſerve to diſtinguiſh the Boeotian currency from that of other ſtates. This is the more remarkable when we remember the fierce political feuds which from the earlieſt times divided Boeotia into ſeveral hoſtile camps.

[1] l. 390, *seqq.*

Here then we have a clear proof that the *Buckler*, which is the type from the earlieſt times to the lateſt of all Boeotian money, is no mere political emblem, but a ſacred ſymbol, which friends and foes alike could unite in reverencing; juſt as in mediæval times all Chriſtians, however hoſtile to one another, and to whatever land they might belong, were ready to pay homage to the ſign of the Croſs. To what divinity this Boeotian ſhield eſpecially belongs we do not know for certain, but the Theban Herakles has perhaps the beſt claim to it.

The cities of Boeotia, however, while they all agreed to accept the buckler as the diſtinctive badge of their money, neverthelеſs aſſerted their ſeparate and individual rights on the reverſe ſide of their coins. On the obverſe we here get uniformity, on the reverſe variety, and yet among all the various types on the reverſes of the coins of the Boeotian cities, there is not one which is not diſtinctly religious, whether it refer to the worſhip of Herakles or Dionyſos at Thebes, to Poſeidon at Haliartus, to Apollo as the sun-god at Tanagra, or to Aphrodite Melainis as a moon goddeſs at Theſpiae. Sometimes the god himſelf is directly portrayed, ſometimes his preſence is veiled under ſome ſymbolic form, as when the amphora or the wine-cup ſtands for Dionyſos, the club for Herakles, the trident for Poſeidon, the wheel for the rolling diſk of the ſun-god, and the creſcent for the goddeſs of the moon.

Proceeding now northwards through Theſſaly Thrace.

and Macedon, we come upon a region where ſilver money was coined in very early times, probably long before the Perſian invaſion, by the mining tribes who inhabited the mountainous diſtrict oppoſite the iſland of Thaſos. Here again we find the ſame cloſe connection between the religion of the people and the types of their coins. The ſubjects repreſented on the money of this northern land are Satyrs and Centaurs bearing off ſtruggling nymphs, rudely but vigorouſly executed, in a ſtyle of art rather Aſiatic than Hellenic.

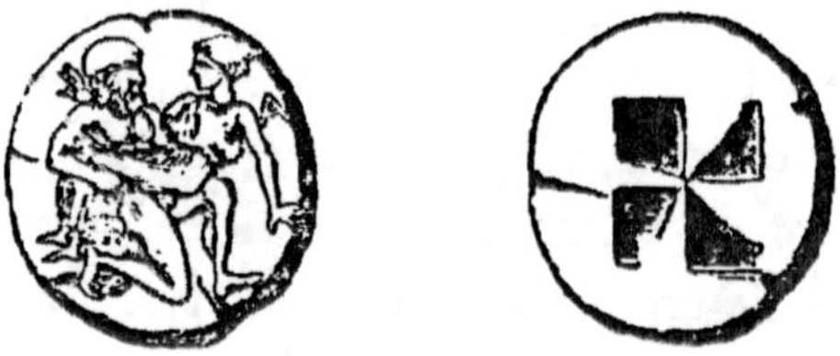

SILVER COIN OF THASOS.

Such types as theſe bring before us the wild orgies which were held in the mountains of Phrygia and Thrace, in honour of the god Sabazius or Bacchus, whoſe myſterious oracle ſtood on the rugged and ſnow-capped height of Mount Pangaeum, while around, among the dark pine foreſts, cluſtered the village communities of the rude mining tribes who worked the rich veins of gold and ſilver with which the Pangaean range abounded.

Ephesus. We will now take an example from Aſia Minor, where we ſhall find the ſame invariable connection between the coinage and the local religious cultus.

The coins of the great city of Epheſus, "firſt

city of Asia," are from very early times marked with a bee on one side, and a stag and palm-tree on the other. The hierarchy of the Ephesian Artemis consisted of a college of priests, at the head of which was a High Priest called 'Εσσήν (the king bee), the leader of the swarm, while his attendant priestesses bore the name of Melissae or Bees; and however difficult it may be for us to seize the exact idea which was intended to be conveyed by this symbol, there can be no doubt that it was one of the most distinctive emblems of the Ephesian goddess in her character of a goddess of nature. The stag is a symbol which every reader of the Greek poets will at once recognise as belonging to Artemis, as is also the sacred palm-tree, *πρωτόγονος φοίνιξ*, beneath which Leto was fabled to have brought forth Apollo and his sister Artemis.

Etruria. In the West, no less than in Greece and Asia, the religious aspect of the coin-types is very striking. Thus on Etruscan coins we meet with the head of the gorgon Medusa and of Hades. Here, too, we see Cerberus and griffins and sphinxes and chimaeras, as well as the head of a priest or augur —types which are symbolical of those gloomy and fantastic ideas connected with death and the world of shades which were peculiarly characteristic of the strange uncanny beliefs of the Etruscans.

Campania In the fertile and vine-growing Campania, on the other hand, the most frequent reverse type is a human-headed bull, a tauriform Chthonian divinity or Earth-god, worshipped very generally throughout

Southern Italy under the name of Dionyſos Hebon; a god whoſe nature partook both of that of Hades and of Dionyſos, and who was aſſociated with a female divinity, reſembling both Perſephone and Ariadne, a perſonification of the eternal renewal of nature in the ſpring-time. The beautiful head of this goddeſs is the conſtant obverſe type of the money of Neapolis (Naples).

SILVER COIN OF TARENTUM.

Magna Graecia. Tarentum

In Magna Graecia the ſplendid ſeries of the money of Tarentum offers the curious type of a naked youth riding on a dolphin. This is Taras, the founder of the firſt Iapygian ſettlement on the Calabrian coaſt, who was ſaid to have been miraculouſly ſaved from ſhipwreck by the intervention of his father Poſeidon, who ſent a dolphin, on whoſe back Taras was borne to the ſhore. At Tarentum divine honours were paid to him as oekiſt or founder, and hence his preſence on the coins. The rider who appears on the reverſe of the coins of Tarentum may be taken as an example

Agonistic Types.

of what is called an *agoniſtic* type, *i.e.*, a commemoration on the ſtate-money of victories in the games held at Tarentum in the hippodrome. All Greek games partook of a religious nature, and were held in honour of one or other of the gods:

at Olympia, for example, in honour of Zeus, at Delphi of Apollo, and at Tarentum probably of Poſeidon.

Another, and a very remarkable early example of one of the agoniſtic types is furniſhed by a coin of Metapontum, in Southern Italy: on the reverſe is the figure of the river Acheloüs in human form, but with the horns and ears of a bull, juſt as he is deſcribed by Sophocles,[1] as ἀνδρείῳ κύτει βούπρῳρος; and around him is the inſcription in archaic characters ΑΧΕΛΟΙΟ ΑΘΛΟΝ, ſhowing that games were celebrated at Metapontum in honour of Acheloüs, king of all Greek rivers, and as ſuch revered from the time of Homer onwards. The coins with this type were doubtleſs ſtruck on the occaſion of the feſtival held in honour of Acheloüs, and may even have been diſtributed as prizes, ἆθλα, among the ſucceſsful athletes. Metapontum.

At leaſt one ſide of every Metapontine coin was always dedicated to Demeter, to whoſe eſpecial favour was attributed the extraordinary fertility of the plain in which the city ſtood. The ear of corn was the recogniſed ſymbol of the worſhip of this goddeſs. On this ear of corn is often ſeen a locuſt, a bird, a field-mouſe, or ſome other creature deſtructive to the crops, which was probably added to the main type as a ſort of propitiation of the daemons of deſtruction, and the maleficent influences in nature.

The Acheloüs on this intereſting coin of Metapontum may ſerve to introduce us to a whole Sicily. River-gods.

[1] *Trach.* 12.

ſeries of river-gods as coin-types on the money of many of the towns of Sicily. River-worſhip would ſeem, indeed, judging from the coins, to have been eſpecially prevalent in that iſland in the fifth century B.C., during which the Sicilian coaſts were girdled by a chain of magnificent Greek cities, all, or nearly all, of which were ſhortly afterwards either deſtroyed by the Carthaginians, or delivered by the tyrants of Syracuſe into the hands of a rapacious foreign ſoldiery.

In Sicily we ſee the river Gelas at firſt as a ruſhing man-headed bull, and later as a beardleſs youth with horns ſprouting from his forehead.

SILVER COIN OF GELA.

The Crimiſſus on a coin of Segeſta takes at firſt the form of a dog, and later that of a hunter accompanied by two dogs. The Hipparis at Camarina is ſeen as a young horned head emerging from the midſt of a circle of waves. The Hypſas at Selinus is a naked youth offering a libation at the altar of the god of health, in gratitude for the draining of the marſh, which had impeded the courſe of his ſtream, and for the cleanſing and purification of his waters. On the reverſe of this coin we ſee Apollo and Artemis in a chariot, the former as ἀλεξίκακος diſcharging his radiant arrows and ſlaying the Peſtilence as he ſlew the Python, while his ſiſter Artemis ſtands beſide him in her capacity of εἰλείθυια or σωώδίνα, for the plague had fallen heavily on the women too, ὥστε καὶ τὰς γυναῖκας δυστοκεῖν.[1]

SILVER COIN OF SELINUS.

From the cultus of rivers we may paſs to that of nymphs, of which we may again find examples among the beautiful coins of Sicily. One of the moſt charming of theſe repreſentations is that of the nymph Camarina on a coin of that city, who is pictured riding on the back of a ſwan, half-flying, half-ſwimming acroſs the waves of her own lake, as ſhe holds with one hand the corner of her peplos or garment, which, filled by the breeze, ſerves the purpoſe of a ſail. Water-nymphs.

More famous ſtill is the fountain-nymph Arethuſa, on a tetradrachm of Syracuſe, a work which, in delicacy of treatment, and in the ſkilful adaptation of the ſubject to the ſpace at the diſpoſal of the artiſt, leaves nothing to be deſired. On this coin the head of the nymph is ſeen facing the ſpectator—a true water-goddeſs—

> With her rainbow locks
> Streaming among the ſtreams;

[1] Diog. Laert., viii. 2, 70.

while dolphins are playing around her, darting and leaping about among the rich maſſes of her floating hair. The artiſt has here ſtriven to convey the idea of the ſweet waters of the fountain in the iſland of Ortygia riſing out of the midſt of the ſalt waves of the harbour of Syracuſe, the ſalt ſea being ſymbolized by the dolphins.

As in the caſe of the river-gods, the head of the nymph is on this coin accompanied by her name, ΑΡΕΘΟΣΑ.

Eagles devouring a Hare.

Another Sicilian coin ſtands out as a truly powerful work. It is a ſilver coin of Agrigentum, on which two eagles are ſeen on a rocky height, the one ſcreaming with uplifted head, the other with raiſed wings and head ſtretched downwards. The two birds ſtand ſide by ſide on the dead body of a hare, which they are about to tear in pieces. As a coin-type, ſuch a ſubject ſeems hard to explain: perhaps it refers to some local myth long loſt; but it is ſcarcely poſſible to conceive that the artiſt

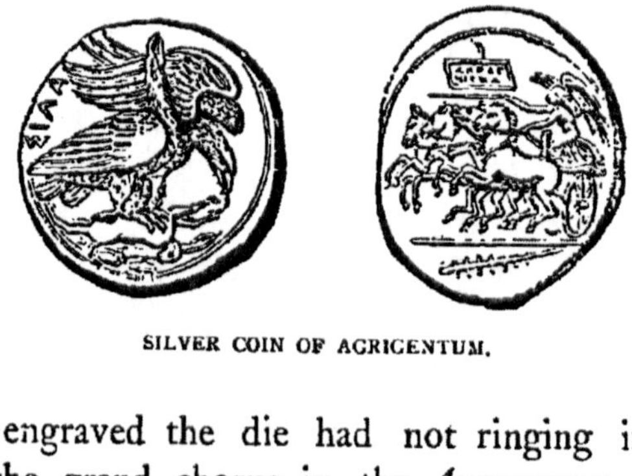

SILVER COIN OF AGRIGENTUM.

who engraved the die had not ringing in his ears the grand chorus in the *Agamemnon* where Aeſchylus depicts the "winged hounds of Zeus" in juſt ſuch a ſcene as the engraver, with equally imperiſhable touches, has handed down to us acroſs the ages:

> On lofty ſtation, manifeſt to ſight,
> The bird kings to the navy kings appear,
> One black, and one with hinder plumage white,
> A hare with embryo young in evil hour
> Amerced of future courſes they devour.
> Chant the dirge, uplift the wail,
> But may the right prevail.[1]

Coinage of Philip and Alexander the Great.

From the coinage of free and autonomous towns, we will now paſs to that of Philip of Macedon, the founder of that vaſt monarchy which was deſtined, in the hands of his ſon and ſucceſſor Alexander the Great, to ſpread the arms, the arts, the literature, and the civilization of Greece as far as the ſhores of the Caſpian and the banks of the Indus and the Nile. But abſolute as was the power of Philip and Alexander, theſe monarchs were ſtill eſſentially Greek, and as Greeks they were careful never to place upon their money any effigy leſs auguſt than that of ſome one of the gods of Greece. Thus Philip, when he had united in his ſingle hand the whole of northern Greece, and when he reorganized the currency of his empire, had recourſe to the two great religious centres of Hellas, Delphi and Olympia, for the types of his gold and ſilver money. On the gold money appears the head of the Pythian Apollo, and on the ſilver that of the Olympian Zeus. The reverſe types are in each caſe *agoniſtic*; that is to ſay, they com-

[1] *Agam.*, 115 (Swanwick).

memorate in a general way Philip's ſucceſſes in the great Greek games, in which, we are told, it was his eſpecial pride to be hailed as a victor. Pallas and her attendant, Victory, with Herakles and the Olympian Zeus, are the gods under whoſe auſpices Alexander's gold and ſilver went forth from a hundred mints over the vaſt expanſe of his heterogeneous empire. But, more than mortal as Alexander was conceived, and perhaps almoſt believed himſelf to be, never once during his lifetime was his own portrait ſeen upon his coins, though it had been the cuſtom in the Eaſt, from the very foundation of the Perſian monarchy which Alexander overthrew, for the great king to place his own effigy upon the royal *Daric* coins. What clearer proof can be required that none but religious ſubjects were at that time admiſſible on the coin?

Introduction of Portraiture.

But after the death of the great conqueror a change is noticeable, gradual at firſt, and then more marked, in the aſpect of the international currency inſtituted by Alexander. The features of the god Herakles on the tetradrachms little by little loſe their noble ideality, and aſſume an expreſſion in which there is an evident ſtriving on the part of the engraver towards an aſſimilation of the god to Alexander, now himſelf regarded as one of the immortals and the recipient of Divine honours.

Alexander's Successors.

The firſt real and diſtinct innovation was, however, made by Alexander's general, Lyſimachus, when he became King of Thrace. The money of this monarch bears most unmistakably a portrait of the great Alexander—of Alexander, however, as a god—in the character which in his lifetime his flatterers had encouraged him to assume, of the son of the Lybian Ammon with the ram's horn over the ear. This was the first step towards the new fashion of placing the head of the sovereign on the coin of the realm; but so antagonistic does this practice seem to have been to the religious susceptibilities even of this late time, that it was only by slow degrees that it came to be adopted. When the centre of gravity, so to speak, of the Greek world was no longer to be found in Hellas, but in the various capitals of those semi-oriental monarchies which arose out of the ruins of the Persian empire, Alexandria, Antioch, and the rest, all Greece received an indelible taint of oriental servility. In comparison with these new self-constituted Βασιλεῖς and their descendants, Philip and Alexander stand forth as Hellenes of the old type. Only in such degenerate times did it become possible for a king to usurp on the coinage the place of honour reserved of old for gods and religious emblems; nay, even to give themselves out as very gods, and to adopt such titles as Θεός ἐπιφανής or Νέος Διόνυσός.

The first of Alexander's successors who substituted his own portrait on coins for that of the deified Alexander was Ptolemy Soter, the founder of the dynasty which ruled Egypt for two centuries and a half. Both he and his queen, Berenice, were deified after their deaths, and appear with the title Θεοί on the money of their ſon, Ptolemy Philadelphus; and the portrait of Ptolemy Soter was perpetuated from generation to generation on the coins of ſucceſſive rulers of Egypt down to the time of the Roman conqueſt, although not to the excluſion of other royal portraits.

Greek coins, from the age of Alexander onwards, poſſeſs an intereſt altogether different from that with which the money of the earlier ages inſpires us. The intereſt of the præ-Alexandrine coins is twofold. In the firſt place, they illuſtrate local myths, and indirectly ſhed much light on the political revolutions of every corner of the Greek world; and in the ſecond place, they are moſt valuable for the hiſtory of art in its various ſtages of development. The intereſt of the poſt-Alexandrine coins is that of a gallery of authentic portraits. "Here," ſays Addiſon,[1] "you ſee the Alexanders, Caeſars, Pompeys, Trajans, and the whole catalogue of heroes who have, many of them, ſo diſtinguiſhed themſelves from the reſt of mankind, that we almoſt look upon them as another ſpecies. It is an agreeable amuſement to compare in our own thoughts the face of a great man with the character that authors have given us of him, and to try if we can find out in his looks and features either the haughty, cruel, or merciful temper that diſcovers itſelf in the hiſtory of his actions."

Portraits— Alexander. Among the fineſt portraits on Greek coins we

[1] *Dialogues upon the Uſefulneſs of Ancient Medals.*

have ſpace only to mention a few. Firſt comes that of the great Alexander himſelf, on the coins of Lyſimachus, idealized no doubt, but ſtill the man in the likeneſs of a god. In many of theſe coins we may note the peculiarities recorded as characteriſtic of his ſtatues by Lyſippus, the ſlight twiſt in the neck and the ardent look in the eyes.

Demetrius Poliorcetes.

Then there is Demetrius Poliorcetes, the deſtroyer of cities, that ſoldier of fortune, terrible in war, and luxurious in peace, whoſe beauty was ſuch that Plutarch ſays no painter could hit off a likeneſs. That hiſtorian compares him to Dionyſos, and as Dionyſos he appears on the coins, with the bull's horn of the god pointing up from out the heavy locks of hair which fall about his forehead.

Philetaerus.

Another highly characteriſtic head is that of the eunuch Philetaerus, the founder of the dynaſty of the Attalid Kings of Pergamus. Here, at laſt, is realiſm pure and ſimple. The huge fat face and vaſt expanſe of cheek and lower iaw carry conviction to our minds that this is indeed a living portrait.

Realism.

To thoſe who are familiar only with Greek art in its ideal ſtage, ſuch faces as this of Philetaerus, with many others that might be cited (Pruſias, King of Bithynia, for example), from among the various Greek regal coins, will be at firſt ſomewhat ſtartling. We have become ſo thoroughly imbued with the ideal conceptions of godlike humanity perpetuated in Greek ſculpture and its derivatives, that when we firſt take up one of theſe portrait-coins of the third or ſecond century B.C., we find it hard to perſuade ourſelves that it is ſo far removed from our own times. This or that uninſpired and commonplace face might well be that of a proſperous modern Engliſhman, were it not for the royal diadem and Greek inſcription which deſignate it as a King of Pontus or Bithynia, of Syria or of Egypt.

Mithradates. Nevertheleſs, although an almoſt brutal realiſm is the rule in the period now under conſideration, there are inſtances where the artiſt ſeems to have been inſpired by his ſubject and carried away out of the real into the ideal. Thus the majority of the coins of the great Mithradates are probably unidealized portraits, ſomewhat careleſsly executed, of a man ſcarcely remarkable unleſs for a certain evil expreſſion of tigeriſh cruelty. But there are others of this ſame monarch on which, it is true, the likeneſs is unmiſtakably preſerved, but under what an altered aſpect! Mithradates is here the hero, almoſt the god, and as we gaze at his head on theſe coins, with flying locks blown back as if by a ſtrong wind, we can picture him ſtanding in his victorious chariot holding well in hand his ſixteen ſplendid ſteeds, and carrying off the prize; or as a runner, outſtripping the ſwifteſt deer, or performing ſome other of thoſe wondrous feats of ſtrength and agility of which we read. This type of the idealized Mithradatic head alſo occurs on coins of Ariarathes, a youthful ſon of Mithradates, who was placed by his father on the throne of Cappadocia. The head, like that of Alexander, was afterwards perpetuated on the money of various cities on the ſhores of the Euxine.

SILVER COIN WITH HEAD OF MITHRADATES.

We have ſpace only to mention one other portrait, that of the famous Cleopatra on a coin of Aſcalon. This is certainly no ordinary face, and yet we look in vain for thoſe charms which faſcinated Caeſar and ruined Antony. The eyes are wide open and eager, the noſe prominent and ſlightly hooked, the mouth large and expreſſive, the hair modeſtly dreſſed and bound with the royal diadem. The evidence afforded by the coins, taken in conjunction with a paſſage of Plutarch, who ſays that in beauty ſhe was by no means ſuperior to Octavia, leads us to the concluſion that Cleopatra's irreſiſtible charm lay rather in her mental qualities and alluring manner, than in any mere outward beauty. Cleopatra.

Quite apart from the intrinſic importance, mythological or hiſtorical, of the ſubjects repreſented on Greek coins, lies their value as illuſtrations of the archaeology of art. Of all the remains of antiquity, ſtatues, bronzes, terracottas, fictile vaſes, engraved gems, and coins, theſe laſt alone Styles of Art and Chronological Sequence.

can, as a rule, be exactly dated. The political conditions and viciſſitudes of the autonomous coin-ſtriking ſtates render it comparatively eaſy for us to ſpread out before our eyes the ſucceſſive iſſues of each in chronological ſequence. In the ſeries of each town we may thus at once obtain a few definite landmarks, around which, by analogy of ſtyle, we ſhall have no great difficulty in grouping the remaining coins. The characteriſtics of Greek art, in the various phaſes which it paſſed through, we do not propoſe, nor indeed is this the place, to diſcuſs. It will be ſufficient to indicate the main chronological diviſions or periods in which the coinage of the ancient world may be conveniently claſſified. Theſe are as follows:

I. Circa B.C. 700-480.	The *Period of Archaic Art*, which extends from the invention of the art of coining down to the time of the Perſian Wars.
II. „ „ 480-415.	The *Period of Tranſitional Art*, from the Perſian Wars to the ſiege of Syracuſe by the Athenians.
III. „ „ 415-336.	The *Period of Fineſt Art*, from the Athenian expedition againſt Sicily, to the acceſſion of Alexander the Great.

IV. Circa B.C. 336-280. The *Period of Later Fine Art*, from the accession of Alexander to the death of Lysimachus.

V. „ „ 280-146. The *Period of the Decline of Art*, from the death of Lysimachus to the Roman conquest of Greece.

VI. „ „ 146-27. The *Period of continued Decline in Art*, from the Roman conquest to the rise of the Roman Empire.

VII. B.C. 27—A.D. 268. The *Period of Graeco-Roman Art*, from the reign of Augustus to that of Gallienus.

It is almost always quite easy to determine to which of the above periods any given coin belongs; and as a rule it is possible to fix its date within the period with more or less precision, by comparing it in point of style with others of which the exact date is known. Even a small collection of well-chosen specimens thus mapped out in periods forms an epitome of the history of art such as no other class of ancient monuments can furnish. It is true that not all coin art is of the highest order for the age to which it belongs. Often, indeed, it is extremely faulty; but, good or bad, it is always instructive, because it is the veritable handiwork of an artiſt working independently, and not of a mere copyiſt of older works. The artiſt may have been unknown, perhaps, even in his own day, beyond the narrow circle of his fellow-citizens; but he was none the leſs an artiſt who expreſſed to the beſt of his ability the ideas of his age and country, and he has handed down to all time, on the little diſk of metal at his diſpoſal, a ſpecimen, on a ſmall ſcale, of the art of the time in which he was at work.

Die Engravers.

There is good reaſon, moreover, to think that the perſons employed to engrave the coin-dies were by no means always artiſts of inferior merit. During the period of the higheſt development of Greek art it is not unuſual, eſpecially in Magna Graecia and Sicily, to find the artiſt's name written at full length in minute characters on coins of particularly fine work; and it is in the laſt degree improbable that ſuch a privilege would have been accorded to a mere mechanic or workman in the mint, however ſkilful he may have been. That artiſts known to fame were (at leaſt in the fourth century) entruſted with the engraving of the coins, is indeed proved by the fact that we find ſeveral cities entirely independent of one another having recourſe to the ſame engraver for their money. For inſtance, Evaenetus, the engraver of the fineſt of thoſe ſplendid medallions of Syracuſe, bearing on one ſide the head of Perſephone crowned with corn-leaves, and on the other a victorious chariot, places his name alſo on coins of two other Sicilian cities, Camarina and Catana; and what is ſtill more remarkable, the Syracuſan artiſt, EYΘ . . . ., appears alſo to have been employed by the mint of Elis in Peloponneſus.

SYRACUSAN MEDALLION.

In Magna Greacia alſo we note that an artiſt, by name Ariſtoxenus, ſigns coins both of Metapontum and Heracleia in Lucania; and another, who modeſtly ſigns himſelf Φ, works at the ſame time for the mints of Heracleia, Thurium, Pandoſia, and Terina.

In Greece proper, artiſts' ſignatures are of very rare occurrence; but of the town of Cydonia, in Crete, there is a coin with the legend in full ΝΕΥΑΝΤΟΣ ΕΠΟΕΙ; and of Clazomenae, in Ionia, there is a well-known tetradrachm, with a magnificent head of Apollo facing, and the inſcription ΘΕΟΔΟΤΟΣ ΕΠΟΕΙ.

Enough has been ſaid to ſhow that in the period of fineſt art there were die-engravers whoſe reputation was not confined to a ſingle town, artiſts of the higher order, whoſe ſignatures on the coin were a credit to the cities for which they worked. Unfortunately, not a ſingle ancient writer has thought of recording the name of any one of theſe great maſters of the art of engraving. How, indeed, could they know that thouſands of theſe, in their time inſignificant, coins would outlaſt the grandeſt works of architecture, ſculpture, and painting, and would go down from age to age, uninjured by the lapſe of time, ſole witneſſes to the beauty of a long-forgotten popular belief, or to the glory of ſome ſplendid city whoſe very ſite is now a deſert or a ſwamp? Yet we muſt not regret that the old Greek engravers worked without any idea of handing down either their own, or their city's, or their ruler's glory to poſterity. Had they thought of theſe things, the coins would have furniſhed far leſs truſtworthy evidence than they now do, and we ſhould probably have had many ancient examples of medals like that famous piece of modern times which Napoleon I. ordered to be ſtruck with the inſcription, *Frappée à Londres.*

Magistrates' Names. Not to be confounded with artiſts' ſignatures on coins are the names of the magiſtrates under whoſe authority the money was iſſued. All ſuch names are uſually written in large conſpicuous characters intended to catch the eye, while the names of artiſts are often purpoſely concealed; and are indeed ſometimes ſo ſmall as to be hardly viſible without a magnifying-glaſs. About the end of the fifth century B.C., at ſome towns, though not generally before the middle of the fourth, magiſtrates begin to place their ſignatures on the money. Sometimes we read their names at full length, ſometimes in an abbreviated form or in monogram; while not unfrequently a ſymbol or ſignet ſtands in place of the name. It is a matter of no ſmall difficulty to diſtinguiſh ſuch magiſtrates' ſignets in the field of a coin from religious ſymbols which are to be interpreted as referring more or leſs directly to the principal type. Thus, for inſtance, an ear of corn might refer to the worſhip of Demeter, or it might ſtand in the place of the name of a magiſtrate Demetrius. As a rule, all ſuch ſmall acceſſory ſymbols before the end of the fifth century have a religious motive; and the ſame ſymbol will be found very conſtantly accompanying the main type. But in later times, while the type remains conſtant, the ſymbol will be frequently varied. It muſt then be underſtood as the private ſeal of the magiſtrate entruſted with the ſuperviſion of the coinage. Unfortunately we know very little of the organization of the mints in the various cities of the ancient world. It has been proved that at ſome cities the chief magiſtrate placed his name on the money iſſued during his tenure of office; thus, in Boeotia, the name of the illuſtrious Epaminondas occurs; and at Epheſus we find the names of ſeveral of the chief magiſtrates, who are mentioned as ſuch by ancient writers or in inſcriptions. This was not, however, the univerſal rule: at Athens, for inſtance, the names of the Archons are not found on the coins; and at ſome cities the high prieſt, and occaſionally even a prieſteſs, ſigns the municipal coinage.

Under the Roman Empire, from Auguſtus to Gallienus, the Greek cities of Aſia, and a few in

Greek Imperial Coinage.

Europe, were allowed to ſtrike bronze money for local uſe. Theſe late iſſues are very unattractive as works of art, and their ſtudy has been conſequently much neglected. In ſome reſpects, however, they are even more inſtructive than the coins of an earlier age, which they often explain and illuſtrate. It is to theſe Greek Imperial coins, as they are called, that we muſt have recourſe if we would know what local cults prevailed in the outlying provinces of the Roman Empire, and eſpecially in what ſtrange and uncouth guiſes the half-Greek peoples of Aſia clothed their gods.

Only in this lateſt period do we find on the coinage actual copies of ancient ſacred images of Aſiatic divinities, ſuch as that of the Epheſian Artemis, with ſtiff mummy-like body, half human, half beſtial, with her many breaſts. It is not to be queſtioned that many ſuch monſtrous ſtatues exiſted in various parts of Greece, ſacred relics of a barbarous age, and that on great feſtivals they were draped in gorgeous attire, and exhibited to public view; but Greek art, as long as it was a living art, ſhrank from the repreſentation of ſuch images, and always ſubſtituted for them the beautiful Greek ideal form of the divinity with which it was cuſtomary to identify them.

Theſe Greek Imperial coins are alſo valuable as furniſhing us with copies of famous ſtatues of the great period of art, ſuch as that of the chryſelephantine Zeus of Pheidias at Olympia, the Aphrodite of Praxiteles at Cnidus, and many others; and they are particularly intereſting for the light which they ſhed upon the ſacred games, Pythia, Didymeia, Actia, Cabeiria, and other local feſtivals and religious ceremonies, of which, but for our coins, little or nothing would have been known.

CHAPTER III.

ROMAN COINS.

THE coinage of Rome falls naturally into two great claſſes: (1) the Family or, as it is often miſcalled, the Conſular ſeries, ſtruck under the Republic; and (2) the Imperial ſeries, of the period of the Roman and Byzantine Emperors, from Auguſtus to the capture of Conſtantinople by the Turks in A.D. 1453.

Introduction of Coinage. The date of the firſt iſſue of a coinage at Rome is uncertain. The preſence of roughly caſt lumps of metal in treaſure offered to divinities of fountains, mixed with large quantities of coins, ſeems to indicate that the firſt attempt at a metal currency at Rome conſiſted of rude lumps or ingots of copper of uncertain weight and ſize, **Aes rude.** called *aes rude*. Theſe pieces are without any mark of authority, and could only have circulated by weight. The introduction of a coinage at Rome has by ancient authority been attributed to Servius Tullius, and he is ſaid to have been "the firſt to mark copper pieces with the representations of an ox or some other animal or symbol." No coins of this remote period have, however, been preserved, and the tradition is doubtless without foundation. Considerably later than the time of the Kings are those quadrilateral or brick-shaped pieces of copper, having on one or both sides a symbol, from which they have been called *aes signatum.* These pieces must have **Aes Signatum.** been issued in considerable quantities, as they are not uncommon at the present time. They are of uncertain sizes and thickness, and were originally cast in large blocks, and afterwards divided into smaller portions. Like the aes rude, these pieces must have circulated by weight. They appear to have been in use up to a late period, even after the coinage had passed into another stage. To these rough pieces there succeeded a much more regular coinage, circular in shape, called *aes grave.* **Aes Grave** It consisted of a large copper coin, the *as*, the unit of the monetary system, and, being of a pound weight, called the *as libralis*, and of a number of fractional parts, called the *semis* (half), the *triens* (third), the *quadrans* (fourth), the *sextans* (sixth), and the *uncia* (twelfth). Multiples of the as were the *dupondius* (double as), the *quincussis* (five-as piece), and the *decussis* (ten-as piece); but these do not appear to have been issued at Rome, but only by the neighbouring cities, which adopted this heavy copper coinage. All the pieces of this new coinage are cast (not struck), in high relief, and without any kind of legend or inscription excepting the marks of value: for the as I, for the ſemis S, and for the other diviſions four, three, two, or one dot or knob. The type of the reverſe, a prow, was the ſame throughout, but that of the obverſe varied with each denomination. On the as was the double-headed Janus, to whom the firſt coinage was mythically attributed; on the ſemis the head of Jupiter, the protector of the Capitol; on the triens the head of Pallas, the protectreſs of Aeneas, or Minerva, the inventreſs of numbers; on the quadrans the head of Hercules, the tutelary genius of the farmyard, and thus in general the god of property and riches; on the ſextans the head of Mercury, the god of traffic and commerce; and on the uncia the head of Roma, herſelf the tutelary goddeſs of the city. The weight of the as was nominally that of the Roman pound of 12 oz., but very few ſpecimens extant come up to the full weight; they range generally from 11 to 9 oz. This may be the reſult of a firſt reduction of a pound of copper from the condition of aes rude, or large quadrilateral pieces of metal, aes ſignatum, circulating by weight, to the form of a real and ſyſtematic currency.

The origin of this libral ſyſtem is aſſigned by Mommſen to the decemvirs, and more particularly to the influence of the Lex Julia Papiria (B.C. 430), which ordered that fines ſhould not be paid in cattle but in money. But in ſtyle and fabric the libral coinage cannot be of ſo early a date. Anyone accuſtomed to the ſtudy of numiſmatics can ſee at a glance that theſe coins bear no trace of archaiſm, and cannot be imitations of types that originated in the fifth century. They belong rather to a time that correſponds with the fine period of Greek coinage. The Romans borrowed all their ideas of painting and ſculpture from the Greeks, and no doubt reſorted to the ſame ſource for the types of their coinage. It muſt therefore be ſuppoſed that the fines ordered by the Lex Julia Papiria were paid in metal by weight, and that the as libralis was an eventual but not an immediate effect of this law.

Early Gold and Silver Coins in Circulation at Rome.

Beſide this rather complicated ſeries of copper coins, no attempt appears to have been made by the State to introduce either of the finer metals, gold, or ſilver. In fixing the as to the weight of a pound, the State had, however, made it poſſible to accept in circulation the gold and ſilver coinages of neighbouring cities. At that period the pound of copper was worth a ſcruple of ſilver, a relative value which had for ſome time exiſted in Sicily, whoſe inhabitants for convenience of trade were deſirous that their ſilver money and the rude copper coins of Latium ſhould have a joint circulation. The coins that chiefly ſupplied this want were the gold and ſilver money of Campania, with the name ROMANO· or ROMA. The gold coin had for the type of the obverſe the head of Janus, and on the reverſe two warriors taking an oath over a youth ſacrificing a pig.[1] The ſilver coins vary in type, but the moſt common have on the obverſe the head of Janus,

Campanian Coins.

[1] Caeſa iungebant foedera porca.—*Aen.*, viii. 641.

and on the reverse Jupiter in a biga, or two-horse chariot, accompanied by the divinity Victory. Both gold and silver coins of these types are inscribed ROMA. The relative value of the coins in gold, silver, and copper is a very difficult question. At this period the usual proportion between gold and silver was 1 to 12, and between silver and copper 1 to 250; but, in order to increase the value of their copper coins, the Romans appear to have estimated them above their usual worth, thus making the silver and copper at a ratio of 1 to 183, and reducing in an equal degree the ratio of the gold.

Reduction of the As Libralis.

Although this large copper coinage must have proved most inconvenient for commercial transactions, a considerable period elapsed before there was any decided change in the Roman monetary system. The authorities of the Imperial age state with a very considerable uniformity of opinion that the change took place during the period of the first Punic war (B.C. 264-241), and that the as libralis fell suddenly to 2 oz., the weight of an as sextantalis. According to Mommsen, however, whose opinion is borne out by the coins themselves, the fall was not so rapid; and what took place appears to have been as follows. From a weight of 10 oz. (nominally 12), the as fell to 8 oz., and at length was reduced to 4, or to that of a triens, and thus became *triental.* This probably occurred about B.C. 269, when the silver coinage of Rome begins. The evidence afforded by the coinages of neighbouring cities subject to

Triental As.

Rome bear out this ſtatement. In B.C. 291 Venuſia was founded, and ſtruck coins of the libral ſtandard; and in B.C. 289 Hatria followed her example; but in B.C. 251, when Lipara became a Roman colony, we find that city iſſuing a triental coinage. It is therefore between theſe dates that the reduction of the as muſt be placed, and in fixing it to B.C. 269 we make it ſimultaneous with the introduction of the new ſilver

SEXTANTAL AS.

coinage. The dupondius (2 aſſes), treſſis (3), and decuſſis (10), were now iſſued at Rome, and alſo the ſemuncia ($\frac{1}{2}$ oz.) and quadruncia ($\frac{1}{4}$ oz.). Theſe two laſt coins, together with the ſextans and uncia, were now no longer caſt but ſtruck, and bore on the reverſe the inſcription ROMA; the other coins were all caſt as before. The triental as did not long preſerve its full weight, but about B.C. 250 fell to 2 oz., and was called the *as ſextantalis*. When the coinage became *ſextantal*, caſting was abandoned, and all coins were ſtruck, and bore the name of the city. Alſo the multiples

Sextantal As.

of the as were discontinued, as well as the semuncia and quadruncia.

First Roman Silver Coinage.

In B.C. 269 the first silver coinage was issued at Rome, and consisted of the *denarius*, its half the *quinarius*, and its quarter the *sestertius*. The legal weight of the early denarius was 4 scruples (72 grains), which gave a convenient number of scruples for each Roman coin. Thus the quinarius = 2 scruples, and the sestertius = 1 scruple, and the Roman pound of silver produced 72 denarii, 144 quinarii, or 288 sestertii. The reason for adopting this new standard for the silver coins is obvious, when we consider what had happened with the copper coinage. This, as has been shown, was reduced to one-third its original value, and the new sestertius was therefore an equivalent to the as libralis, of which many specimens must have still remained in circulation. In all indications of sums fixed at the period of the introduction of the new coinage, the Latin writers use as synonymous terms the words *sestertius* and *aes grave*. The relative value of silver and copper was by this arrangement maintained, although it did not long keep so, as the weight of the copper coins soon fell, and they became mere pieces of account or tokens, like the bronze coinage of the present day. In B.C. 217 the standard of the silver was reduced, and the as became uncial. The denarius was struck at 80 to the pound, and the quinarius at 160. The issue of the sestertius ceased, and was not again struck in silver, excepting at occasional intervals during the first century B.C. The quinarius, after a very short time, fell into disuse, and was only occasionally reissued. The denarius remained at this new standard for nearly three centuries, and maintained its purity throughout.

Another silver coin was also in circulation: this was the *victoriatus*, so-called from its type, which showed on the obverse the head of Jupiter, and on the reverse Victory crowning a trophy. This coin was first issued in B.C. 228; it was in weight 3 scruples, or three-fourths of the denarius, and was originally a Campanian coin; but after the fall of Capua, B.C. 211, the coinage of the Victoriatus was transferred to Rome, itself, where it continued to be coined for the use of the Provinces. It was also current at Rome, perhaps, however, to no great extent. When the weight of the denarius fell in B.C. 217, that of the victoriatus was reduced in like proportion, but after a few years its issue ceased. The type was afterwards adopted for the quinarius. Victoriatus.

When the as fell from sextantal to uncial, its value was also changed from one-tenth to one-sixteenth of the denarius. As the soldiers were paid after the old standard of ten asses to the denarius, that coin retained its mark of value X. By this reduction the relation of silver to copper fell to 1 to 112, less than half the original ratio. Thus the copper coinage became still more a money of account; and when in B.C. 89 it was again reduced to a *semuncial* standard no ill-effects were produced. In B.C. 80 the copper coinage Uncial As.

ceaſed; and, excepting a few pieces ſtruck in the eaſtern and weſtern provinces, it was not revived during the period of the Republic. In B.C. 16 Auguſtus introduced a new copper coinage conſiſting of a ſeſtertius of four aſſes, a dupondius of two aſſes, an as, a ſemis, a triens, and a quadrans.

Gold Coins, after B.C. 269. The only other pieces which remain to be mentioned are the gold. The early coins of 3, 2, and 1 ſcruple, marked LX., XXXX., and XX., with the helmeted head of Mars on one ſide and an eagle ſtanding on a thunderbolt on the other, are uſually conſidered a Campanian iſſue. Theſe were firſt ſtruck ſoon after B.C. 269; but from their extreme ſcarcity their iſſue could only have extended over a very ſhort period. The firſt purely Roman gold money was ſtruck by Sulla in B.C. 84-82. They bear his own name and that of his proquaeſtor, L. Manlius, and from their fabric appear to have been iſſued in Greece, probably as rewards to his veterans. The gold coins ſtruck by Julius Caeſar in B.C. 49 are of the ſame character as thoſe of Sulla; and it is not till after Cæſar's death that a gold coinage is firmly eſtabliſhed, which conſiſted of an *aureus* and a *half-aureus*, the former ſtruck at forty to the pound, and repreſenting in value twenty-five denarii.

Types. The original type of the denarius is, on the obverſe, the head of Roma wearing a helmet adorned with wings, and a griffin's head for the creſt; behind is the mark of value X; and on the reverſe, the Dioſcuri on horſeback, charging, their ſpears couched, their mantles floating behind, and their conical hats ſurmounted each by a ſtar, emblematic of the morning and evening; below, is the inſcription ROMA.

DENARIUS OF THE FIRST ISSUE.

This is no doubt a repreſentation of theſe demigods as they were ſeen, according to the legend, fighting for the Romans at the battle of Lake Regillus. Any change of type was at firſt very gradual. After a time the mark of value is removed from behind the head of Roma and placed under her chin, and the inſcription is transferred from the reverſe to the obverſe. About B.C. 125 the mark of value changes to X̶., and in one inſtance to XVI., the latter to repreſent ſixteen aſſes, the true value of the denarius at that time. About B.C. 90 the mark of value is no longer ſtamped on the ſilver coins. The firſt inſtance of a change in the head on the obverſe can be fixed with certainty to B.C. 100. In that year the Quaeſtors Piſo and Caepio, having been ordered by the Senate to purchaſe corn and to ſell it to the people below the market value, received a ſpecial privilege to iſſue coins to cover this extraordinary expenditure. To diſtinguiſh their coins from thoſe ſtruck by the officers of the mint, they varied the type by placing on the obverſe the head of Saturn, probably in allufion to L. Appuleius Saturninus, who had propofed the Lex Frumentaria. Seven years later, in B.C. 93, the monetarii iffued two fets of coins having the fame reverfes; but on the obverse of one fet was the head of Roma, and on the other that of Apollo. After this time the head on the obverfe changed year by year, being either that of a divinity, fometimes but rarely of Roma, or of a traditional or hiftorical perfonage. Thefe types were generally in fome way connected with the family of the monetarius. In B.C. 44, by order of the Senate, the head of Julius Caefar was placed upon the coins; and after a few years the ufual type is that of fome living perfonage, generally of him who iffued the coins.

The firft change in the type of the reverfe occurred about B.C. 217, when Diana in a two-horfed chariot is fubftituted for the Diofcuri. But this was an exception, and it is not till after a further interval of more than fifty years that we again meet with any variation. From about B.C. 160 the coins fhow a delight in recording the great deeds of Rome's heroes in the paft, in reprefenting the mythological and hiftorical traditions of the nation, and in illuftrating public events after the manner of medals. One of the earlieft hiftorical types is to be found on the coins, already referred to, of the Quaeftors Pifo and Caepio, who are reprefented diftributing largeffe to the public. A ftill more remarkable coin is that ftruck by Brutus after the murder of Julius Caefar, having on one fide his own head, and on

Historical and traditional types.

the other a cap of Liberty between two daggers, and the inſcription EID. MAR.

DENARIUS OF BRUTUS.

Brutus had already, when a monetary triumvir, recorded the famous deed of his anceſtor L. Junius Brutus, the baniſher of the Tarquins, by placing his head upon the coins. To the ſame claſs belong the coins of Sextus Pompeius, who for a time defied the efforts of Octavius to ſuppreſs his piratical excurſions. Theſe have on one ſide the pharos of Meſſana ſurmounted by a figure of Neptune, and on the other the monſter Scylla, half-dog, half fiſh, ſweeping the ſea with her rudder. They refer either to the defeat of Octavius at Meſſana in B.C. 38, or to the deſtruction of his fleet off the Lucanian promontory in the following year, on which occaſion Pompeius offered ſacrifices to Neptune for his timely aſſiſtance, and even ſtyled himſelf the ſon of Neptune. Of the traditional types, perhaps one of the moſt intereſting is that on a coin of the Poſtumia gens, with the buſt of Diana on the obverſe, and on the reverſe a rock on which is a togated male figure before a lighted altar extending his hand towards a bull. It illuſtrates the worſhip of that goddeſs at Rome, to whom, for the uſe of the inhabitants of Latium, then under Roman rule, Servius Tullius founded a temple on the Aventine. At their annual feſtival the augurs foretold the domination of Rome over all the Latin race, which was accompliſhed by Aulus Poſtumius at the battle of Lake Regillus B.C. 496. In conſequence of this victory, the Poſtumia gens claimed for itſelf the fulfilment of the prophecy. On a coin of the Marcia gens are the heads of Numa Pompilius and Ancus Marcius, and a naked warrior (*deſultor*) riding two horſes; theſe allude to the traditional deſcent of the Marcia gens from Mamerces, ſon of Numa, and the celebration of the games in honour of Apollo, which were inſtituted by the ſoothſayer Marcius. We have alſo ſuch legendary ſubjects as Tarpeia cruſhed beneath the bucklers, Aeneas carrying Anchiſes on his back and holding the Palladium, Ulyſſes returning from Troy and recogniſed by his dog, and the rape of the Sabines. Still more numerous are the ſimple repreſentations of the divinities of the Roman Pantheon.

The gold coins of Sulla and ſubſequent iſſues have types ſimilar to thoſe of the denarius. The copper coins of the reduced ſtandard preſerved their original types.

Moneyers' Marks and Names.

An important feature in the gradual development of the types is the moneyers' marks and names, which serve to indicate the ſucceſſive iſſues from the mint. At firſt this mint officer only placed a ſymbol, a fly, cap, ſpear, or prow, to diſtinguiſh his iſſue from thoſe of previous years. Later on he added his initial, then his name, firſt in monogram and finally in full, the prenomen on the reverſe, and the cognomen on the obverſe. Theſe inſcriptions are always in the nominative caſe. They cease about B.C. 36, when, after the defeat of Sextus Pompeius, and the ſubmiſſion of the triumvir Lepidus, amongſt the many honours which Octavius received from the Senate, not the leaſt was the commemoration of his victories in the types on the coins. To theſe was added his portrait, and from B.C. 29, when he was created Imperator, the coinage becomes imperial.

The right of iſſuing the coinage at Rome, as elſewhere in all Republics, belonged to the State, which fixed by decrees the ſtandard and the various denominations. At an early period the duty of carrying into execution theſe regulations was delegated to three officers, who were called the *tresviri auro*, *argento*, *aere*, *flando*, *feriundo*. The word *flando* may ſhow that theſe officers were nominated before the reduction of the as to the sextantal ſtandard. The office certainly exiſted before the adoption of the uncial as in B.C. 217, as we begin to meet with the initials and monograms of the moneyers before that change took place. It was an occaſional office at firſt, and appears only to have been filled up when freſh iſſues were needed for the uſe of the State. About B.C. 104, the more frequent occurrence of the moneyers' names ſhows that theſe officers were then appointed at cloſer intervals. Julius Caeſar increaſed the number of this magiſtracy to four, and theſe continued to be nominated annually till the diſ- Constitution of the Mint, Officers, etc.

ſenſions cauſed by the ſecond triumvirate. In B.C. 39 the office was quite ſuſpended, and does not appear to have been reinſtituted till B.C. 16, when Auguſtus, before his departure for Gaul, re-appointed the quatuorviri. The office was aboliſhed about the year B.C. 3, and the Roman coinage then entered on a new phaſe. According to law, each officer of the mint was independent of the other, and could iſſue his coins ſeparately or in conjunction with his colleagues. Theſe monetarii were not the only magiſtrates who could ſtrike money. The urban quaeſtors, ediles, and praetors were ſometimes charged with extraordinary commiſſions; but theſe caſes were exceptional, and generally in virtue of ſome unuſual expenditure. Such pieces were marked with a ſpecial formula, as Ex. S. C. (*Ex Senatus Conſulto*), or S. C. (*Senatus Conſulto*), formulas never uſed by the regularly appointed monetarii. The curule ediles were alſo occaſionally all wed to ſtrike coins to cover the expenſes of the great public games.

Local Mints and Issues. Beſides the coins iſſued in Rome, there were others ſtruck outſide the city. Theſe may be divided into two claſſes: the coinage of the neighbouring cities, and the *monetae caſtrenſes* or *nummi caſtrenſes*. It is evident from monograms and letters on certain pieces of rude fabric that a few cities, after they came under Roman juriſdiction, were allowed to retain the right of coinage. Amongſt theſe places were Luceria, Canuſium, Crotona, and Hatria. Theſe coins were of the ſame ſtandard as thoſe ſtruck at Rome. This privilege appears to have ceaſed during the ſecond Punic War, or ſhortly afterwards. The monetae caſtrenſes or nummi caſtrenſes are coins iſſued by the general for payment of his ſoldiers, whether as dictator, conſul, proconſul, or imperator. This right could be delegated by the commander to his quaeſtor or proquaeſtor, who uſually added his own name, and in ſome inſtances placed it alone, without that of his ſuperior officer. Theſe coins circulated throughout the Republic with the State coinage, although the authority of the Senate was not uſually inſcribed on them. Finds in Spain, Ciſalpine Gaul, and elſewhere, ſhow that the nummi caſtrenſes were ſtruck as early as the middle of the ſecond century B.C.; but their iſſue was ſuſpended for a time after the outbreak of the Social War. They are again found in large quantities from the time of the Civil War between Pompey and Caeſar till the death of Mark Antony. They may be claſſed under the following diſtricts: Sicily, Spain, Africa, Gaul, the Eaſt, which includes Greece and Aſia Minor, and Cyrenaica.

To the coins iſſued *extra muros* belong thoſe ſtruck by the revolted Italian States during the Social or Marſic War. Theſe are of the denarii claſs, and many bear the ſame types as the State coinage of the time, but they are of rude fabric. The greater portion have the inſcriptions in the Oſcan character, and bear the names of the leaders, Papius Mutilus, Pompaedius, Minius Jegius, and Numerius Cluen- Oscan Coins.

tius. Others, ſimply inſcribed ITALIA, are eaſily recogniſable as belonging to this claſs.

Classification. The coins of the Roman Republic may be claſſified in two ways, (1) by families, under the name of the gens to which the monetarius belonged, or (2) chronologically. In large collections for facility of reference, the arrangement under families is perhaps the more practicable, but by this ſyſtem the hiſtorical intereſt of the coinage is almoſt entirely loſt. There are a large number of pieces which have no moneyer's name, others with only a ſymbol, a letter, or a monogram. In the arrangement by families, many of theſe coins would find no diſtinct place. By a chronological arrangement, each coin has its place, and we are able not only to trace the ſequence of the coinage, and ſee how the types gradually developed, but alſo to follow the extenſion of Roman domination, as it ſpread throughout Italy to the Weſt, to the Eaſt, and onwards into Aſia, and acroſs the Mediterranean into Africa. The large ſeries of coins of Julius Caeſar, Pompey, Brutus, Caſſius, and the triumvirate, would teach us very little if arranged under the Julia, Pompeia, Junia, Caſſia, Antonia, and Aemilia gentes. For aſſiſtance in a chronological arrangement, we have the evidence afforded by the growth of the types, by hiſtory, and by the various finds. To this ſtudy Mommſen has given much attention, and the reſults of his labours are embodied in his learned work on the Roman coinage.[1] But more can be accompliſhed than

[1] *Geſchichte des Römiſchen Münzweſens.*

even Mommsen has done as regards a local classification, and this was done by the late Count de Salis, who arranged the Roman coins in the British Museum, both republican and imperial, in chronological and geographical order.

When Augustus in B.C. 3 abolished the office of the monetarii, he reserved to himself all rights connected with the gold and silver coinages, and these remained with all succeeding emperors. To the Senate, however, belonged the power of striking the copper money, and its authority was denoted by the letters S. C. (*Senatus Consulto*), which also served to distinguish the copper coins of Rome from those issued in the provinces. **Imperial Coinage.**

The coinage in circulation in Rome from that time was—in gold, the aureus, of forty to the pound, and the half-aureus; in silver, the denarius, of eighty-four to the pound, and its half, the quinarius; and in copper, the sestertius, of four asses, its half the dupondius, the as, the semis or half-as, the triens or one-third-as, and the quadrans or quarter-as. The aureus was worth twenty-five denarii, and the denarius sixteen asses. The as was nearly equal in weight and size to the dupondius, but it was distinguished by being of red copper; whilst the sestertius and the dupondius were of yellow brass or *orichalcum*, being a composition of copper and zinc. The earliest deteriorations in the Imperial coinage took place in the reigns of Nero and Caracalla; and in A.D. 215 the aureus was only the fiftieth of a pound, and the denarius became so debased that it contained

Argenteus. only 40 per cent. of pure ſilver. When Caracalla had thus corrupted the coinage, he introduced a new ſilver piece, called the *argenteus Antoninianus*, of ſixty to ſixty-four to the pound, which was worth a denarius and a half, and which ſoon became the principal coin of the Empire. This piece may be eaſily diſtinguiſhed from the denarius by its having the head of the emperor radiate and the buſt of the empreſs upon a creſcent or half-moon.

From the reign of Caracalla to that of Diocletian the greateſt diſorder prevailed in the coinage, and the period of the ſo-called Thirty Tyrants was one of complete bankruptcy to the State. Each Emperor debaſed the coinage more and more, ſo that the intrinſic value of the ſilver currency was not one-twentieth part of its nominal value. The argenteus ſupplanted the denarius, and after a ſhort time, from a ſilver coin became only a copper one waſhed with a little tin; and, having driven the copper money out of currency, became itſelf the only piece in circulation with the exception of the gold. Diocletian, in A.D. 296, put an end to this confuſion by withdrawing from circulation all the coinage, and iſſuing another entirely freſh one, baſed on the ſtandard of the currency of the firſt

Diocletian's Reforms. century A.D. The aureus was ſtruck at ſixty to the pound, and a new coin in ſilver, called the *cententionalis*, took the place of the denarius; whilſt in copper two new pieces were iſſued, called the follis and the denarius. Special intereſt is attached to this new coinage, as it affords the means of explaining the prices marked in the great tariff of the Roman Empire which was publiſhed in A.D. 301, and which fixed the "maximum" price of almoſt every article of food or produce that found its way into the market. It was the abrogation of this tariff which occaſioned a ſlight modification in the monetary ſyſtem during the reign of Conſtantine, who reduced the weight of the aureus to ſeventy-two to the pound, and gave to this new coin the name of *ſolidus* in Latin and *nomiſma* in Greek. This piece remained in circulation ſo long as the Empire laſted, maintaining its full weight; and when current at a later period in Weſtern Europe, it received the name of bezant or byzant. Conſtantine added two freſh ſilver coins to the currency, the *miliarenſis*, and its half, the *ſiliqua*, twelve of the former being equal in value to the ſolidus. Except ſome ſlight modifications in the copper money made by Anaſtaſius and by Baſil I., no further important changes remain to be mentioned. **The Solidus.**

The obverſe of the Imperial coinage had for its type the head or buſt of the Emperor, the Empreſs, or the Caeſar, and occaſionally that of a near relative, ſuch as the Emperor's mother or ſiſter. The type varied with the period. In Pagan times the head or buſt was laureate, *i.e.* bound with a wreath, or radiate, *i.e.* wearing a radiated crown, ſometimes bare, but rarely helmeted; in the Chriſtian and Byzantine period it is uſually adorned with a diadem or a creſted helmet. The portraits, too, may be divided into two claſſes, **Imperial Types.**

realiſtic and conventional. The early Caeſars, and their ſucceſſors to Gallienus, fall under the firſt claſs, and the remaining Emperors, including the Chriſtian and Byzantine, under the ſecond. The types of the reverſe are commonly mythological (divinities), allegorical (perſonifications), hiſtorical (events connected with the hiſtory and traditions of Rome), and architectural (the principal public

SESTERTIUS OF VESPASIAN.

buildings, eſpecially thoſe at Rome). On the coins of Veſpaſian and Titus is recorded the conqueſt of Judaea, figured as a woman ſeated weeping beneath a palm-tree, near which ſtands her conqueror, or elſe the ferocious Simon, who headed the revolt and only ſurvived to adorn the triumph of his enemies. On the large braſs of Titus is to be ſeen a repreſentation of the Flavian Amphitheatre, begun by his father and completed by himſelf, ſtanding between the Meta Sudans and the Domus Aurea, with its many ſtoreys or arcades, and its vaſt interior filled with ſpectators witneſſing the magnificent dedication feſtival of a hundred days. The coins of Trajan record his conqueſt of Dacia, Armenia, Meſopotamia, and his deſcent down the Euphrates and the Tigris to the Indian Ocean, the only Roman general who accompliſhed this feat. There are repreſentations of the Forum, the moſt memorable of all Trajan's works; the Circus Maximus, which he embelliſhed with the obeliſk of Auguſtus; and the Aqua Trajana, by which he turned a portion of the pure and limpid Aqua Martia into the Aventine quarter of the city. The coins of Hadrian, beſides bearing allegorical repreſentations of divinities, countries, and cities, are of ſpecial intereſt as illuſtrating his extenſive journeys into every Roman province, from Britain to the far Eaſt.

Such is the ſucceſſion of types till the reign of Gallienus, when their intereſt flags, and for the moſt part we meet with badly executed repreſentations of mythological perſonages.

The coins of the Chriſtian Emperors differ much in their character. At firſt the types are generally allegorical; and though free from Pagan intention are not without Pagan influence, as may be ſeen in the types of Victory inſcribing the Emperor's *vota* on a ſhield, or two Victories holding a wreath, or the ſeated figures of Rome and Conſtantinople. Though the coins of Conſtantine the Great are of a ſomewhat Chriſtian character, yet purely Chriſtian types are at firſt unuſual. After a while, however, Victory no longer holds a wreath, but ſtands graſping a croſs, and in place of repreſentations of ſome mythological perſonage we find the monogram of Chriſt formed of X and P. In the purely Byzantine period all the Pagan

Christian Types.

influence diſappears, and Chriſtian types prevail, the moſt common being that of the Holy Croſs raiſed high on ſteps.

Iconographic Types. The coins of the later Emperors of the Eaſt are ſpecially intereſting for their iconographic types. Repreſentations of a large number of ſacred figures are to be found upon them, and theſe repreſentations are far ſuperior in execution, and, therefore, of much greater value for the ſtudy of Chriſtian iconography than any to be found on the mediaeval coins of Weſtern Europe. The figures of Chriſt and the Virgin offer a variety of different attitudes. The former is moſt frequently ſeated, holding in one hand the goſpels and with the other giving the Greek benediction. The Virgin is frequently ſeated; ſometimes ſhe holds in her arms the infant Saviour, ſometimes ſhe crowns the Emperor who ſtands beſide her, often with both hands raiſed in the attitude of prayer. In one very intereſting type ſhe ſtands amidſt the walls of Conſtantinople. A number of Saints are alſo repreſented, among which may be cited St. George, St. Michael, St. Demetrius, St. Theodore, and (St.) Conſtantine the Great; alſo in one famous inſtance we ſee depicted the worſhip of the Magi.

Inscriptions. The inſcriptions on the coins of the Pagan emperors are either deſcriptive, giving the Emperor's name and the date, partly on the obverſe, and partly on the reverſe; or elſe they are of a dedicatory nature, adding to the name of the Emperor a reference to the type. From Titus to Severus Alexander the chronological character of the inſcription is maintained, giving the current conſulſhip of the Emperor, or his laſt conſulſhip, and the year of his tribuneſhip; but in the latter half of the third century we meet with the Emperor's name alone on the obverſe, and a dedicatory inſcription on the reverſe. Very little change occurs under the early Chriſtian Emperors, except that the legend on the reverſe loſes its mythological character, and it is ſome time before the gradual transformation of the Roman State into the Eaſtern Empire is traceable in the coinage. Anaſtaſius was the firſt who uſed Greek letters to indicate the value of the coins; yet although under Juſtinian I. the Greek language was much uſed by the people, it is not till the reign of Heraclius that the Greek legend ΕΝ ΤΟΥΤΩ ΝΙΚΑ is found upon the coins. In the eighth century the Greek titles of *Baſileus* and *Deſpotes* make their firſt appearance in the place of *Auguſtus*, and under the Baſilian dynaſty Greek inſcriptions occupy the field of the reverſe of both ſilver and copper coins; but the reverſe of the ſolidus retains its Latin form till the latter part of the eleventh century, when it is found for the laſt time on the coins of Michael VII., A.D. 1078. Alexius I. was the firſt Emperor who adopted entirely Greek legends for his coins, and after his acceſſion Latin never appears again on the coinage of the Roman Empire, which now loſes all trace of its Weſtern origin, and becomes purely Byzantine. The moſt remarkable change in the coinage of the late Byzantine period was the introduction of concave pieces, *scyphati nummi.* This form was introduced as early as the close of the tenth century, but did not become the prevailing type of the gold, ſilver, and copper coinages till the end of the eleventh.

Local Mints. When the Roman Empire came under the ſway of Auguſtus, the Roman monetary ſyſtem was impoſed as the official ſtandard in financial buſineſs throughout the Empire, and no mint was allowed to exiſt without the imperial licence. This permiſſion was, however, conceded to many Greek cities, which for the moſt part ſtruck only copper coins; a few iſſued ſilver, but the only local mint of which gold coins are known is that of Caeſarea in Cappadocia. Theſe coins are uſually deſignated Greek Imperial.[1] Pure ſilver coins do not appear to have been iſſued to any great extent; and, if we except the large ſilver pieces ſtruck in the provinces of Aſia, and uſually called medallions, the local currencies in this metal may be ſaid to have ended with the reign of Nero, when the abundance of copper money placed the ſilver at a premium, and gradually drove it out of circulation.

The copper coinage of the Provinces had for the type of the obverſe the head of the Emperor, etc., and for the reverſe ſome mythological or hiſtorical ſubject: the inſcriptions were always in Greek. In the ſecond century the iſſues of this copper money increaſed very rapidly; but as the Roman denarius became more and more debaſed, and the local mints could no longer make a profit by iſſuing coins on any local ſtandard, one city after

[1] See Chapter II., page 40.

the other gradually ceaſed to exerciſe the right of coining, and by the end of the reign of Gallienus almoſt the only provincial mint of importance remaining was that of Alexandria, which continued to iſſue its coins till the reign of Diocletian. This mint was able to hold out longer than the others, becauſe it adopted the ſame tactics as the imperial mint at Rome: as the denarius became more and more debaſed, Alexandria, to keep pace, lowered the ſtandard of all her coins, and the ſilver became potin, and the potin, copper. Alexandrian Coinage.

Apart from theſe mints there exiſted from time to time others, which iſſued gold and ſilver coins after the Roman types and ſtandard. It is probable that theſe coins were of the ſame nature as the *nummi caſtrenſes* of the time of the Republic, their iſſue being ſuperintended by the military or civil governors of the provinces. One of theſe mints was eſtabliſhed at Antioch in the time of Veſpaſian and continued through the ſucceeding reigns to Gallienus. Its coins, the aureus and denarius, are of a peculiarly rude fabric. The denarius was alſo ſtruck at Epheſus during the reigns of Veſpaſian and Domitian. In the weſtern part of the Empire Spain ſtruck coins of the Roman ſtandard and types in conſiderable numbers from the reign of Auguſtus to that of Titus, and in Gaul we find a large number of aurei iſſued during the ſame period. The coinages of Clodius Macer in Africa, of Clodius Albinus in Gaul, of Pacatianus, Regalianus, and Dryantilla at Siſcia, and ſimilar iſſues, muſt be conſidered as exceptional and as having no legitimate authoriſation.

When the baſe ſilver State coinage had driven the Greek Imperial copper coins out of circulation, Gallienus eſtabliſhed local mints throughout the whole Empire, which ſtruck money after the Roman types and ſtandard. The number of theſe mints was further increaſed by Diocletian, and they continued to exerciſe their rights till the extinction of the Roman rule in the Weſt and afterwards in the Eaſt. At firſt there was no indication on the coin that it was ſtruck out of Rome; but Diocletian placed on all the coins, both of Rome and elſewhere, a monogram or initial letter of the city whence they were iſſued.

Medallions and Tickets.

Beſides coins proper, there are certain pieces in metal which reſemble money in appearance, but which were never meant to paſs as currency. Theſe are the medallions, which correſpond to medals of the preſent time, and the tickets, which ſerved as paſſes to the public entertainments, etc.

The types of the medallions reſemble thoſe of the copper ſeſtertius, having on one ſide the portrait of an imperial perſonage, and on the other ſome mythological, dedicatory, hiſtorical, or architectural ſubject, which more often than in the caſe of the coinage has ſome ſpecial reference to the imperial family. The ſize of the medallion is uſually ſomewhat larger than that of the ſeſtertius, and it is eaſily diſtinguiſhed from the coins by the abſence of the letters s.c., by its finer workmanſhip, and by being in high relief. Theſe pieces were ſtruck in gold, ſilver, and eſpecially copper. The ſilver and copper medallions were apparently firſt iſſued in the reign of Domitian ; but the firſt gold ſpecimen extant is of the reign of Diocletian, after whoſe time gold and ſilver medallions are more general than thoſe of copper. The fineſt pieces were iſſued by Antoninus Pius, Marcus Aurelius, and Commodus ; but the quality of the work was fairly maintained at a later period, when the coinage had much deteriorated in ſtyle and character. Even during the reigns of Conſtantine the Great and his ſucceſſors, the execution of the medallions is throughout much ſuperior to that of the current coins. It is probable that theſe pieces were all ſtruck as honorary rewards or memorials, and were preſented by the Emperor to his troops or to thoſe about the court. It has been ſuppoſed that they were intended to be placed on the ſtandards, becauſe ſome are provided with deep outer rims, but this ſeems doubtful, as in all repreſentations of ſtandards on the column of Trajan and other buildings it may be ſeen that the medallions, with which they are adorned, have the buſt of the Emperor facing, whereas on exiſting pieces it is always in profile.

Of the tickets the moſt important are the *contorniates*, ſo called becauſe they have the edge ſlightly turned over. Theſe pieces are of copper, of the ſize of the ſeſtertius, but ſomewhat thinner, and they have for types on one ſide ſome mythological, agoniſtic, or hiſtorical ſubject, relating to the public games or to the conteſts which took place for the honours of the amphitheatre, the circus, the ſtadium, or the odeum; and on the other ſide, a head or buſt, imperial or regal, or of ſome philoſopher, author, or poet. The queſtion of the object of theſe pieces, and the time when they were ſtruck, has provoked much diſcuſſion, but theſe two points ſeem now to have been fairly ſettled. It appears that they were made for preſentation to the victors at the public games and conteſts, who uſed them as a kind of check, on the preſentation of which at ſome appointed place and time they were awarded the allotted prizes; and, judging from the fabric, their iſſue appears to have begun in the reign of Conſtantine the Great, and to have been continued to about that of Anthemius, A.D. 464-472, that is, for a ſpace of about 150 years.

Medallic Art. In the maſſive and rude forms of the early coinage of Rome, bold in relief, and not without ſome knowledge of the laws of perſpective, we ſee illuſtrated the ſtern, hard character of the Roman, whoſe entire attention was given either to univerſal conqueſt abroad or to agricultural purſuits at home. Art to him poſſeſſed no charm; he was devoid of elegance and taſte, and even the nobles prided themſelves on their natural deficiency in matters of art, which they conſidered unworthy of a warlike and free people. This feeling, at the end of the ſecond century B.C., became ſomewhat ſoftened by the preſence in Rome of the vaſt ſpoils of Greece, conſiſting chiefly of ſtatues and paintings; and if the people ſtill deſpiſed the practical cultivation of the arts, they were in general delighted with the beauty, or perhaps the novelty, of theſe acquiſitions. This increaſing taſte for art may be traced in the types of the coins, which during the Republic acquire a pictorial character. If compared artiſtically with the earlier period, this may be called progreſſive.

With the Auguſtan age came a viſible change, and Greek artiſts were encouraged to visit Rome, not only to adorn the temples of the gods, but alſo to embelliſh the villas of the rich, into many of which numerous original works from Greece, Aſia, and Egypt had already found their way. As the taſte increaſed, and it was impoſſible to furniſh all with original Greek works, there aroſe a great demand for copies of the moſt famous and beſt-known objects. Inſtances of theſe copies may be ſeen in the Britiſh Muſeum in ſuch works as the Diſcobolus, which is ſuppoſed to be taken from a bronze figure by Myron; the Townley Venus, which, if not a work of the Macedonian period, may be a copy of one; and the Apollo Citharoedus, probably adapted from ſome celebrated original, ſince two other nearly ſimilar figures exiſt. Though we cannot claim much originality for the Roman artiſts at this period, they are not mere ſervile copyiſts; by a frequent modification of the original deſign they give a ſtamp of individuality to their works. What has been ſaid of ſculpture applies alike to medallic art, and the effect of this Greek influence is very marked on the coins of the Auguſtan age, and eſpecially on thoſe of the two Agrippinas, Caligula, and Claudius. The mythological figures which we meet with on theſe coins often ſtrike us very forcibly as copies of Greek ſtatues. Jupiter ſeated holding his thunderbolt and ſceptre; Minerva leaning on her ſpear and ſhield ornamented with the ſerpent; Spes tripping lightly

MEDALLION OF ANTONINUS PIUS.

forward, holding a flower and gently raiſing her dreſs; and Diana ruſhing onward in the chaſe, her bow in her outſtretched hand, and her hound at her heels—are all repreſentations of Greek ſubjects. The coins of Nero ſhow the perfection which portraiture had attained, the growth of his paſſions being traceable in the increaſing brutality of his features; whilſt the coinages of Trajan, Hadrian, Antoninus Pius, and Aurelius diſplay the higheſt ſtate of Roman medallic art. With the decay of the Empire comes an immediate decline in the workmanſhip of the coinage; from Commodus to Diocletian it was one continued downward courſe. The coins of the early Chriſtian Emperors ſhow a ſlight artiſtic revival, and when, in later times, the artiſts of the Weſt poured into Conſtantinople, carrying with them all that remained of artiſtic life in the ancient world, they imported into the coinage that ſtyle of ornament ſo peculiarly Byzantine, the traces of which are ſtill to be ſeen in the architecture of the Greek Church both in Europe and Aſia.

CHAPTER IV.

THE COINAGE OF CHRISTIAN EUROPE.

UNDER this title is included the coinage of all that portion of Europe which was not ſubject to the rule of Mohammedan princes, from the fall of the Weſtern Empire to our own day. When we conſider what vaſt fields of ſpace and time are covered by this branch of numiſmatics, it will be ſeen to be too large a ſubject to be fully dealt with in a ſingle chapter. The difficulty is found to be increaſed when we take into account how many different intereſts the ſtudy touches. The mere economiſt, the hiſtorian, the ſtudent of the hiſtory of art, and the ſtudent of Chriſtian iconography, might each expect to have his enquiries anſwered were there an entire volume at our diſpoſal. The only circumſtance which makes it poſſible to deal with the ſubject briefly as a whole is the fortunate tendency which in all ages the different countries of Europe have ſhown to bring their coinage into ſome ſort of common conformity.

Of this tendency we have plenty of examples in our own day, as, for instance, the practical uniformity which by the "Monetary Convention of the Latin Nations" was established in the coinages of Belgium, France, Switzerland, and Italy; in the recently-established uniformity of coinage throughout the German Empire; and in the inclination which the establishers of this coinage have shown to model their currency upon that of England. The same kind of tendency among contemporary nations is to be detected throughout the numismatics of the Middle Ages, and in truth by no means diminishes in force the further we retreat toward the beginnings of mediaeval history; a fact which will seem strange to those who are accustomed to look upon the Europe of these days as a mere collection of heterogeneous atoms, and its history as nothing better than a "scuffling of kites and crows."

It is thus possible in some degree to study the numismatics of the Middle Ages, and of more modern times, as a whole; and in a very rough way to divide its history into certain periods, in each of which the most striking characteristics numismatically and the most important events can be pointed out, without any attempt to follow in detail the history of the currency in each land. When in a subsequent chapter we come to speak of the English coinage, a more minute treatment of that special branch will be possible. **Division of the Subject.**

The periods into which I propose to divide the numismatic history of Christian Europe are these:

Period I. Tranſition between the Roman and the true mediaeval: let us ſay, from the depoſition of Romulus Auguſtulus (A.D. 476) to the acceſſion of Charlemagne (A.D. 768).

Period II. From the riſe of the new currency which was inaugurated by the houſe of Heriſtal, and which attained its full extenſion under Charles the Great, for all the time during which this currency formed practically the ſole coinage of Weſtern Europe.

Period III. From the re-introduction of a gold coinage into Weſtern Europe, which we may date from the ſtriking of the *Fiorino d'oro* in Florence, in 1252, to the full development of Renaiſſance Art upon coins, about 1450.

Period IV. From this year, 1450, to the end of the Renaiſſance Era, in 1600.

Period V. That of modern coinage, from A.D. 1600 to our own day.

Special Points of Interest belonging to each Period.

This diviſion of our ſubject may ſerve at once to give the ſtudent ſome general notion of the ſort of intereſt which pre-eminently attaches to the numiſmatics of each period. If he is concerned with the earlieſt hiſtory of the Teutonic invaders of Roman territory, with what may almoſt be called the *prehiſtoric* age of mediaeval hiſtory, he will be diſpoſed to collect the coins which belong to our firſt diviſion. The coins of the ſecond period are of great value for the ſtudy of the true Middle Ages, not only as illuſtrations of that hiſtory, but for the light which they ſhed upon the mutual relations of the different nations of

Chriſtendom, upon the economical hiſtory of this age, and laſtly upon the iconography of this, the dominant, era of mediaeval Catholiciſm. The coinage of the third period illuſtrates, among other things, the riſe in wealth and importance of the Italian cities, the greater conſideration which from this time forward began to attach to the purſuits of wealth and commerce, and a conſequent growth of art and of intellectual culture. The coins of the fourth period, beſide their deep hiſtorical intereſt for the portraits which they give us of the reigning ſovereigns or rulers, are pre-eminent in beauty above thoſe of any other of the five periods, and alone in any way comparable with the money of Ancient Greece. Finally, the fifth period will be moſt attractive to thoſe whoſe hiſtorical ſtudies have lain altogether in the age to which it belongs.

Period I. From Augustulus to Charlemagne.

It is generally found that a monetary change follows ſome time after a great political revolution. People cannot immediately forego the coinage they are uſed to, and even when this has no longer a *raiſon d'être*, it is ſtill continued, or is imitated as nearly as poſſible. Thus, though from the beginning of the fifth century (A.D. 405) a ſteady ſtream of barbarian invaſion ſet into the Roman Empire, from the Viſigoths in the ſouth and from the Suevi and Burgundians and their allies in the north (in Gaul), no immediate change in the coinage was the reſult. The money of the Roman Empire in the Weſt and in the Eaſt circulated among theſe barbarians, and was imitated as cloſely as poſſible by them. The new-comers did not even venture to place their names upon the money; but the names of their Kings were ſometimes ſuggeſted by obſcure monograms. The firſt coin which bears the name of any Teutonic conqueror is a ſmall ſilver coin which ſhows the name of Odoacer (A.D. 476-490), and this piece is of great rarity. The Oſtrogothic Kings in Italy, after the acceſſion of Athalaric to the end of their rule (A.D. 526-553), and the Vandal Kings in Africa ſubſequent to Huneric (*i.e.* from A.D. 484-533), placed their names upon coins, but only upon thoſe of the inferior metals. The full rights of a coinage can ſcarcely be claimed until the ſovereign has ventured to iſſue coins in the higheſt denomination in uſe in his territory. Theſe full rights, therefore, belonged, among the people of the Tranſition Era, only to three of the conquering Teutonic nationalities: (1) to the Viſigoths in Spain, (2) to the Franks in Gaul, and (3) to the Lombards in Italy.

The Viſigothic coinage begins with Leovigild in 573, and ends with the fall of the Viſigothic kingdom before the victorious Arabs at the battle of Guadaleta in 711. The coins are extremely rude, ſhowing (generally) a buſt upon one ſide, on the other either another buſt or ſome form of croſs. Three main types run throughout the ſeries, which conſiſts almoſt excluſively of a coinage in gold.

The Frankiſh coinage is likewiſe almoſt excluſively a gold currency. It begins with Theodebert, the Auſtraſian (A.D. 534), and, with unimportant intervals, continues till the acceſſion of the houſe of Pepin. At firſt the pieces were of the ſize of the Roman *ſolidus* (*ſolidus aureus*), but in latter years more generally of the ſize of the *tremiſſis*. Below is a ſpecimen of a Frankiſh tremiſſis, ſtruck by Chlovis II. (A.D. 638-656), and with the name of his treaſurer, St. Eloi. It is noticeable that in this ſeries only a few pieces bear the names of the monarchs, while the reſt have ſimply the names of the towns and the moneyers by whom they were ſtruck.

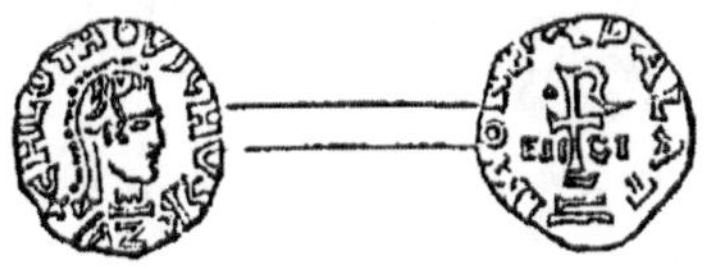

COIN OF CHLOVIS II.

The Lombardic coinage of North Italy—of the Kings of Milan and Pavia—begins with Cunipert (A.D. 687), and ends with the defeat of Deſiderius by Charlemagne, 774, in which year the Frankiſh king aſſumed the crown of Lombardy. The coinage is generally of gold, and of the type of Coins of the Lombards.

COIN OF CUNIPERT (680—702).

the coin of Cunipert repreſented in the figure, ſhowing on one ſide the buſt of the King (imitated from the Roman money), and on the reverſe the figure of St. Michael, legend SCS MIHAHIL. This ſaint was, we know, eſpecially honoured by the Lombards.[1] Another Lombardic coinage was that of the Dukes of Beneventum, who ſtruck pieces upon the model of the money of the Eaſtern Emperors.

The figure below repreſents the earlieſt papal coin, that ſtruck by Pope Adrian I. after the defeat of Deſiderius in A.D. 774.

COIN OF POPE ADRIAN I. (772—795).

PERIOD II. True Mediaeval Period.

The ſecond age is the true Middle Age, or what is ſometimes called the Dark Age; for with the beginning of our third period, which it will be ſeen is nearly that of the laſt cruſade, the firſt dawn of the Renaiſſance is diſcernible. It follows that in the ſcarcity of printed monuments of this age, the coinage of the period is one deſerving of a very attentive ſtudy, and of a much more detailed treatment than I am able to beſtow upon it.

The coinage inaugurated by the houſe of Pepin has the peculiarity of being totally unlike any currency which preceded it. The three chief autonomous barbarian coinages which we have enumerated above conſiſted almoſt excluſively of gold money; the coinage inaugurated by the

[1] Paul. Diac., *Hiſt. Lang.*, iv. 47; v. 3, 41.

Carlovingian dynasty was almost exclusively of silver. Silver from this time forth, until the end of our second period, remained the sole regular medium of exchange; a gold coinage disappeared from Western Europe, and was only represented by such pieces as were imported thither from the east and the south. Such gold coins as were in use were the bezants or *byzantii*, *i.e.*, the gold coins of the Roman Emperors of Constantinople, and (much less frequently) the *maravedis*, or gold coins struck in Spain by the Moorish dynasty of Al-Moravides (El-Murábitín). When Charles extended his Empire to its greatest limits, he introduced almost everywhere in Europe the new silver coinage, which was known as the new denier (*novus denarius*), or possibly in German as *pfenning*.[1] This denarius was the first coinage of Germany. In Italy it generally superseded the Roman denarius, or the coinage of the Lombards.

The usual type of this *New Denarius* was at first (1) simply the name or monogram of the Emperor, and on the reverse the name of the mint or a plain cross; (2) the bust of the Emperor, with a cross on the reverse; or (3) the bust of the Emperor on the obverse, and on the reverse a temple inscribed with the motto XPISTIANA RELIGIO. The pieces engraved on the next page, probably of Charles the Bald, are good examples of the earliest New Denarius.

[1] Our word *penny* (orig. *pending*, *pening*) is equivalent to the Old High German *Phantine*, whence *Pfenning*, *Pfennig*, and is derived from the Anglo-Saxon *pand* (German *Pfand*), a pledge. So Sanders and Skeat; but F. Kluge (*Etym. Wörterb.*, 1883) speaks doubtfully concerning the derivation of Pfennig.

types of denarii. One of the firſt documents referring to this coin is a capitulary of Pepin the Short (755), making its uſe compulſory in his dominions. In imitation of the new denarius, the *penny* was introduced into England by Offa, King of Mercia (757-794). The only exceptions to the general uſe of this denarius in Weſtern Europe were afforded by thoſe towns or princes in Italy which imitated the money of the Byzantine Empire.

CARLOVINGIAN DENARII.

This was the caſe with ſome of the earlier Popes, as is ſhown by the coin of Adrian I., repreſented on p. 80, which is quite Byzantine in type. Venice, which at firſt ſtruck denarii of the Carlovingian pattern, after a ſhort time changed this currency for one cloſely modelled upon the Byzantine pattern, while other neighbouring cities followed her example.

Mediaeval Coins of France. After the acceſſion of the race of Capet to the throne in France, the denarii continued little changed; and not only in the diſtricts over which ruled the early kings of this dynaſty, but over the greater part of what is now France. The number of feudal diviſions into which the country was ſplit up is ſhown by the numerous princes' names which appear upon the currency, but they did not cauſe much variety in the type of the money. The types continued to be various combinations of (1) an inſcription over all the face of the coin; (2) a rude buſt, ſometimes ſo degraded as to be barely diſtinguiſhable; (3) the conventional equal-limbed croſs; (4) a changed form of the temple, made to take the appearance of a Gothic arch between two towers. This type in its moſt altered ſhape has been ſometimes taken for the ground-plan of the fortifications of Tours.

Of Germany.

In Germany, the Carlovingian Emperors were ſucceeded by the Saxon dynaſty, which in its turn gave place to that of Franconia. During all this period (A.D. 919–1125), the denarius continued the chief, and almoſt the ſole, coin in uſe in Germany. Here, however, the variety of types was much greater, though moſt of theſe varieties may be ſhown to have ſprung out of the old Carlovingian types. The right of coinage was at this time even more widely extended in Germany than in France; but in the former country the nominal ſupremacy of the Emperor was generally—though far from univerſally—acknowledged, and his name was placed upon the coinage.

Of Italy.

In Italy, moſt of the towns which poſſeſſed the right of a coinage derived it directly from the

Emperor: thus Genoa obtained this right from Conrad III.; Venice (at firſt), Piſa, Pavia, Lucca, Milan, are among the cities which ſtruck coins bearing the names of the early German Emperors.

The firſt change which took place in the coinage of this our ſecond period aroſe in Germany from the degradation of the currency. This reached ſuch a pitch (eſpecially in the eccleſiaſtical mints) that the ſilver denarius, of which the proper weight was about 24 Engliſh grains, was firſt reduced to a ſmall piece not more than one-third of that weight, and next to a piece ſo thin that it could only be ſtamped upon one ſide. This new money, for ſuch it was in fact, though not in name, aroſe about the time that the dynaſty of Hohenſtaufen obtained the imperial crown, that is to ſay, in the middle of the twelfth century. The pieces were called ſubſequently *Pfaffen-Pfennige* (parſon's pennies), becauſe they were chiefly ſtruck at eccleſiaſtical mints; they are now known to numiſmatiſts as *bracteates*.

Pfaffen-Pfennige or Bracteates.

Beſide the coinages of France, Germany, Italy, and England, we have alſo briefly to notice thoſe of Scandinavia and of Spain, both of which were inaugurated during the ſecond age of mediaeval numiſmatics.

Arabic Currency in the North.

It is a curious fact that in the north, during the ninth and tenth centuries, we find that a large number of the contemporary Arabic ſilver coins (*dirhems*) were current. It ſeems at firſt ſight extraordinary that they ſhould have travelled ſo far, but leſs ſtrange when we bear in mind the extenſive

Viking expeditions which took place during the ſame period. As has been well ſaid by a recent writer,[1] the Vikings gave a ſort of reality to the popular notion that Chriſtian Europe was an iſland; for, ſtarting on one ſide to the weſt, they crept down all that coaſt of the continent until they reached the Straits of Gibraltar, and thence made their way into the Mediterranean, while on the other ſide, mounting the rivers which emptied themſelves into the Baltic—the Viſtula or the Dvina—with but a few miles of land-carriage they brought their boats to the Dnieper, and by that route upon the eaſtern ſide ſtole down into the ſame Mediterranean. It was in this way that the Vikings came in contact with the Arab merchants, and carried Arab money to the far North. It happened that this ſilver coin, the dirhem, was in weight juſt double that of the denarius current in Europe. Carlovingian denarii, Engliſh pennies, and Arab dirhems were alike hoarded by the Norſe pirates. It was not till the end of the tenth century that the Danes and Scandinavians began to make numerous imitations of the contemporary coinage of England. On the acceſſion of Canute the Great to the Engliſh throne, A.D. 1016, a native currency obtained a firm footing in Denmark.

Between the battle of Guadaleta (A.D. 711) and the union of the crowns of Caſtile and Aragon (A.D. 1479), the Chriſtian coinage of Spain was repreſented by the coins of theſe two kingdoms, Spain.

[1] Steenſtrup: *Normannerne*, page 1.

the reſt of the peninſula being in the hands of the Arabs or Moors. The coinage of Caſtile begins with Alfonſo VI. (1073-1109); that of Aragon with Sancho Ramirez of Navarre (1063-1094). The money of theſe countries is a denarius of the ſame general module as the contemporary denarii of France. The uſual types of theſe coins, as of all the contemporary coinage of Europe, conſiſt of ſome combination of a profile head and a croſs. Some pieces have a buſt, facing.

Iconography. The beſt ſpecimens of Chriſtian iconography contained upon coins are to be found in the ſeries of Byzantine coins. Of theſe mention has been already made. In Italy we have S. Michael on the coins of the Lombards; S. Peter on the Papal money; S. Mark on that of Venice; and S. John upon the coinage of Florence. The Virgin and Child appear on the copper coins of the Norman Kings of Sicily, and S. Matthew on thoſe of the Norman Dukes of Apulia. The *Sanctus Vultus* or holy icon of Chriſt, ſtill preſerved at Lucca, is repreſented on the money of that town. Upon the denarii of Germany and the Low Countries the iconographic types are alſo numerous, but the repreſentation of the perſons is very rude. Beſides the ſymbols of the Three Perſons of the Trinity—the Hand, the Croſs, and the Dove—the ſecond univerſal, the third comparatively rare—we ſee repreſentations of numerous ſaints, each on the money of the town of which he was the ſpecial patron. Thus we have S. Lambert for Liège and Maeſtricht, S. Servatius for Maesſtricht, S. Martin for Utrecht, S. Remachus (Stablo), S. Maurice (Magdeburg), S. Charlemagne (Aix la Chapelle), S. Boniface (Fulda), S. Kilian (Würzburg), S. Stephen (Metz and other places in Lorraine), SS. Simon and Jude (Magdeburg, Goſlar), S. Peter (Lorraine, Toul, Cologne, Berg, Trèves, etc.), the Virgin (Lower Lorraine, Huy, Hildeſheim, Spier, Augſburg).

On the coins of France ſacred types and ſymbols, excepting the croſs, which is all but univerſal, are leſs frequent during this age. The head of the Virgin occurs upon ſome coins. On the money of the Cruſaders iconographic types are very common.

The general revival of a gold coinage in Europe followed, as we have ſaid, the coining of the *fiorino d'oro* in 1252. But the firſt attempt to inſtitute a currency in the moſt precious metal was made in Apulia by the Norman Dukes of that place. Roger II., who had long made uſe in Sicily of Arabic gold coins of the Fátimy type, at length ſtruck gold coins of his own, which having his name and title, DVX APVLIAE, were called *ducats*. Theſe pieces were ſtruck about A.D. 1150. After the Hohenſtaufen dynaſty had ſucceeded the Norman Dukes in Apulia and Sicily, Frederick II., beſides ſtriking ſome gold pieces for his Arab ſubjećts, iſſued a very remarkable coinage modelled upon the old Roman ſolidus and half ſolidus: on the obverſe the buſt of the Emperor in Roman dreſs, and on the reverſe an eagle with wings

PERIOD III. Return to a Gold Currency.

difplayed. The legend was (obv.) FRIDERICVS, (rev.) IMP. ROM. CESAR AVG. The next State to follow this example was Florence, which in A.D. 1252 ftruck the gold florin, bearing on one fide the figure of S. John the Baptift, and on the other the lily of the city. The correfponding filver coin bore the rhyming Latin verfe,

The Fiorino d'Oro.

> "Det tibi florere
> Chriftus, Florentia, vere."

Owing in part to the great commercial pofition of the city, in part to the growing want felt

FIORINO D'ORO.

throughout Europe for a gold coinage, the ufe of the gold florin fpread with extraordinary rapidity—

> "La tua città . . . .
> Produce e spande il maladetto fiore
> Ch'a difviate le pecore e gli agni
> Però c'ha fatto lupo del pastore." [1]

So general was the currency obtained by this coin in Europe that we prefently find it largely copied by the chief potentates in France and Germany, as, for example, by the Pope John XXII. (at Avignon), the Archbifhop of Arles, the Count of Vienne and Dauphiny, the Archduke Albert of Auftria, the Count Palatine of the Rhine, the

[1] *Paradifo*, ix. 127-131.

Archbiſhop of Mainz, the free town of Lübeck, the Kings of Hungary and Bohemia, and the King of Aragon; while in other places, as France and England, where the firſt gold coinage was not ſo diſtinctly an imitation of the florin, it was obviouſly ſuggeſted by it.

The town of Italy which rivalled Florence in the extent of its iſſues was Venice, which firſt ſtruck its gold coin, the ducat, about A.D. 1280. The piece was afterwards called *zecchino* (ſequin). It bore on one ſide a ſtanding figure of Chriſt, on the other the Doge receiving the ſtandard (*gonfalone*) from S. Mark. The motto was of the ſame kind as that on the ſilver florin:

> "Sit tibi, Chriſte, datus,
> quem tu regis, iſte ducatus."

Genoa alſo iſſued a large currency in gold, as did the Popes (when they returned to Rome), and the Kings of Naples and Sicily.

The country north of the Alps which firſt iſſued an extenſive gold coinage was France. This was inaugurated by S. Louis, of whom we have numerous and various types. Of theſe the *agnel*, with the Paſchal Lamb, is the moſt important. Louis's gold coins are, however, now ſcarce, and it is poſſible that the iſſue was not large. It became extenſive under Philip the Fair.

Other changes were introduced into the money of Northern Europe at this period. Large denarii, *groſſi denarii*, afterwards called *groſſi* (gros), and in Engliſh *groats*, were coined firſt at Prague, afterwards chiefly at Tours. We have already ſpoken of the ſo-called *bracteates* of Germany. Theſe at this time became larger, to correſpond in appearance with the groſſi of France and the Low Countries. The uſe of gold coins and of groats became general in England during the reign of Edward III.

Fourteenth Century.

We have now arrived at the fourteenth century. The coinage of this period has certain marked characteriſtics, though the exact types are far too numerous to be even mentioned. The general characteriſtics of the fourteenth century money are theſe. In the firſt place it reflects the artiſtic, ſpecially architectural, tendencies of the time. The architecture of this period, leaving the ſimplicity of the earlier Gothic, and approaching the Decorated or Flamboyant ſtyle, when more attention is paid to detail, is very well ſuggeſted by the coins, where we ſee the effects of the ſame minute care and beautiful elaboration. Nothing can in their way be more ſplendid than the gold deniers of Louis IX. But as time paſſes on, this elaboration becomes extreme, the croſſes loſe their ſimple forms, and take every imaginable variety ſuggeſted by the names fleury, fleurt, quernée, avellanée, etc., while the cuſps and treſſures around the types are not leſs numerous and varied. The iconographic types are fewer upon the whole, eſpecially in compariſon with the number of types in exiſtence at this time; the croſſes themſelves are rather parts of the ſtructure of the coins than religious ſymbols, while now for the firſt time ſhields and other heraldic devices, ſuch as creſts, caps of maintenance, mantlets, etc., become common. The coin below may ſerve as a ſample of the coinage of the early years of the fifteenth century. Anyone who is acquainted with the hiſtory of this century, the white dawn, as we may call it, of the Renaiſſance, will diſcern in theſe characteriſtics of the coinage the ſigns of the times.

GROS OF THE FIFTEENTH CENTURY.

From the time of the iſſue of the fiorino d'oro, the initiative in moſt of the great changes which were wrought in the coinage of Europe belonged to Italy. It is naturally on the coinage of Italy that the firſt riſe of the artiſtic renaiſſance is diſcernible. It is in the fifteenth century that we firſt have portraits upon coins which are diſtinctly recogniſable, and no longer merely conventional. This century is the age of the greateſt Italian medalliſts, of Piſano, Sperandio, Boldu, Melioli, and the reſt; and though theſe earlieſt medalliſts were not themſelves makers of coin dies, it was impoſſible that their art could fail before long to influence the kindred art of the die-engraver. Portraits begin to appear upon the Italian coins about 1450. In the ſeries of Naples we have

PERIOD IV. The Renaissance Era.

Portraits.

during this century money bearing the heads of Ferdinand I. and Frederick of Aragon, and later on of Charles V. and Philip of Spain. The Papal ſeries is peculiarly rich in portrait coins, which were engraved by ſome of the moſt celebrated artiſts of the fifteenth and ſixteenth centuries, as by Franceſco Francia and Benvenuto Cellini. The portraits of Alexander VI., Julius II., and Leo X., are eſpecially to be noted. Cellini alſo worked for Florence, and we have a fine ſeries of the Dukes and Grand Dukes of this city, beginning with the Aleſſandro il Moro. In Milan we have coins with the heads of Aleſſandro Sforza, of Galeazzo Maria and the younger Galeazzo, of Bona, the mother of this laſt, and of Ludovico, and again, after the French conqueſt, of Louis XII. and Francis; later ſtill, of Charles V. and Philip. The coins of Mantua, Ferrara, Modena, Bologna, Parma, and Mirandola, are all worth a lengthy ſtudy. Venice and Genoa alone among the great towns of Italy kept their money almoſt unchanged, probably from commercial conſiderations, like thoſe which prompted Athens to adhere to the archaic form of her tetradrachms.

In France, authentic portraits upon coins firſt appear in the reign of Louis XII., and the beauty of the medallic art in France is well illuſtrated by the money of Francis I. and Henry II., and only one degree leſs ſo by that of Charles IX. and Henry IV. The celebrated engravers Dupré and the two Warins worked during the latter part of the ſeventeenth century. In England, the moſt beautiful portraits are thoſe on the coins of

Henry VII. and Henry VIII., though those of Mary and Edward VI. are only one degree inferior. The first Scottish coins with portraits are those of James IV. The German coins show traces of the peculiar development of German art. Those of the Emperor Maximilian are the most splendid and elaborate. Some of these are worthy of the hand of Dürer, to whom they have been attributed—though without much authority. Next to these, the series of Saxony, of Brunswick, of Brandenburg, and the coins of some of the German and Swiss towns, are to be noted. Even the remote northern lands, Sweden and Denmark, did not escape the influence of the age.

We must not omit to mention that the first rude coinage of Russia begins during this period. The country, however, possessed no properly ordered monetary system before the reign of Peter the Great.

PERIOD V. Modern Coinage.

The coinage subsequent to 1600, though it receives more attention from collectors than any other, must be pronounced, upon all historical grounds, by far the least interesting. And for this reason, if for no other, that our historical documents for this period are so voluminous that the coins can serve little purpose, save as illustrations of these documents; we cannot hope to gain from them any important light upon the times. Still, it cannot be denied that they have an interest regarded as illustrations merely, and some phases of this interest must be briefly indicated.

And first, in a general way, the modern coinage

illuſtrates well the riſe of the commercial ſpirit of the Weſt, which, taking a freſh ſtart with the diſcovery of America in the fifteenth century, has ſince become perhaps the chief determining force of our modern civilization. For now the coinage of all countries becomes as much improved for commercial purpoſes as it is artiſtically debaſed. The introduction of the "mill" in the manufacture of coins, in place of the older device of ſtriking them with a hammer, greatly improved their ſymmetry and the facility with which the money could be counted, while the uſe of an indented edge (commonly called "a milled edge") prevented the practice of clipping, which was ſo frequent in earlier times, and thus tended to keep coins to a juſt weight, and ſo greatly to ſimplify exchange.

Portraits of Sovereigns.

In a more particular way the coins of each nation are intereſting, as now always, or nearly always, bearing the head of the reigning ſovereign of the country. By this means we get a ſeries of hiſtoric portraits, which, if not of much artiſtic excellence, are, on the whole, truſtworthy. Theſe are the better from the fact that large ſilver coins (crowns or thalers) were now generally current in Europe, having been introduced during the preceding epoch. Guſtavus Adolphus, Frederick the "Winter King" of Bohemia, and other heroes of the Thirty Years' War; Chriſtina, Queen of Sweden; the "Great Elector" of Brandenburg; Charles XII. and Peter the Great; Louis XIV. and the contemporary Emperors of the Houſe of Austria; Frederick William I. of Prussia; Frederick the Great and Maria Theresa; an excellent series of the Popes; and finally the English sovereign, may be cited as the coin-portraits most likely to interest the historical student. The money of the Czar Peter deserves, indeed, a special attention, as it is the first regularly ordered series of coins issued in Russia, and, when compared with the money which preceded it, is a type by itself of the improvements which Peter introduced into the condition of the country.

Another feature connected with the large silver coins is a certain tendency which we find to make use of these for medallic purposes. This is especially the case in Germany. Among the earliest examples of this use may be cited the Luther celebration medals, issued in Saxony on the jubilees of the Reformation held in 1617 and 1630. The latest is the *Sieges-Thaler*, struck after the Franco-German War in 1870. The thalers issued by Ludwig, King of Bavaria, father of the present King, almost all of which commemorate either some event of his reign or the erection of some public building, form the largest series of coins of this medallic kind. The *schütz-thäler*, issued in Germany and Switzerland as rewards to those who had been successful in the national or cantonal shooting-contests, deserve mention in this place. The Papal coins are also frequently commemorative of historical events or of the erection of public monuments. Medallic Character.

Finally, in some of the towns of Germany

Views of Cities.

and Switzerland, the reverſes of the coins bear views of theſe towns, which are ſometimes ſo drawn as to form a very pleaſing deſign. Bâle, Lucerne, Zurich, Augsburg, Cologne, Conſtance, Danzig, Hamburg, Magdeburg, and Nuremberg, give examples in various degrees of excellence of this ſtyle of decoration. Thus, while the coinage of England, as we ſhall have occaſion to remark in the next chapter, toward the end of the ſeventeenth century loſes all artiſtic merit and originality of deſign, and ceaſes to perform any function ſave that of a medium of exchange, the ſame fate does not till more than one hundred years later overtake ſome of the continental iſſues. The lateſt coins which can boaſt of artiſtic beauty are thoſe of Napoleon I., eſpecially the ſeries ſtruck for Italy, on which the head is finely modelled. Some of the coins ſtruck during the French Revolution are intereſting from their containing alluſions to contemporary hiſtorical events.

Weights and Denominations.

The ſtudent of European hiſtory muſt be upon his guard againſt the danger of confounding *money of account* with coined money. As we have ſaid, the *new denarius* of Charlemagne was, from the time of its introduction till the thirteenth century, practically the only piece coined in weſtern continental Europe. The Roman gold coin, the *ſolidus*, however, continued to be uſed for ſome time, and for a much longer period it remained in uſe as a money of account. The ſolidus was tranſlated in the Germanic languages by *ſchilling*, *ſhilling*, *ſkilling*. Thus when we read of ſolidi and ſhillings it does not in the leaſt follow that we are reading of actual coins. The real coins which paſſed current on the occaſion ſpoken of were very probably ſimply the denarii, or pennies, but they were reckoned in the ſhilling or ſolidus of account which contained (generally) twelve denarii.

Other moneys of account were in reality ſimply weights, as (1) the *pound*, which was the Roman weight, the *libra*, containing twelve ounces, and in ſilver reckoned as equal to 240 denarii ; and (2) the German (Teutonic) weight, the *mark*, equal to two-thirds of a pound, *i.e.*, eight ounces and 180 denarii. It need hardly be ſaid that the actual weight of the denarius ſoon fell below this nominal weight of twenty-four grains. The recollection of the three denominations of *libra*, *ſolidus*, and *denarius* is preſerved in our abbreviations *£ s. d.* for pounds, ſhillings, and pence.

We have already ſpoken of the *groſſus*, or groat. The gold coins in France received a variety of names, of which the moſt uſual and the wideſt ſpread was *écu*. In Germany the earlieſt gold pieces ſeem to have been called *ducats*, and this name was continued in the ſubſequent gold coinage of the ſixteenth and ſeventeenth centuries. The weight of the ducat was founded upon the weight of the *fiorino* of Florence and of the *ducat* or *zecchino* of Venice, uſually about fifty-four grains, and theſe equal to about one hundred denarii of the old value. As, however, the ſilver coins contemporary with theſe ducats, though nominally denarii, were exceedingly debaſed, the relative value of the gold was very much higher.

One other coin-name of wide extenſion is the *thaler*, or dollar. The origin of this name lies in the Joachimsthal near the Harz Mountains, the mines of which furniſhed the ſilver from which theſe large pieces were firſt ſtruck.

CHAPTER V.

COINAGE OF THE BRITISH ISLANDS.

IN the laſt chapter a brief ſketch was given of the general numiſmatic hiſtory of Europe in Chriſtian times. In the preſent chapter we confine our attention altogether to the coinage of our own iſlands; not, however, from Chriſtian times only, but from the earlieſt period in which a coinage was known here. During the greater part of this ſketch it will be neceſſary to keep in mind the character of the currency in the other lands of Europe, for the monetary hiſtory of the Middle Ages—we might add the political hiſtory alſo—can only be properly ſtudied as a whole. The different epochs into which the hiſtory of the coinage of Europe has been divided will therefore ſerve us again in the preſent caſe. Our firſt period, however, precedes any of theſe epochs, for here we have to do with a currency in uſe in Britain before the introduction of Chriſtianity.

The circumſtances attending the firſt introduc-

The Coinage of the Britons.

tion of a coinage into these islands require some explanation. For the remote causes of this event we have to go back as far as to the times of Philip of Macedon, and to the acquisition by him of the gold mines of Crenides (Philippi). The result of this acquisition was, as is well known, to set in circulation an extensive gold currency, the first which had been widely prevalent in the Greek world. The gold staters of Philip obtained an extensive circulation beyond the limits of Greece—a much wider circulation than could have been obtained by any silver currency. Through the Greek colony of Massalia (Marseilles), they came into the hands of the Gauls. Massalia was, we know, the chief trading centre for the western lands, and for the barbarian nations of Northern Europe. It was not long after the death of Philip that Pytheas, the great "commercial traveller" of Marseilles, made his voyages to Britain and the coasts of Germany, as far as the mouth of the Elbe, or even, some think, the Baltic. We may readily believe that Marseilles was then in some relation with Northern Europe through Gaul; and it would seem that at this time the Gauls began to appreciate the use of a coinage, and to make one for themselves. The pieces thus manufactured were simply imitations of the gold stater of Philip. That coin bore on the obverse a beardless head laureate, generally taken to be the head of Apollo, but by some the head of young Heracles, or of Ares. On the reverse is a two-horse chariot (*biga*). The Gaulish coins were copies of this piece, gradually becoming more rude as time went on, and about the middle of the ſecond century B.C., the ſouthern coaſt of Britain adopted from Gaul the ſame habit. The earlieſt Britiſh coins were thus of gold, and though immediately only copies of the Gauliſh money, they were in a remote degree copies of the ſtaters of Philip of Macedon. The copies have, in nearly every caſe, departed ſo widely from the original, that, were it not that the Gauliſh money affords us examples of an intermediate type, we ſhould have

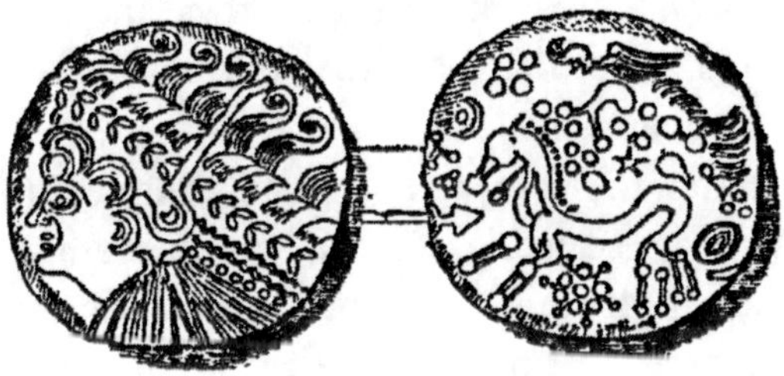

BRITISH GOLD COIN.

great difficulty in recogniſing the relationſhip of the Britiſh to the Macedonian coin. This is the hiſtory of the introduction of a coinage into the Britiſh Iſles.

The earlieſt coins of Britain were excluſively of gold, and were devoid of inſcription; any ſign which has the appearance of a letter being in reality only a part of the barbarous copy of the Greek coin, and without meaning in itſelf. About the time of Caeſar's invaſion, however, the coins begin to carry inſcriptions upon them—the name of ſome chief or tribe, the former being in moſt cases unknown to history save from his coins. One or two historical names do occur—as Commius, possibly the King of the Atrebates, who may be supposed to have fled into England ; and certainly Cunobelinus, King of the Trinobantes, the Cymbeline of Shakespeare. After the Roman conquest of Gaul, the native currency there was exchanged for the imperial coinage, and the change soon affected the coinage of Britain, which from about the Christian era began to make coins upon the Roman pattern. This fact is symbolical of the Romanising influence in the southern districts, which in this country, and in so many others, preceded the actual subjugation of the land by Roman arms.

Roman Mints.

After the complete Roman conquest the native currency ceased. Roman mints were not established in Britain until the time of Carausius (A.D. 287-293), who was Emperor in Britain only. Carausius' mints were Londinium and Camulodunum (Colchester). Between the time of Allectus and that of Constantine the Great no money was coined in Britain. The latter Emperor did not use a mint at Colchester, and struck at London only. The last imperial coins struck in Britain were those of Magnus Maximus (died A.D. 388).

Coinage of the Saxons.

From this period till after the beginning of the seventh century there is an almost total want of numismatic documents. There can be no question that the Britons continued to use the later Roman coins, especially those of Constantine and his immediate successors, which seem to have been ſtruck in large numbers. Such coins as came into the hands of the Saxon invaders would probably be cheriſhed rather as ornaments than for any other purpoſe. This would at any rate be the caſe with the gold coins. We find that Roman gold coins were very extenſively uſed as ornaments by the northern nations during the Viking age, and that they were imitated in thoſe peculiar diſc-like ornaments known as bracteates.[1] In the ſame way we find an imitation of a gold coin of Honorius engraved with Saxon runes. But gold belonged rather to the chiefs than to the great body of the people, and for the uſe of theſe laſt a regular coinage of ſilver appeared ſoon after the beginning of the ſeventh century.

The earlieſt Saxon coins, like the earlieſt Britiſh, The Sceat.
are anonymous, the only trace of letters upon moſt of them being nothing more than a blundered imitation of the coin-legend which the engraver was endeavouring to copy; and for this reaſon it is impoſſible accurately to determine their date. Theſe early Saxon coins are generally known to numiſmatiſts as *ſceattas*, and it ſeems probable that at one time they were diſtinguiſhed by that name. But *ſceat* properly ſignifies only treaſure,[2] and it is not likely that the word was at firſt used to denote any ſpecial denomination of coin.

The anonymous ſceattas, hardly poſſeſſing an

[1] Theſe bracteates are not to be confuſed with the German ſilver bracteates ſpoken of in the laſt chapter. Theſe were of gold, were made in the Scandinavian countries, and uſed as ornaments, not as coins.

[2] Primarily, *treaſure*; ſecondarily, *tax*.

hiſtoric, or, in the ſtrict ſenſe, a numiſmatic intereſt, have ſuffered too much neglect at the hands of collectors. For they are, in ſome reſpects, the moſt curious and noteworthy coins which have been iſſued ſince the Chriſtian era. In no other ſeries of coins do we find among ſo ſmall a number of individual pieces ſo great a variety of deſigns. The only ſeries of coins which can in this reſpect be compared with the ſceattas is that of the electrum pieces ſtruck in Aſia Minor in the fifth and fourth centuries B.C. The larger number of actual pieces among the ſceattas are indeed copied from Roman coins; many alſo from Merovingian ſilver pieces. But among thoſe which remain there are a great number of deſigns which ſeem perfectly original, and which far outnumber the *types* taken from any other ſource. Of theſe apparently original and native works of art we may count between thirty and forty diſtinct deſigns; and as they are probably earlier than moſt of the extant remains of Saxon or Iriſh architecture, and earlier than moſt of the Saxon and Iriſh manuſcripts, the intereſt which belongs to theſe pieces is very great. It is impoſſible to deſcribe theſe deſigns here; a great number conſiſt of ſome fantaſtic bird, or animal, or ſerpent, ſimilar to the animals which appear in ſuch profuſion in the Saxon manuſcripts, and at a later period in architecture.

It is evident that the Germanic peoples had a ſpecial partiality for a coinage in ſilver; and this may have dated back to quite early days, when the old consular denarii (*serrati, bigatique*[1]) were current among them. Mommsen tells us that when the silver coinage of Rome was debased, the old pieces of pure metal were almost absorbed for the purpose of exchange with the barbarian nations of the North. We find further evidence of this partiality in the fact that the silver sceattas were current in England before the grand reform made by the introduction of the new denarius into Europe,[2] and in the fact that this very reform was due to the most Teutonic (last Romanised) section of the Frank nationality. When, therefore, the great reform was brought about on the Continent, of which we have spoken in the preceding chapter, the effect was less felt in England than in any other land; it resulted merely in the exchange of the sceat for the silver penny, the former standing probably to the latter in the proportionate value of 12 to 20 ($=\frac{3}{5}$), though according to some documents they were in the proportion of 24 to 25.

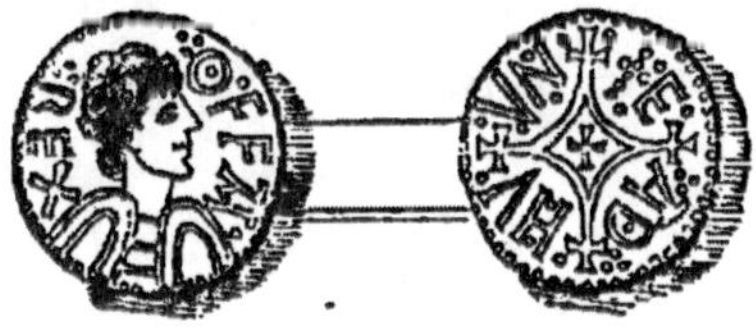

PENNY OF OFFA.

The penny, introduced about 760, differed from the sceat in appearance. The latter was small and thick, the penny much broader but thin. The The Penny

[1] Tacitus, *Germ.*, c. 5.
[2] See Chapter IV., p. 81.

pennies of Offa are remarkable for the beauty and variety of their deſigns and an artiſtic excellence which was never recovered in after years. The uſual type of the penny conſiſts of, on one ſide, a buſt, a degraded form of the buſt on Roman coins, and on the reverſe a croſs; but a very large number of coins have no buſt, and the croſs is by no means an invariable concomitant. The legend gives the name of the King as OFFA REX, AELFRED REX, or with the title more fully given, OFFA REX MERCIORUM. On the reverſe appears the name of the moneyer, that is to ſay, the actual maker of the coin; at firſt the name ſimply, as EADMUUN, IBBA, later on with the addition of MONETA (for *monetarius*), and later ſtill with the name of the town at which the piece has been ſtruck, as GODMAN ON[1] LUND. Town names begin to appear on coins in the reign of Egberht, King of Weſſex. They are not infrequent on the pennies of Aelfred, and univerſal from the time of Aethelred the Unready.

It is to be noticed that the treaſure plundered from England by the Vikings ſeems firſt to have given to the Northern people the notion of iſſuing a currency. Rude imitations of Saxon money are frequently diſcovered in the Weſtern Iſles of Scotland, and were doubtleſs iſſued by order or for the behoof of the Daniſh or Norwegian Kings of thoſe parts. In the ſame way we find that the Norſe Kings in Ireland iſſued a coinage in imitation of that of Aethelred II. Moſt of the early coins of Norway are likewiſe copied from the coins of this King. When the Daniſh dynaſty of Cnut

[1] Probably for [M]ON[ETARIUS].

(Gormsson) supplanted the English line of Kings, it made no change in the coinage of this country, though it was instrumental in introducing an improved coinage into Denmark.

Nor, again, did the Norman conquest make any immediate change in the English currency. The penny long remained the sole English coin. The variety of towns at which money was struck, of moneyers employed for this work, and of types made use of by them, reach their maximum in the reign of Edward the Confessor; but those of William I. and William II. (for the coins of these two Kings cannot with certainty be distinguished) are little less numerous. After the reign of William II., however, all these begin steadily to decline, until we find, in the reign of Henry II., only two different types, and the latter of the two extending, without even a change in the name of the King, into the reign of Henry III. This simplification in the appearance of the penny corresponds with a certain amount of centralization in the regulation of its issues. It would seem that down to the middle of the reign of Henry II. each separate moneyer was responsible for the purity of his coins, but that shortly after this date a general overseer was appointed, who was responsible to the King's Government. Norman Coinage.

In this approach to uniformity the general types which survive are those which have on the obverse the head or bust of the King facing, and on the reverse some kind of cross. At the beginning of the reign of Henry II. the latter is a cross *patée* cantoned with crofflets. This changes to a ſhort croſs voided (that is, having each limb made of two parallel lines, very convenient for cutting the coin into halfpence and farthings), and that again changes to a longer croſs voided. But in the reign of Edward I. the forms of both obverſe and reverſe become abſolutely ſtereotyped. And this ſtereotyping of the coin into one ſingle pattern is the firſt very important change in the penny which took place ſince its introduction. The ſtereotyped form henceforward until the reign of Henry VII. is as follows: *obverſe*, the King's head (ſometimes with ſlight traces of buſt), crowned, facing; *reverſe,* a long croſs *patée* with three pellets in each angle. In this reign, too, the names of moneyers ceaſe to be placed upon coins. Robert de Hadleye is the laſt moneyer whoſe name appears. Finally we have to notice that Edward I. re-introduced a coinage of halfpence, unknown ſince Saxon times, and firſt ſtruck the groat and the farthing. The groats were not in general circulation till the reign of Edward III.

Groat, Halfpenny, Farthing.

We have many documents ſhowing that in making theſe changes of coinage Edward I. alſo reformed the conſtitution of the mint in many particulars. His pennies obtained a wide circulation not only in this country but on the Continent. where they preſently (much as the *fiorino* did) gave riſe to imitations. The cloſeſt copies are to be ſeen in the money of the various ſtates of the Low Countries, as the Dukedom of Brabant, the Counties of Flanders, Hainault, etc. Other imitations are to be found in the denarii of the

Emperors of Germany and the Kings of Aragon. The English money never followed the rapid course of degradation which was the lot of the continental coinages; wherefore these English pennies (also called *esterlings*, *sterlings*, a word of doubtful origin) were of quite a different standard from the continental denarii. The English penny did, indeed, continually diminish in size, so that before the type introduced by Edward I. was radically changed (in the reign of Henry VII.), the penny had shrunk to not more than half of its original dimensions. But this degradation was slow compared to that which was undergone by the continental coins.

We have now for a moment to retrace our steps to the latter part of the reign of Henry III. In the preceding chapter we spoke of the re-introduction of a gold currency into Western Europe. Only a few years after the first issue of the *fiorino d'oro*, namely, in 1257, we find the first record in the annals of the English coinage of the issue of a gold currency. In this year Henry III. struck a piece called a gold penny. It represented on one side the King enthroned, on the other bore a cross voided cantoned with roses; and was at first valued at twenty pence, afterwards at twenty-six. The innovation was premature, and the coin being unpopular had soon to be withdrawn from circulation. It was not till nearly ninety years afterwards that a regular gold coinage was set on foot.

Introduction of a Gold Coinage.

In 1343 or 1344 Edward III. issued this new gold coinage. It at first consisted of pieces

Florins. called *florins*, half and quarter florins. The obverſe types of theſe three orders of coins were—(1), the monarch enthroned between two leopards; (2), a ſingle leopard bearing the Engliſh coat; (3), a helmet and cap of maintenance with ſmall leopard as creſt; a croſs formed the reverſe type in every caſe. Theſe pieces were rated too high, and were almoſt immediately withdrawn from circulation; after which were iſſued coins of a new type and denomination, *nobles*, half-nobles, and quarter-nobles.

Nobles.

NOBLE OF EDWARD III.

The nobles and half-nobles were the ſame in type; on the obverſe they ſhowed the King ſtanding in a ſhip; the quarter-noble contained a ſhield merely on the obverſe. The type of the noble is perhaps commemorative of the naval victory off Sluys. The legend on the noble was IHS [JESUS] AVTEM TRANSIENS PER MEDIVM ILLORVM IBAT (S. Luke iv. 30), a legend which long continued on the Engliſh money, and which has given riſe to a good deal of abſurd ſpeculation. The legend was a charm againſt thieves, but poſſibly bears ſome further reference to the victory commemorated by the type. The noble was made equal to half a mark (a money of account), or 80 pence English; in weight it was exactly that of the modern English sovereign, 120 grains. As it was of very pure gold, and perhaps the finest coin then current in Europe, it was, like the penny of Edward I., a good deal imitated abroad (always, we may be sure, to the advantage of the imitator), and laws were constantly being enacted, without much success, to hinder its exportation.

Anglo-French Coinage.

Before we leave the reign of Edward III. we must cast one glance at a class of coins which now began to assume considerable dimensions, namely, the *Anglo-French* money, or coins struck for the English possessions in France. These naturally followed French types and denominations. As early as the reign of Henry II. we have deniers struck for Aquitaine; Richard I. struck for Aquitaine, Poitou, and Normandy; Edward I. coined for Aquitaine and Bordeaux. But under Edward III. and the Black Prince (Governor of Guienne) quite a large issue of Anglo-French coins, both in gold and silver, appeared. The gold coins of Edward III. were the *guiennois* (standing figure in armour), *leopard*, *chaise* (King enthroned), and *mouton* (Paschal Lamb), and in silver the *hardi* (half-figure holding sword), *double-hardi*, *gros*, *demi-gros*, *denier*, *demi-denier* (also apparently called *ardit* [*sic*]). Edward Prince of Wales struck guiennois, leopard, chaise, demi-chaise, hardi (d'or), and *pavillon* (prince under a canopy), and in silver money the same as his father. Edward III. began, too, the iſſue of Calais ſilver groats, which (as Calais was really henceforth an Engliſh town) can ſcarcely be counted among the Anglo-French coinage. In every reſpect, this coin, as well as the Calais half-groat, penny, etc., exactly correſponded to the Engliſh money. In order to end the ſubject we may add that Richard II. ſtruck gold and ſilver hardis and demi-hardis as well as deniers and half-deniers. Henry V. ſtruck in gold moutons and demi-moutons, and poſſibly *ſalutes* (the angel ſaluting Mary), and gros. Henry VI. ſtruck ſalutes, *angelots*, and *francs*, and in ſilver grand and petit *blancs*. He alſo continued an extenſive iſſue of Calais money. With Henry VI. the Anglo-French coinage really comes to an end.

Edward IV. introduced ſome important changes into the gold coinage. He ſeems to have ſtruck a few nobles of the old type; but he very ſoon made an alteration in the type of the noble by ſubſtituting on the reverſe a ſun for the older croſs, and on the obverſe, placing a roſe upon the ſide of the ſhip, in the form of which laſt ſome other changes were introduced. From the roſe on the obverſe the coins came to be called *roſe*

Rose Noble.

nobles, and owing to changes in the relative values of gold and ſilver they were now worth 10s. (120 pence), inſtead of 6s. 8d. (80 pence) as before. To ſupply a coin of the old value of half a mark, a new gold piece was ſtruck, called at firſt the

Angel.

angel-noble, but ſoon ſimply the *angel*. On one ſide it repreſented a ſhip, bearing (inſtead of the King) a croſs; on the other was S. Michael overcoming Satan. The motto was PER CRVCEM TVAM SALVA NOS XPE (CHRISTE) REDEMPTOR.

> They have in England
> A coin that bears the figure of an angel
> Stamped in gold, but that's insculped upon:
> But here an angel in a golden bed
> Lies all within.[1]

Shakespeare is much given to playing upon this word,[2] and we find frequent allusions of the same kind in other writers, his contemporaries.

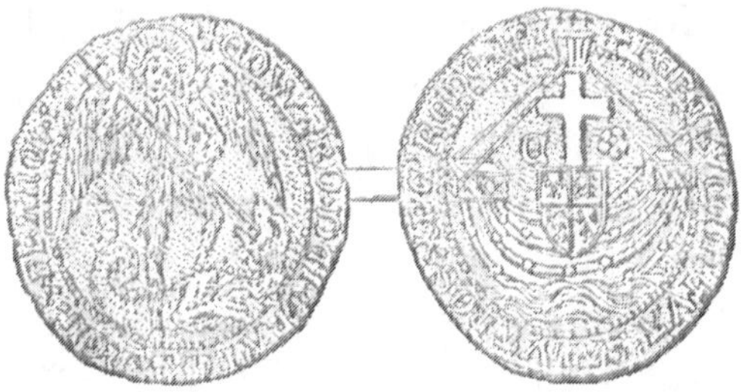

ANGEL OF EDWARD IV.

We have spoken of some coins probably struck by the Norsemen in the western isles. The regular coinage of Scotland does not begin before 1124 (David I.), when an issue of pennies (or *sterlings*, as they were generally called in Scotland) began. Even yet we find that offences were more frequently punished by fines of cattle than of money. At first the money of Scotland copied very closely the contemporary currency of England. Thus the pennies of David resemble those of Henry I.; the next coinage, that of William the Lion, grandson of David (1165-1214) resembles the money of

Scottish Coinage.

Sterling.

1 *Merchant of Venice*, ii. 7.
2 Cf. *Merry Wives of Windsor*, i. 3; *King John*, ii. 1.

Henry II.; the pennies of Alexander II. have ſhort and long voided croſſes, like thoſe of Henry III., and the coins of Alexander III. are like thoſe of Edward I. This King, like Edward, added halfpennies and farthings to the currency of pennies. But both the moneyers and the places of mintage are far leſs numerous in Scotland than in England. We count no more than ſixteen of the latter. The coinage of John Baliol and of Robert Bruce followed the type of Alexander III. The mint-records for theſe reigns are loſt: they begin again in the reign of David II. This King iſſued nobles after the pattern of Edward III.'s nobles. He alſo ſtruck groats and half-groats, pennies, halfpennies, and farthings.

All this time it will be ſeen that, deſpite the war between the two countries, Engliſh influence was paramount in determining the character of the Scottiſh coinage. There was preſent a certain French influence as well, which may be detected in minor marks upon the coins (fleurs-de-lis, and ſuch like), and which was exerciſed alſo in a very unhappy direction towards a degradation of the currency. Scotland followed the continental faſhion in this reſpect, and the commercial relations of the two bordering countries are marked by a perpetual chorus of complaint on the part of England of the debaſed character of the Scottiſh money. Thus in 1372 we find both Scottiſh gold and ſilver forbidden in England, and as if the prohibition had been relaxed, it is repeated in 1387. In 1390 Scottiſh money is admitted at half its nominal value; in 1393 it is forbidden again, ſave as bullion, and in 1401 there is a decree of Parliament to the ſame effect.

In the reign of Robert II. Scotland took a new departure by coining ſome gold pieces of an original type (no longer borrowed from England), viz., the *Lion* and *St. Andrew*. The firſt had Lion. St. Andrew the ſhield of Scotland with rampant lion, the ſecond the figure of St. Andrew with a ſhield on the reverſe. In the reign of Robert III. we note a further ſign of continental influence in the introduction of *billon* (baſe metal) coins. James I. ſtruck the *demy* (Obverſe, arms in lozenge; Re- Demy. verſe, croſs in treſſure) and *half-demy*; James II. ſtruck demies, St. Andrews, and half St. Andrews. James III. introduced two new types of gold coins, viz., the *rider* (knight on horſeback) and the Rider. *unicorn*, which ſhows a unicorn ſupporting the Unicorn. Scottiſh ſhield. The ſame King iſſued ſeveral denominations of billon coins, as *placks*, *half-placks*, Plack. farthings.

Hoards of Engliſh coins of the ninth century The Coinage of Ireland. have been found in Ireland, and were doubtleſs taken there by the Norſemen ſettled in the land. The actual coinage of theſe Norſe Kings, however, does not begin till the end of the tenth century. It copies almoſt invariably a peculiar type of the coinage of Aethelred II. (978-1016), having on one ſide a buſt uncrowned, and on the other a long voided croſs. After that we have no Iriſh coinage until ſubſequent to the conqueſt of a portion of the country by Henry II. Henry made his ſon John governor of the iſland, and John ſtruck in his own name pennies, half-pennies, and farthings, having on the obverſe a head (ſuppoſed to be that of John the Baptiſt) and on the reverſe a croſs. During his own reign John coined pennies having the King's buſt in a triangle on one ſide; on the other the ſun and moon in a triangle. Henry III.'s Iriſh pennies are like his Engliſh long croſs type, ſave that the King's head is again ſurrounded by a triangle. This diſtinction once more ſerves to ſeparate, in point of type, Edward I.'s Iriſh from his Engliſh coins, the reverſe types of the two being the ſame. John ſtruck at Dublin and Limerick, Henry III. at Dublin, and Edward I. at Dublin, Cork, and Waterford. One or two Iriſh pennies of Henry V. or VI. have been ſpoken of, but there was no extenſive coinage for Ireland between the reigns of Edward I. and Edward IV. The Iriſh coins of Edward IV. were very numerous, and conſiſted of double-groats, groats, half-groats, pennies, and (in billon) halfpennies and farthings. The types of theſe coins are varied; ſome are but ſlight divergences from the correſponding Engliſh coins; others have for reverſe a ſun in place of the uſual croſs; others again have a ſingle crown on obverſe, on the reverſe a long croſs; and another ſeries has three crowns, with the Engliſh ſhield for reverſe. The mints are Dublin, Cork, Drogheda, Limerick, Trim, Waterford, and Wexford. No gold coins were ever ſtruck for Ireland.

Hen. VII. We have thought it beſt to diſpoſe of the

Middle Age coinage of all Great Britain and Ireland before we come to ſpeak of any currency ſtruck in more modern days. We have thus carried our enquiries down to the acceſſion of Henry VII. The diviſion which has been thus made in our ſubject is not, indeed, an equal diviſion in reſpect of time nor even of recorded hiſtorical events; but it is obviouſly the moſt ſuitable which could be found. It correſponds generally with the line of demarcation ſeparating modern from mediaeval hiſtory, and with what we may call the inſtallation of the Renaiſſance. The line is always more or leſs ſhadowy and indefinite, but nowhere is it leſs ſo than in England. The Wars of the Roſes were the final act in the drama of mediaeval Engliſh hiſtory. When theſe ended in the Battle of Boſworth the new era definitely began.

We have ſeen[1] that this age of the Renaiſſance was for the whole of Europe, ſo far as the coins were concerned, notable chiefly as being the era of portraiture. Portraits begin on Engliſh coins with Henry VII. Up to his nineteenth year this King continued the older forms of ſilver currency, but in 1504 he made a complete change. He coined ſhillings in addition to the groats, half-groats, **Shilling.** pennies, etc., which had up to that time been current; and on all the larger pieces, in place of the conventional buſt facing which had prevailed ſince the days of Edward I., he placed a profile

[1] Chapter IV., pp. 91-93.

buſt which had not been ſeen on coins ſince the days of Stephen.[1] The buſt appears upon all coins of higher denomination than the penny. A new type was invented for the latter coin, the full-length figure of the monarch enthroned. The portrait of Henry VII. is a work of the higheſt art in its own kind. Nothing ſuperior to it has appeared ſince, nor anything nearly equal to it except upon ſome of the coins of Henry VIII.
Art. and Edward VI. The artiſtic merit of theſe pieces is ſo conſiderable that on that account alone they are worthy of peculiar ſtudy. It has been well pointed out by archaeologiſts that one intereſt belonging to the ſtudy of Greek coins lies in the fact that they are tokens of the artiſtic work of many places of which no other ſuch monuments remain. The ſame may almoſt be ſaid of the coinage of England during the Renaiſſance. In the great artiſtic movement of thoſe days, England ſeems at firſt ſight to take no part. While Italy, France, and Germany had each its own ſchools of artiſts, and each its ſeparate character of deſign, the conſpicuous monuments made in England were the work of foreigners; they were the ſculptures of Torrigiano or the paintings of Holbein. But as ſmaller monuments the contemporary coins are an evidence of native talent,

[1] It is worth noticing that Henry VII. was the firſt King ſubſequent to Henry III. who uſed a numeral upon his coins. Some of his ſhillings read HENRIC VII., others HENRIC SEPTIM. James IV. in the ſame way introduced (for the firſt time on Scottiſh coins) the word QUART. after his name.

for moſt of the engravers to the mint during theſe reigns bear genuinely Engliſh names.[1]

Increase of Wealth.

Next to the evidence of art-culture which the coins afford, comes the evidence of greater wealth, of larger trade and manufacture, and of an increaſed demand for a medium of exchange. When Henry VII. aſcended the throne, although the country had juſt been ſuffering from a bitter and prolonged civil war, the great maſs of the community was far from having been impoveriſhed thereby. It was during all this period ſteadily acquiring wealth, and the wealth of the country, as a whole, was upon the increaſe.[2] The careful reign of Henry VII. foſtered this increaſe. It need not ſurpriſe us, therefore, to find an addition made to the coinage of the previous reigns.

SOVEREIGN OF HENRY VII.

Henry VII. ſtruck the principal gold coins which were current in former reigns; that is to say,

[1] Nicholas Flynte, John Sharpe, and —— Demaire, are the names of the engravers during the reigns of Henry VII. and Henry VIII., as given by Ruding; the third may, likely enough, be a French name.

[2] Rogers' *Hiſt. of Prices*, vol. iv., Intr., p. 22.

the ryal, or roſe-noble (now worth ten ſhillings), the angel, and the angelet. In addition to theſe pieces he ſtruck for the firſt time the pound ſovereign, or double ryal, worth twenty ſhillings, a large gold coin repreſenting the King enthroned, and on the reverſe a double roſe charged with the Engliſh ſhield. The piece meaſured more than one-and-a-half inches, and weighed two hundred and forty grains; that is to ſay, twice as much as the preſent ſovereign. It was without queſtion the fineſt gold coin then current in Europe. It does not appear, however, to have been iſſued in large quantities.

Sovereign.

Hen. VIII. As we follow the hiſtory of coinage under the Tudors, we ſee the currency gradually increaſing in quantity and in the variety of its denominations. Henry VIII. did not indeed make any decided ſtep in this direction, and in one reſpect, preſently to be noticed, he made a conſpicuous retrogreſſion. Nevertheleſs he ſtruck ſome two-ſovereign pieces, and he largely increaſed the number of ſovereigns. At firſt this coin followed the type inſtituted by Henry VII., but later on a ſecond type was introduced, having the King ſeated on a throne upon one ſide, and on the other the Engliſh ſhield ſupported by a lion and a griffin. Henry coined half-ſovereigns of the ſame type. He coined crowns or quarter-ſovereigns and half-crowns in gold, having on one ſide the Engliſh ſhield, and on the other the Tudor roſe. He likewiſe ſtruck roſe-nobles or ryals, angels, and angelets of the types formerly in uſe. The

Crown.

older nobles had given place to the ryals which, at firſt meant to be current for ſix-and-eightpence like their predeceſſors, had at once riſen to be worth ten ſhillings. Henry VIII. now iſſued a new ſeries of nobles at the leſſer value. They were called George nobles, from having on the obverſe the figure of St. George on horſeback ſlaying the dragon. In ſilver Henry ſtruck pieces of the ſame denomination as thoſe of his father—namely, ſhillings, groats, half-groats, pennies, halfpennies, and farthings. The earlier groats ſhowed a profile buſt like the groats of Henry VII., but in 1543 for this was ſubſtituted a buſt facing or turned three-quarters towards the ſpectator, and the ſhillings of Henry VIII., which were firſt coined at this date, were of the ſame pattern. George Noble.

It has been noticed how in the continental coinage heraldic devices begin during the fourteenth century to take the place of the ſimpler croſſes which generally decorate the mediaeval coins. Owing to the ſtereotyped character of the Engliſh coinage between Edward I. and Henry VII., the ſame change could not be ſo early diſcovered here. But it is very noticeable in the currency of the Tudor dynaſty. From the time of Henry VII. the Engliſh ſhield (quartering France) is rarely abſent from the coins. It is laid over the croſs on the reverſe, which in many caſes it almoſt completely hides from view. A great number of the heraldic devices, with which we are ſo familiar in the chapel and tomb of Henry VII. in Weſtminſter Abbey, are introduced upon his coins or thoſe of his immediate ſucceſſors, as the lion, the griffin, the double roſe, the portcullis. The laſt device was derived from the Beaufort family (the legitimated children of John of Gaunt and Catherine Swynford), from which Henry could claim deſcent.

Wolsey's Groat.

One coin of Henry VIII. has a ſpecial hiſtorical intereſt. It is the groat ſtruck at York by Cardinal Wolſey when Archbiſhop of York. On the piece he placed his cardinal's hat; and as this act was accounted illegal, and even treaſonous, it was included in the bill of indictment againſt him:

> That out of mere ambition you have cauſed
> Your holy hat to be ſtamped on the king's coin.[1]

In the actual articles of indictment he is only blamed for, "of his pompous and preſumptuous mind," ſtamping the hat upon the *groats* ſtruck at York, as if the offence lay eſpecially in the iſſuing of ſuch large pieces with the inſignia of his office. Several prelates before his time had placed their own initials and ſome ſymbol of their dignity upon the pennies of York, Durham, etc. It may, however, have been conſidered part of the offence for which, as a whole, Wolſey was held to have incurred the penalties of a *praemunire*; namely, the endeavour to exalt unduly the poſition of his holy office, and to ſpread an impreſſion among the people that his legateſhip gave him a power independent of the power of the Crown. The groats and half-groats ſtruck by Cardinal Wolſey

[1] *Henry VIII.*, iii. 2.

have, beneath the ſhield on the reverſe, a cardinal's hat, and on either ſide of the ſhield the letters T. W.

Edward VI. ſtill further increaſed the gold coinage, eſpecially the coinage of ſovereigns. He ſtruck triple, double, and ſingle ſovereigns. The latter at firſt followed the type of Henry VII., and the earlier ſovereigns of Henry VIII., and Edward's double ſovereign was of that type alſo. Other pieces ſhowed the king with ſhorter robes, and of this type was the triple ſovereign. Later Edward adopted a new deſign—the half-length figure of the King to right, crowned, and holding the ſword and orb. On the reverſe was a ſhield. The half-ſovereign was either of this type, or elſe preſented only the buſt of the King, with head either crowned or bare, and the reverſe as before. In ſilver Edward VI. coined for the firſt time crowns, half-crowns, and ſixpences. The firſt two denominations repreſented the King riding to right, and the Engliſh ſhield on the reverſe. The ſhillings and ſixpences contained a buſt crowned, either in profile to right or facing. The coins of this reign are the firſt of Engliſh coins which bear a date. Edw. VI. Sixpence Date.

Mary coined ſovereigns of the earlieſt (Hen. VII.'s) type, the ryal of the old type—only that the figure in the ſhip is the Queen—as well as angels and angelets. Her groats, half-groats, and pennies were all of the ſame type, having a crowned buſt of the Queen to right upon the obverſe, and on the reverſe a ſhield. After her marriage with Philip, Mary ſtruck half-crowns and ſhillings. Mary.

The former have the buſt of the King and Queen upon the two ſides of the piece, while the latter have the two together, facing one another, "amorous, fond, and billing," on the obverſe, and on the reverſe a ſhield.

Elizabeth.

The number of coin denominations reaches its maximum in the reign of Elizabeth, from whoſe mints were iſſued no leſs than twenty diſtinct kinds of coin; that is to ſay, in gold, the ſovereign, ryal, half-ſovereign, quarter-ſovereign, half-quarter-ſovereign, angel, half-angel, quarter-angel; in ſilver, the crown, half-crown, ſhilling, ſixpence, groat, threepenny, half-groat (or twopenny), three-halfpenny-piece, penny, three-farthings, half-penny, farthing. Fortunately the varieties of type were much leſs numerous. It is enough to ſay that, of the firſt iſſue, the ſovereign, the ryal, and the angel did not materially differ from the correſponding coins of Mary, and that the ſovereign of the ſecond iſſue, with all its diviſions, ſhowed ſimply a crowned buſt to left, with hair flowing behind; on the other ſide, the ſhield, as before. The ſilver crown and half-crown had a crowned profile buſt to the left holding a ſceptre; and all the other denominations of ſilver coins had a crowned profile buſt without the ſceptre. The ſixpence and its diviſions were diſtinguiſhed by a roſe placed at the back of the head.

Three-penny, Two-penny, Three-half-pence, etc.

Another ſeries of coins ſtruck by Elizabeth deſerves particular mention. By virtue of a commiſſion, dated January 11th, 1600, or 1601, a coinage was ordered, "unknown to the Engliſh mint, either before or since her time, for it was by law exportable, and intended for the use of the East India Company." This is, in fact, the first appearance of a colonial coinage for England. This coinage consisted of silver pieces, the size of the Spanish coins of eight, four, and two ryals. The coins had on one side the royal arms, on the other a portcullis. The reasons which induced the Queen to take this step were sound and statesmanlike. The East India Company had applied for leave to export Spanish dollars, representing that these coins alone were familiarly known, and therefore readily accepted, in the East. The Queen determined to issue a currency which was genuinely English, in order "that her name and effigies might be hereafter respected by the Asiatics, and she be known as great a Prince as the King of Spain."

Coinage for East India Company.

All the facts which we have here summarised witness to the growth of fiscality throughout the prosperous reigns of the Tudor dynasty. With this growth a number of economic questions came to the front, which long continued to tax the sagacity of statesmen. We are too ready to congratulate ourselves on our supposed superiority over our ancestors in the art of statecraft. But there can be no question that in one respect we stand in a position of immense advantage over them—in respect, that is, to our mastery of the most important laws of economy and finance. There can be nothing more melancholy than to follow the enactments of successive reigns concerning the ſupply of bullion, and to note the radically falſe conception which the laws ſhow touching the nature of wealth. Thus, in the reign of Henry VII., an Act was paſſed forbidding "any perſon dwelling in the realm to pay to any alien for merchandiſe, or other thing, any piece of gold coined in *that or any other realm*," etc. And the ſame kind of enactments follow one another with weariſome iteration. A ſtill more important example of the ignorance of economic laws was ſhown in the liberties which the Government took with the purity and weight of the currency.

In earlier times, though men were no better inſtructed in economic ſcience, a certain healthy moral inſtinct had long kept the rulers from degrading the title of the coins they iſſued. Men's inſtinct had taught them that ſuch an act was fraudulent and unworthy, though in many caſes, eſpecially among the petty Princes (and ſtill more eſpecially the Prince Prelates) of Germany, this inſtinct had not been very efficient. Philip the Fair, of France, was one of the firſt who perſiſtently debaſed his coinage, and Dante's ſcornful deſcription of Philip—

> Lì ſi vedrà lo duol che ſopra Senna
> Induce, falſeggiando la moneta,
> Quei che morrà di colpo di cotenna[1]—

ſhows in what way his acts were regarded by healthy minds. But at the age at which we are

[1] *Paradiſo*. xix. 118.

now arrived, no traditional laws of morality could hold their force unquestioned. Why, it was said, seeing that a pound or a shilling gains its value through the royal sanction, may not the same sanction and the same value be given to a piece of much lower metallic value, and thus the Government be the gainer, and yet the subjects not the losers? From the time of Philip the Fair the degradation of the coinage had proceeded rapidly in France and in most other European countries, including Scotland; but the purity of the English money had been hitherto unassailed. Henry VIII. was the first of English monarchs who debased the sterling fineness of the coin. Some of his shillings and groats contained only one-third silver to two-thirds copper. Some of his gold coins consisted of about five-sixths of gold to one-sixth of silver. This evil continued through the two successive reigns, and was finally reformed by Elizabeth. Even Elizabeth, however, did not do her work completely, as, instead of withdrawing the base coins completely from circulation, she passed them over St. George's Channel for the use of her subjects in Ireland. It is a curious fact, and one which reflects credit upon the Queen and her advisers, that her reform of the coinage, wise, and indeed necessary as it was for the welfare of her subjects, was by no means forced upon the Queen by public opinion, but was on many sides viewed with great dislike. The opposite state of things would, of course, confer some slight and temporary advantages upon the producer, while the chief ſufferers would be, as Elizabeth's proclamation ſaid, "All poor people that lived of their hand-labour, as well artificers in cities and towns as labourers in huſbandry, or men that took dayetall wages, either by land, by ſea, or by freſh waters, and all mean gentlemen that lived upon penſions and ſtipends, ſoldes and wages."

Another reaſon why the old ſtate of things was favoured by ſome was that it would tend to bring into circulation a large number of pieces of low denomination. So ſoon as men had come to an underſtanding that a penny and a halfpenny were each not worth more than half their nominal values, a large number of what really were half-pennies and farthings would be found to be in circulation, and the making of ſmall purchaſes would be greatly facilitated. There is no doubt that theſe facilities were very much deſired by the poor, and the want of a lower currency was much felt. Up to this time no regular copper coinage had been introduced. The place of it was firſt ſupplied by the iſſue of tokens by private perſons. Theſe appear firſt to have been of lead. Eraſmus ſpeaks of the *plumbei Angliae*, apparently referring to leaden tokens in the reign of Henry VII. In the reign of Elizabeth there was a very extenſive iſſue of private tokens in lead, tin, latten, and leather. At length propoſals were made for the iſſue of a copper coinage—propoſals not then carried into effect, though ſome patterns were ſtruck.

Tokens.

To bring this ſubject to a cloſe, we may add

that in James I.'s reign the uſe of copper tokens was fully recogniſed, but that the monopoly of ſtriking them was conferred upon certain individuals, at firſt upon Lord Harrington. The ſame cuſtom was continued in the reign of Charles I., but in the abolition of privilege, which reſulted from the Civil War, the monopoly lapſed, and the reſult was an iſſue of copper tokens by the principal tradesmen of almoſt all the towns of England. Thus aroſe the *ſeventeenth century tokens*, which are much prized by their collectors, and which are often of conſiderable value to the local hiſtorian. In 1672 an authorized copper coinage of halfpennies and farthings was undertaken, and in conſequence the iſſue of copper tokens, though it did not immediately ceaſe, fell gradually into diſuſe. It revived again for a ſhort time at the end of the laſt century, and the early years of this; that is to ſay, from 1787 to 1795, and again from 1811 to 1815, owing to a ſcarcity in the copper money of the realm.

In order to diſmiſs the hiſtory of copper coinage, we have advanced far beyond the period with which we had been dealing. Before we again return to it—that is, to the Engliſh coinage immediately ſubſequent to the death of Elizabeth —we will take one glance at the Scottiſh coinage during the intervening period between the acceſſion of James IV., already ſpoken of, and that of James I.

Scotland.

The coinage of Scotland during this period follows the ſame general lines as the Engliſh

currency, but in many reſpects it likewiſe ſhows clear traces of French influence. Such influence is moſt apparent in matters belonging to art. We have ſaid that the firſt coins with portraits are ſome groats of James IV. Theſe pieces are noticeable from the fact that the type of buſt does not reſemble the type on any Engliſh contemporary coin. It is a three-quarter face to left. James V. at firſt ſtruck groats nearly reſembling thoſe of Henry VII.'s later coinage; that is to ſay, having a crowned buſt to right. The moſt artiſtically beautiful among the Scottiſh coins belong to this reign and the early part of the ſucceeding one—
Bonnet Pieces. the reign of Mary. Few coins are more beautiful than the bonnet-piece of James V., a gold coin in weight 88½ grains, midway between the Engliſh half-ſovereign and the angel, and having on the obverſe the buſt of the King wearing a ſquare cap or bonnet, or than the ryal of the early years of Mary's reign. The ſame influences which were at work bringing about an immenſe extenſion of the Engliſh coinage, are traceable, though in a leſs degree, between the reigns of James IV. and James VI. A large number of gold coins was iſſued during theſe reigns. James IV. ſtruck *St. Andrews*, *riders*, and *unicorns*, with the diviſions of theſe pieces; James V., *écus* and *bonnet-pieces*; Mary, écus or crowns, *twenty-ſhilling pieces*, *lions*, *ryals*, and *ducats*, with the diviſions of moſt of theſe coins. The ſame Queen ſtruck ſilver ryals, a much larger coin than had been iſſued by any of her predeceſſors. Her other ſilver coins were the

two-third and third ryal, and the testoon and half-testoon.

We have said that the Scottish monarchs went far beyond the English both in degrading the title and in debasing the material of their money. No professedly *billon* coins were ever issued from the English mint: the Scottish had long established a currency in this base metal standing between silver and copper.[1] Moreover, the Scottish penny had long fallen in value far below that of the English penny. The Kings of Scotland from time to time made efforts to establish a currency which should be exchangeable with that of the neighbouring country, and we find orders taken for the making of certain special denominations of money designed to serve this end. In 1483, for example, it was ordered that a gold coin should be struck of the fineness and weight of the English rose noble, and groats of the value of the English groat. The first of these designs was never carried into effect, but in 1489 a groat of the desired standard was coined. We find that it was equal to fourteen-pence Scottish, so that the Scottish penny was between a quarter and a third of the English coin. When James VI. came to the English throne, however, the Scottish penny had sunk to be one-twelfth of the English.

James I. of England and VI. of Scotland had to James I.

[1] Among these billon pieces the *bawbee* (corrupted from *bas pièce*, in Scottish French) was the longest remembered, and is the most worthy of notice. The name is expressive of the influences under which the base money was introduced into Scotland.

maintain a double currency. In fact, the coinages of the two realms were not brought into entire uniformity until the reign of Anne, when the complete union was effected. For Scotland James ſtruck in gold the *twenty-pound piece*, the ducat, the lion noble, the thiſtle noble, and the rider, before his acceſſion to the Engliſh throne; and in ſilver, the *ſword dollar*, the *thiſtle dollar*, and the *noble*, with the diviſional parts of moſt of theſe coins, as well as pieces of two, four, five, eight, ten, ſixteen, twenty, thirty, and forty ſhillings, and ſeveral billon pieces. After his acceſſion his peculiarly Scottiſh coins were the ſword and ſceptre piece, and the thiſtle mark.

The Engliſh coins of James were the ſovereign, and the double or roſe ryal. Theſe were during his reign generally current for thirty ſhillings. The type of the ryal was that of the ſovereigns of Henry VII. The half of this was the ſpur ryal, which at firſt followed the old type of the roſe nobles or ryals, but afterwards ſhowed on one ſide a lion ſupporting the Engliſh ſhield (quartering Scotland and France), on the reverſe the ſpur, or ſun as on the roſe nobles. The angel ſhowed ſome variety of type from that of the previous reign. But the moſt diſtinctive coin of James I., and that which ſuperſeded all the others, was the *unite* or

Unite.

broad, a piece of twenty ſhillings, and deſigned to paſs current in both countries. The type was at firſt a half figure holding ſword and orb; ſubſequently a buſt, either crowned or laureate. This laſt type prevailed, and earned for the piece the name *laurel*, while the motto FACIAM EOS IN GENTEM UNAM was the origin of its older name. The laurel wreath had never appeared upon the head of any previous Englifh monarch upon his coins. As it is commonly worn by the Roman Emperors on their money, it was moft likely adopted by James with the object of proclaiming his imperial rank as King of England, Scotland, and Ireland; for we find that he alfo, for the firft time, adopted the title Imperator upon fome of his medals.

It is noticeable that in the reign of James I. we for the firft time have the values of the coins given upon them. His thirty, fifteen, ten, and five-fhilling pieces in gold, and his fhillings, fixpences, half-groats and pennies, are marked with numerals expreffing their value. The cuftom was continued in the reign of Charles I., and during the Commonwealth. Value.

The variety of coin denominations reaches, as has been faid, its maximum under Elizabeth. From the time of the introduction of the unite this number begins rapidly to decline; fo that in the reign of Charles I. it almoft reached the fame fimplicity which it now has. A comparifon might, in truth, be inftituted between the refpective coinages of the Tudor and the Stuart dynafties and their refpective literatures. The greateft artiftic excellence belongs to the coinage (as to the literature) of the firft era, while that of the fecond era ftands next to it, and fuperior to anything which was fubfequently produced. In the fecond clafs we Number of Denominations.

find a marked tendency toward ſimplicity and adaptability to the ordinary needs of life.

Thus the ſilver coinage of the Stuarts is practically the ſame as that which now exiſts, with the exception that James I. did not ſtrike the ſmaller pieces, and that Charles I., in the midſt of the Civil War, ſtruck ſome large coins which were never afterwards reproduced. The crowns and half-crowns of James I. repreſent the King on horſeback, the ſhillings the crowned buſt of the King, the ordinary ſhield (now without any appearance of a croſs) forming the reverſe in each caſe.

Charles I. Charles I.'s uſual gold coinage is the unite, half-unite, and crown. Theſe pieces have the King's buſt on the obverſe, and on the reverſe a ſhield. His ſilver coins of higher denominations were like thoſe of his father, and the lower denominations follow the type of the ſhilling. After the outbreak of the Civil War, Charles adopted for the reverſe of his coins, both in gold and ſilver, what is called the Declaration type, namely the legend RELIG. PROT. LEG. ANG. LIBER. PARL. (The Proteſtant Religion, the Laws of England, and the Liberty of Parliament), written in two lines acroſs the field of the reverſe. Of this type he ſtruck ſome pieces of three pounds, as well as large ſilver coins worth twenty and ten ſhillings, made out of the plate which was brought by his adherents to the royal mints.

Charles I. eſtabliſhed mints at a great number of towns during the Civil War. Altogether we have coins ſtruck during his reign at the following places: Aberyſtwith, Briſtol, Cheſter, Cork, Dublin, Edinburgh, Exeter, London, Oxford, Shrewsbury, Weymouth, Worceſter, York. Beſide the regular coinage, there was during the Civil War a large iſſue of *ſiege-pieces* ſtruck in towns or caſtles which were in a ſtate of ſiege. Theſe are of Beeſton Caſtle, Carliſle, Colcheſter, Newark, Pontefract, and Scarborough. Some of the Pontefract pieces may count as the earlieſt coins ſtruck in the name of Charles II. The caſtle ſtill held out after the death of Charles I. Accordingly the governor placed upon the ſiege-pieces the legend CAROLUS SECUNDUS, or CAROL. II., etc., and on the other ſide POST MORTEM PATRIS PRO FILIO.

Various Mints.

Siege Pieces.

In artiſtic merit the coinage of Charles I. is

OXFORD CROWN OF CHARLES I.

only inferior to that of the earlier Tudor ſovereigns. This King, whoſe taſte in art is well known, employed upon his money ſeveral engravers of diſtinguiſhed merit. Among theſe were Thomas Rawlins and Nicholas Briot. The latter had firſt been engaged at the French mint, and while there had invented ſeveral improved methods of ſtriking coins; but finding no appreciation of his talents, he came to England, and was at once employed by Charles. Rawlins was for a long time engraver at the Tower mint, and on the outbreak of the Civil War he removed with the mint to Oxford. While there he executed the famous *Oxford Crown.* The coin, though it does not differ materially from the crowns of Charles I. of the Declaration type, ſhows, behind the figure of the King on horſeback, a view of the city of Oxford, in which the fortifications and ſome of the chief buildings, notably Magdalen tower, are very clearly pourtrayed.

Commonwealth. The Commonwealth employed as their engraver the famous medalliſt, Thomas Simon, whoſe medallic portraits, made in conjunction with his brother Abraham, are among the fineſt art products of that age. The extreme ſimplicity of the types upon the coins did not, however, give Simon room for any great diſplay of artiſtic talent. The coin bore upon one ſide a ſhield charged with St. George's croſs (England), on the other ſide two ſhields, one with St. George's croſs, and the other with the harp of Ireland. Preſumably the figure of the ſaint would have been conſidered more idolatrous than his emblem preſented in the baldeſt form. It is remarkable, too, that during the Commonwealth was adopted for the firſt, and alſo unhappily for the laſt time, the ſenſible device of having the legends both on obverſe and reverſe in Engliſh inſtead of Latin. On the obverſe was ſimply THE COMMONWEALTH OF ENGLAND, on the reverſe the motto GOD WITH US. In 1656, when Cromwell had been raiſed to the rank of Lord Protector of the Commonwealth, he entruſted to Thomas Simon the taſk of preparing dies for a new coinage, which had on one ſide the profile buſt of the Protector, on the other the ſhield of England, Scotland, and Ireland, and as an eſcutcheon of pretence that of Cromwell himſelf. The motto was appropriate and expreſſive, PAX QUAERITUR BELLO; and the whole piece was one of the fineſt of Thomas Simon's works.

All this time the coinage had been wonderfully ſimplifying its character. We have ſeen that James VI. definitely ſettled the ſilver currency upon the baſis (ſo far as the number of pieces is concerned) which it has ſince reſted upon. In the time of the Commonwealth there were, in reality, only two regularly current gold coins—the broad and half-broad. During the reign of Charles II. further changes were made, which had the effect of definitely ſettling the denominations of coins down to the middle of the reign of George III. So that all that is really worth record in the hiſtory of Engliſh money comes to an end in the courſe of the reign of Charles II.

After his reſtoration Charles II. continued for ſome little time to employ the engraver of the Commonwealth, Thomas Simon, and this artiſt executed the sovereigns and shillings of the first years of the reign, which are the most beautiful of Charles II.'s coins, in truth the last really beautiful coins which were issued from English mints. Simon was superseded by the engraver Blondeau, who had produced some patterns for Commonwealth coins, and Blondeau was succeeded by the Roettiers. Simon, in order to obtain his recall, executed his famous *petition crown*, in which the King is besought to compare the likeness upon that piece with any that was issued by the Dutch engraver to the Royal Mint. And in truth there can be no question that this pattern is in delicacy of treatment superior to any other English coin.

Guinea. In the same year the twenty-shilling pieces began to be called guineas, from the fact that most of them were made from gold brought from Guinea by the African Company. The pieces actually made of this gold were stamped with an elephant below the bust, but the name which properly belonged to them was transferred to all, and by accident the value of the piece increased from twenty to twenty-one shillings. The earliest coinage of Charles had consisted of twenty and ten-shilling pieces and crowns: but in 1662 this issue was exchanged for a coinage of pieces made by the mill, which were five guineas, two guineas, guineas, and half-guineas. This currency became henceforth stereotyped, so that from the reign of Charles II. to that of George II. inclusive, the English coinage consisted of five guineas, two guineas, guineas, half-guineas, in gold; of crowns, half-crowns, shillings, sixpences, groats, three-pennies, two-pennies, and pennies, in silver. The last four denominations were only struck for issue as Maundy money. The copper coinage during these reigns was much less fixed. It generally consisted of halfpennies or farthings. Five-guinea and two-guinea pieces were not coined after the reign of George II., and in the course of the reign of George III. a twenty-shilling piece was once more introduced, bearing the older name of sovereign.

Irish Coins of James II.

The only coins struck subsequent to the reign of Charles II. which are of interest to the historian are those issued in Ireland, by the authority of James II., after his abdication of the English crown.

The King began first, in order to meet his pressing necessities, to strike bronze (or gun-metal) sixpences. Subsequently he issued shillings, half-crowns, and crowns in the same metal. The value of these pieces was of course a purely fictitious one, the real worth of a crown being no more than a penny, and the loss to the nation when the money was recalled by William III., and paid for at its actual value, was very great, It was found that the total issue amounted nominally to £22,489, of which the actual value was £642.

The silver coins of Anne, made from the treasure seized in the Vigo Bay expedition, and in consequence marked with the word VIGO; the coinage of George I., marked with the letters

S S C, becauſe ſtruck from ſilver furniſhed by the South Sea Company; and that of George II., with the word LIMA, becauſe made from treaſure which had come from thence, are worthy of a paſſing notice.

The copper coinage of Queen Anne conſiſted of a limited number of farthings ſtruck in the year 1714. Several patterns for farthings were likewiſe made in this and the preceding year. They would ſcarcely claim mention here, but that through ſome unexplained cauſe a ridiculous notion has gained currency that theſe pieces are of immenſe value. Their real value is from 10s. to £1, if in fine condition.

CHAPTER VI.

EARLY ORIENTAL COINS.

THE art of coinage was, as has been already pointed out, of Oriental invention. The firſt coins ſeem to have been iſſued at about the ſame time, the ſeventh century B.C., by the Lydians in the weſt of Aſia, and by the Chineſe in the extreme eaſt. When the Perſians under Cyrus conquered Lydia they adopted the uſeful art of coinage; but choſe a ſimpler ſyſtem than the Lydian. If we exclude money iſſued by Greek cities under Perſian rule and by Perſian ſatraps on the occaſion of ſome military expedition, there were in uſe in the length and breadth of the Perſian Empire but two claſſes of coins—the gold *darics* and the ſilver *ſigli*, or *ſhekels*. The daric bore on one ſide as type a figure of the King ſhooting with the bow; on the other ſide a mere punch-mark or incuſe: it weighed rather more than a ſovereign, and was of almoſt pure gold. The ſhekel was of nearly the ſame ſize, and ſtamped with the ſame type; but was

Persia.

Darics and Sigli.

only two-thirds as heavy; in fact, almoſt exactly of the weight of a ſhilling. Twenty ſhekels were equivalent to a daric. It is intereſting to find the equivalents of pounds and ſhillings circulating throughout Weſtern Aſia at a period ſo early.

Until the Perſian Empire fell, darics and ſigli were probably the only officially recogniſed currency between the Halys in Aſia Minor and the borders of China. Other coins were, however, ſtruck in ſome places. The Greek cities of the coaſt were not allowed to iſſue gold coin ; but the Perſian rulers did not interfere with their autonomous iſſues of ſilver and copper money, which bore types appropriate to the ſtriking cities. And ſome of the ſatraps of the Perſian King were allowed, more eſpecially on the occaſion of military expeditions, to iſſue ſilver coins, the types of which curiouſly combine Perſian and Greek mythology, one of them, for inſtance, preſenting on one ſide the figure of Hormuzd, on the other that of Zeus. And there were certain ſtates which enjoyed, among other privileges of partial autonomy, the right of ſtriking coins. Such was the Lycian league, conſiſting of moſt of the cities of Lycia, all of which impreſſed on one ſide of their money a circular three-membered ſymbol, which moſt writers conſider to be of ſolar meaning. And ſuch were ſome of the kingdoms of Cyprus which were ſaved by the intervening ſea from complete ſubſerviency to the Perſian Empire, and the coins of which bear Greek legends written in the curious Cyprian character, of cuneiform appearance.

It is a curious fact that coinage in Phoenicia, one of the most commercial of ancient countries, should have been late in origin, and apparently not very plentiful. There are, in fact, no coins of earlier period than the third century which we can with certainty attribute to the great cities of Tyre and Sidon. Some modern writers, however, consider that many of the coins generally classed under Persia—notably those bearing the types of a chariot, a galley, and an owl respectively—were issued by those cities in the fifth and fourth centuries B.C. But it is certain, in any case, that the Phoenicians were far behind the Greeks in the art of moneying. **Phoenicia.**

With the invasion of Persia by Alexander the Great came a great change; and all the ancient landmarks of Asiatic government and order were swept away. During the life of Alexander the Great the coins bearing his name and his types circulated throughout Asia; and after his death the same range of currency was attained by the money of the early Seleucid Kings of Syria—Seleucus I., Antiochus I., and Antiochus II., who virtually succeeded to the dominions of the Persian Kings, and tried in many respects to carry on their policy. Of these monarchs we possess a splendid series of coins, beginning with Seleucus, the general of Alexander, and going down to Tigranes. Their features are thoroughly familiar to us, and by the help of their portraits we can **Successors of Alexander.**

judge more ſatisfactorily of their appearance in hiſtory as recorded by Juſtin and Appian. At firſt their rule extended from the Aegean Sea to the great deſert of Gobi; and their coins were iſſued by numberleſs mints throughout Aſia, and copied by the barbarous tribes of the Chineſe and Indian frontiers.

In the reign of Antiochus II., however, the Syro-Greek kingdom began to fall to pieces; and with its decay Oriental coinage, as oppoſed to Greek, may properly be ſaid to commence. About B.C. 250 the Greek ſatraps of the wealthy provinces of Bactria and India became independent; and the Parthian Arſaces raiſed the ſtandard of a ſucceſſful revolt on the ſouthern ſhores of the Caſpian. In the next century ſmaller kingdoms aroſe in Arabia, Armenia, and Meſopotamia; and the Jewiſh people wreſted their independence from the hands of Antiochus Epiphanes. In the far Eaſt rude tribes of Sacae and Huns from the borders of China ſwept down on the eaſtern provinces of the Perſian Empire, and founded dynaſties which ſeem, however, to have ſoon paſſed away.

Beginning of Oriental Coinage.

I ſhall not ſpeak of Aſia Minor on the weſt, for that diſtrict was dominated by Greek and Roman influences; nor of China on the eaſt; each of theſe regions is treated of elſewhere in this volume. The vaſt ſpace between theſe two extremes may be divided into three regions: (1) Armenia, Syria, and the country to the weſt of the Tigris and the Caſpian; (2) Central Aſia;

(3) India and Afghaniſtan. We will ſpeak in turn of the coins of the two former regions, during the whole period which elapſed between the break-up of the Syro-Greek kingdom and the conquering ſpread of Iſlam—that is to ſay, from the third century before, until the eighth century after, the Chriſtian era. India is reſerved for a ſeparate chapter.

The earlieſt coins which we poſſeſs which belong diſtinctively to Central Aſia are thoſe recently diſcovered in Bokhara, bearing the name of Andragoras, who muſt have been a revolted Greek ſatrap of Parthia or Media. Central Asia.

In the courſe of the ſecond century the Parthians, under their great King Mithradates, occupied all Mid-Aſia, or rather gained a ſort of lordſhip over it, and defended it for centuries from the attacks of the Greeks and Romans on the one ſide, and of the Huns on the other. The Parthian ſilver coins conſiſt of two diſtinct claſſes—regal and civic. The regal coins are of ſilver, of the weight of an Attic drachm, 60-65 grains, and bear during the whole of Parthian hiſtory uniform types—the head of the ruling King on one ſide, and on the other the firſt King, Arſaces, ſeated, holding a bow. The civic coins were iſſued by the semi-Greek cities of Perſia and Meſopotamia. They are four times as heavy, and preſent a greater variety of type. Subſidiary copper pieces accompany each ſeries. Parthians.

As the Parthians were conſtantly at war with the Syro-Greek kingdom ſo long as it laſted, it may at firſt ſurpriſe us to find that the legends of the Parthian coins, except in the caſe of a few of the lateſt, are in Greek. The date of them is indicated by the increaſing complexity of theſe legends as time goes on. All the ſucceſſors of the firſt Arſaces keep his name as their dynaſtic title, juſt as all the Kings of Egypt are ſtyled Ptolemy, and the Roman Emperors Auguſtus; but they add to this dynaſtic name a conſtantly increaſing number of epithets. In fact, the number of theſe epithets which are to be found on a coin is uſually the readieſt means of aſſigning its date. The earlieſt pieces bear only the legend Ἀρσάκου or βασιλέως Ἀρσάκου; but already the ſecond King Tiridates aſſumes the title of Great King, βασιλεὺς μέγας; his ſucceſſors add a variety of epithets, θεοπατὼς, ἐπιφάνης, εὐεργέτης, and the like, until, under Orodes the Great, we reach the formula βασιλέως μεγάλου Ἀρσάκου εὐεργέτου δικαίου ἐπιφάνους φιλέλληνος, which remains uſual until the end of the dynaſty. The laſt-mentioned title, Philhellen, is intereſting, and records the fact that, at all events after the fall of the Syro-Greek kingdom, the Parthian Kings were anxious to ſecure to themſelves the goodwill of the ſemi-Greek population which dwelt in many of the large towns under their rule.

The title of "Great King" was not in the ſtyle of the Parthian monarchs a mere parade or an unmeaning phraſe. It ſignified that he was maſter of a number of under-kings or ſatraps, who ruled under his authority the various diſtricts of Central Aſia, and in compariſon with whom he might well be called great. Some of the rulers adopt the alternative title, "King of Kings," which has much the ſame meaning. The coins ſupply us with full and truſtworthy information as to the dreſs and armour of thoſe Parthian horſemen who more than once ſpread the terror of their name as far as Rome.

The great cities of Meſopotamia, ſuch as Charax and Seleucia on the Tigris, in all probability iſſued the large coins already mentioned. The type of theſe is more varied. Before

AN EARLY PARTHIAN KING.

the time of Orodes it is like that of the regal money; but after that time it uſually repreſents the Parthian King ſeated, receiving a wreath either from the goddeſs Nike (Victory), or from Pallas, or more often from a City perſonified in a female deity who holds a cornucopiae. The head of a perſonified City appears on the copper pieces which go with the civic coins. Both ſilver and copper bear a date, the year in which the coin was ſtruck according to the Seleucid era, which begins in B.C. 312; ſometimes even the month of that year. We thus gain moſt valuable means of checking the dates of the events of Parthian history, at all events of the accession and deposition of the Kings. Once in the series we have a portrait of a woman, Musa, an Italian girl presented by Augustus to Phraates IV., who made so good a use of her talents that she persuaded the King to declare her son Phraataces his heir, and reigned in conjunction with that son until he lost his life in a revolt. She wears a jewelled head-dress, and is clad in Oriental splendour.

The district of Persia proper seems to have enjoyed partial independence in Parthian times; and we may feel justified in assigning to this district a long series of small silver coins which are usually called sub-Parthian; bearing on one side the head of a king, on the other usually a fire-altar, and inscriptions in Pehlvi characters, which have as yet been very imperfectly read.

Sassanian Dynasty.

About A.D. 220 the princes of Persia revolted against their Parthian masters, and succeeded in wresting from them the supremacy of Asia. A great Persian dynasty then arose, beginning with Artaxerxes or Ardeshir the Sassanian, and ruled the East until the rise of Mohammadanism. The coins of the Sassanian Kings present a great contrast to those of the Parthians. Their execution is far neater and more masterly, and they show in all respects a reaction of the more manly tribes of Southern Asia alike against the debased Hellenism which had invaded the cities of Western Persia, and against the barbarous Parthian hordes, who seem to have passed out of history with their overthrow, leaving scarcely a trace on the art, the religion, or the customs of Asia.

The great bulk of the Sassanian issues is in silver, and consists of flat, well-wrought pieces, of the weight of an Attic drachm, 67 grains. There are also gold coins weighing 110-115 grains, rather heavier than the contemporary solidi of Rome, and a few copper pieces. Gold and silver coins are of similar legends and devices, and throughout the whole of Persian rule preserve an almost unchanged character. On the obverse is universally the head of the King. The various monarchs have different styles of crown and coiffure, sometimes of a very extravagant character, the hair being rolled into huge balls and

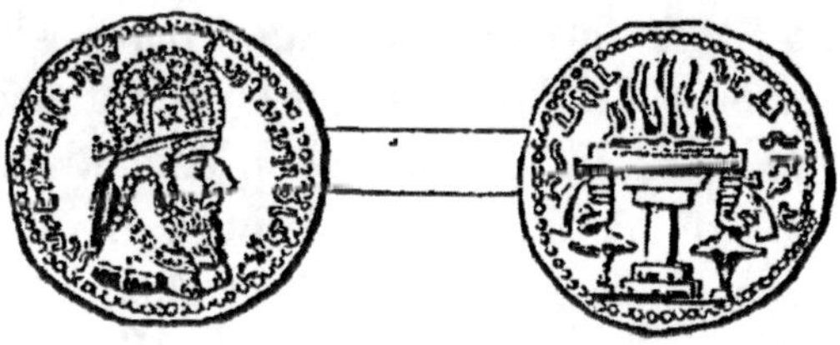

ARTAXERXES I.

tufts. On his earliest coins, Artaxerxes' head is closely copied from that of Mithradates I., the greatest of the Parthian monarchs, whom the Persian King seems thus to claim as prototype and model. Around the King's head on all the Persian coins is his name and his titles in Pehlvi letters. Artaxerxes is termed the worshipper of Ormazd, the divine King of Kings of Iran. Later monarchs vary the formula; on the money of some of the latest, the mint where the coin was iſſued and the year of the reign are written in Pehlvi characters in the field of the reverſe. The reverſe type of all Saſſanian coins is the ſame, the fire-altar, the ſymbol of the worſhip of Ormazd, uſually guarded by ſoldiers, or approached by the King in humble adoration.

Western Asia. Between Armenia on the north and Arabia on the ſouth, coins were iſſued during Parthian times by a number of ſmall ſtates which maintained a precarious autonomy againſt the Romans on the one hand, and the Parthians on the other. Moſt of them diſappear before the revived force of the empire of the Saſſanians. **Armenia.** Armenia was, until the time of the Parthian Mithradates (B.C. 160), the ſeat of ſeveral ſmall dynaſties. We hear of Arſames, a king of Arſamoſata, who received the Syrian prince Antiochus Hierax when he fled from his brother Seleucus; and of one Xerxes, who ruled in the ſame diſtrict, and reſiſted the arms of Antiochus IV. Both of theſe rulers have left us coins of Greek faſhion, but bearing on the obverſe a head of the King in peaked Armenian tiara. But Mithradates, if we may truſt the hiſtory of Moſes of Khoren, overran Armenia, and ſet on the throne his brother Vagharſhag or Valarſaces, who was the firſt of a line of Arſacid Kings of Armenia, under whom the country reached a higher pitch of proſperity than ever before or ſince. We poſſeſs coins of ſeveral of theſe Kings—of Tigranes, who became King of Syria and ſon-in-law of Mithradates of Pontus, and whoſe numerous ſilver coins ſtruck at Antioch bear as type the Genius or Fortune of that city ſeated on a rock; of Artaxias, who was crowned by Germanicus; and of Artavaſdes, who was for a brief period maintained by the arms of Auguſtus. We alſo have a long ſeries of coins in copper iſſued by the Kings of Oſroene or Edeſſa, whoſe dynaſtic names were Abgarus and Mannus, and who flouriſhed during the firſt three centuries of the Chriſtian era, living in independence by no means complete, for the one ſide of their coin is generally occupied by the effigy of a Roman emperor.

The Arab tribes to the eaſt of Paleſtine at ſome periods enjoyed independence under kings of their own. We have a ſeries of coins of the firſt century B.C. ſtruck by the Nabathean Kings Malchus and Aretas, partly at Antioch, partly at Petra. The inſcriptions and types of theſe coins are in earlier times Greek, and one of the Kings who bore the name Aretas calls himſelf Philhellen; but later the legends are written in local alphabet and dialect, and the portraits aſſume more of a native aſpect. The ſhort-lived Palmyrene Empire, founded by Odenathus and Zenobia, and put down by Aurelian, has alſo left numiſmatic traces of its exiſtence in money quite identical in fabric, weight, and types, with the contemporary coins iſſued by Roman emperors at Alexandria. Some of the effigies of Zenobia on theſe coins may, however, be conſidered fairly good portraits for the time.

Nabathea.

Palmyra.

Further ſouth, in Arabia, we find at leaſt two

Arabia

tribes who iſſued abundance of coin before the birth of Mohammad. The Himyarites circulated great quantities of imitations of the Athenian coins of various periods, and at a later age of the money of Auguſtus. Types of their own they ſeem not to have uſed, but they impreſsed on their imitations of civilized coins an inſcription which identifies them as Himyarite. The people of Characene, a ſmall diſtrict on the Perſian Gulf, began in the ſecond century B.C. a ſeries of tetradrachms of Greek ſtyle, the general appearance and types of which are copied from the coins of contemporary Greek Kings of Syria and Bactria. The names of a ſeries of theſe monarchs, Tiraeus, Attambelus, and ſo forth, together with their order of ſucceſſion, are preſerved to us by coins.

One of the moſt curious facts noticeable in the coins of Arabia is the frequency with which the heads of queens occupy the obverſes, in conjunction with thoſe of their huſbands and ſons. This peculiarity illuſtrates the hiſtorical fact, known from other ſources, that before the days of Mohammad women not unfrequently ruled among the Arabian tribes, either alone or conjointly with ſome male relative. The abundance of the known money of this country, and the purity of the metal of which it is compoſed, ſhow that while the Ptolemies ruled in Egypt, a briſk trade went on between Arabia and the countries to the eaſt and weſt of it. But for art the Arabs ſeem never to have had a taſte. They merely copied the coins which passed current most freely in their neighbourhood.

Most people will take a greater interest in the coins of Judaea, although none of these are very ancient, nor are they artistically pleasing. It would seem that, until the middle of the second century B.C., the Jews either weighed out gold and silver for the price of goods, or else used the money usually current in Syria, that of Persia, Phoenicia, Athens, and the Seleucidae. Simon the Maccabee Judaea.

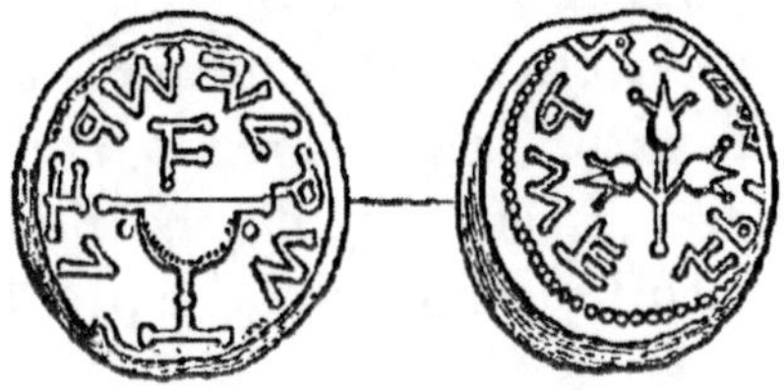

EARLY JEWISH SHEKEL.

HALF SHEKEL.

was the first to issue the Jewish shekel as a coin, and we learn from the Book of Maccabees that the privilege of striking was expressly granted him by King Antiochus VII. of Syria. We possess shekels of years 1–5 of the deliverance of Zion; the types are a chalice and a triple flower.

The kings who succeeded Simon, down to Antigonus, confined themselves to the issue of copper money, with Hebrew legends and with types calculated not to ſhock the ſuſceptible feelings of their people, to whom the repreſentation of a living thing was abominable—ſuch types as a lily, a palm, a ſtar, or an anchor. When the Herodian family came in, ſeveral violations of this rule appear. For example, we find objects of heathen cultus, ſuch as a tripod and a caduceus; and money was even ſtruck in Judaea bearing the effigies of men, ſometimes of the reigning Roman Emperor, sometimes even of the Jewiſh King. Both the Agrippas are guilty of this violation of principle. The Roman Procurators of Judaea alſo iſſued coin with Greek legends, and carefully dated, ſo that we can diſtinguiſh the money iſſued during the eventful years of the riſe of Chriſtianity at Jeruſalem.

Both of the deſperate but unſucceſsful revolts

SIMON BAR COCHAB.

of the Jews againſt their Roman maſters—that in the reign of Veſpaſian under Simon and Eleazar, and that in the reign of Hadrian under Bar Cochab—have left a deep impreſſion on the Jewiſh coin. In both periods the iſſue of ſhekels was reſumed, and Roman denarii were freely reſtruck by the revolted leaders with their own types and names. With these coins the Jewish money comes to an end. Jerusalem became a Roman colony under the name of Aelia Capitolina, and all money issued in that region bears witness in its types only to the defeat and slavery of the Hebrews.

CHAPTER VII.

MOHAMMADAN COINS.

IN the ſtudy of Greek coins we are unceaſingly faſcinated by their artiſtic excellence and the lights they throw on the mythology of the moſt intereſting people of antiquity. Roman and mediaeval coins have their importance in ſhowing us the ſource of our monetary ſyſtem, and poſſeſs an added charm in the many hiſtorical aſſociations they awake, though they ſeldom increaſe our actual knowledge of hiſtory. Engliſh coins we ſtudy becauſe we are Engliſhmen, and like to know what our anceſtors bartered their ſouls for. None of theſe attractions belong to Mohammadan coins. Art we ſhould ſcarcely look for, ſince we all know that the Bleſſed Prophet declared that "every painter is in hell-fire," and ſtraitly forbade the making of "ſtatues" (by which he probably meant idols) and images of living things, on pain of the artiſt's being compelled to put a ſoul into his creation on the Day of Judgment. Hence true believers have always been very cautious of repreſenting human or even animal forms as an aid to decoration, and we ſhall find that it is only when barbarous Tartars or heretical Perſians enter the field that figures of living things appear in the art of Mohammadan countries, and then very rarely upon their coins. The Eaſtern draughtsman, being debarred from the moſt fruitful of artiſtic materials, took refuge in the elaboration of thoſe beautiful arabeſque deſigns and geometrical patterns which are characteriſtic of ſo-called Arabian work, and even turned the natural grace of the Arabic writing to account as an element in decoration. Thus, on coins, as in moſques, we find the Kufic character uſed as a thing of beauty, and diſpoſed to the beſt advantage, where a European artiſt would have relegated the letters to an obſcure corner, and devoted all his ſpace to the head or other figure that occupied the face of the coin. It was a matter of neceſſity rather than of choice, but it had a good effect in developing the graceful and elſewhere little cultivated art of calligraphy.

Calligraphy

Nor muſt we expect any very intereſting metrological data to be derived from Mohammadan coins. Their metrology, ſo far as it is known, is borrowed—like moſt other ſo-called Arabian things, whether philoſophical, artiſtic, literary, or even religious—from the more cultivated nations the Muſlims conquered, and the ſcience ſtill reſts in deep obſcurity, chiefly becauſe no one, except my indefatigable friend M. Sauvaire,[1] has had the patience to work ſo dreary a vein. Hiſtorical aſſociations it were vain to call up at the ſight of a Muſlim coin, ſince the great majority of even well-educated and reading folk are profoundly ignorant of everything oriental, except what is Biblical or Japaneſe. There are, perhaps, three or four Mohammadan celebrities known by name to a fair proportion of ordinary readers. "The good Haroun Al-Raſchid" owes his popularity to the *Arabian Nights* and Lord Tennyson, and coins bearing his name, together with that of the ill-fated Vizir Jaafar, of which there are many examples in the Britiſh Muſeum and every other large collection, might touch a chord of remem-

Historical Associations.

brance; while a piece iſſued by the famous Saladin, though in itſelf unintereſting, carries upon its ſurface a long train of Cruſading aſſociations for the hiſtorical ſtudent. The currency of the great fighting Sultans of Turkey, the Amuraths and Mahomets, the Selims and Solimans—to adopt the barbarous kakography of Weſtern writers—has its memories, and ſo have the large gold pieces, with their uncompromiſing declaration of faith, iſſued by "Bobadil" and the other heroes of the dying kingdom of the Moors in Spain. To a very few the ſolitary piece of gold ſtruck

Coin of a Mamlûk Queen.

by the Mamlûk Queen, Shejer ed-Durr (which, being interpreted, means Tree of Pearls), may

[1] *Matériaux pour ſervir à l'Hiſtoire de la Numiſmatique et de la Métrologie Muſalmanes;* and ſeveral profound papers in the *Journal of the Royal Aſiatic Society.*

recall the fact that it was this apparently fascinating but not quite irreproachable lady who first made the pilgrimage to Mekka in the palanquin or mahmal, which has ever since been a notable feature of the departure of the pilgrims from Cairo, and which, being inextricably confused with the Holy Carpet, severely exercised the British conscience during the triumphal ceremonies that followed hard upon the battle of Tell-el-Kebîr.

The coin in question is a good example of the rich genealogical material to be extracted from an Arabic half-guinea. On one side, in the margin, is the profession of faith, testifying that "there is no God but God, and that Mohammad is His Prophet,"—a formula which appears on the majority of Mohammadan coins, often accompanied by other expressions of religious orthodoxy, and by sentences from the Korân. This very marginal inscription goes on to tell, in the words of the Korân, how God "sent Mohammad with the guidance and religion of truth, so that he might make it triumph over all other creeds." Encircled by these pious words, the field shows a long string of titles, all belonging to Queen Shejer ed-Durr, from which a sort of outline of her life may be constructed. In the first place she is called El-Musta'simîyeh, which means that she was once a slave-girl of the 'Abbâsy Khalif El-Musta'sim. Her next title is Es-Sâlihîyeh, showing that she was transferred from the Khalif's harîm to that of Es-Sâlih, the grand-nephew of Saladin, who had Genealogical data.

succeeded to the kingship of Egypt after the deaths of his grand-uncle, grandfather (the scarcely less famous "Saphadin" El-'Adil), and father. Further, this coin gives her the title of "Queen of the Muslims," and "Mother of El-Mansûr Khalîl," a son who, we know from the historians, died in infancy. On the other side are the name and titles of the reigning 'Abbâsy Khalif El-Musta'sim, the Queen's former husband, round which is arranged a marginal inscription which records how, "in the name of God, the compassionate, the merciful," the coin was struck at Cairo in the year of the Hijreh 648, *i.e.*, A.D. 1250.

Crusade of St. Louis.

This year was a very critical one for the Mohammadan supremacy in Egypt. In 1249 Es-Sâlih had died, and the French army of the last Crusade, under St. Louis, was in occupation of Damietta, and already advancing upon the capital. In this position of affairs, the Slave-queen undertook the government. She concealed the death of her husband, and subdued the panic which the Frank invasion was exciting. Then the tide of fortune changed; the Bahry Mamlûks, under the command of Beybars of the lion-crest, won a complete victory over the French at Mansûrah; St. Louis and his army were made prisoners of war; and, on the death of the heir to the throne, Shejer ed-Durr was proclaimed Queen of Egypt. For two months and a half she reigned alone, and then, on the remonstrance of the Khalif, first of her three husbands, at the impropriety of a woman exercising royal power, she associated the Emîr Eybek and another nominal colleague with her in the sovereignty. But from the first moment she took the reins of government into her hands till the day of her death, she was sovereign mistress of Egypt, let who would enjoy the name of Sultan. She made Eybek Sultan, and married him; but she retained the absolute authority she had held before, and when her colleague showed symptoms of independence, and seemed inclined to enlarge the circle of his affections, she had him murdered in his bath, under her own eyes. Three days afterwards "Tree of Pearls" herself was beaten to death with wooden bath-clogs by the slaves of a divorced wife of the murdered man.

The unique coin described above must have been issued during these two stirring months of female autocracy, of which it is the only numismatic evidence we possess, in corroboration of the statements of the historians, which it confirms in the most minute particulars, in every detail of the long string of titles attached to the Queen's name; and it derives a peculiar interest from having been struck at the very moment when St. Louis received his final discomfiture at the hands of the infidels, and by the very Queen whose treasury was enriched by a million gold bysants, which formed the ransom of the King of France.

Wealth of Historical Information.

In the wealth of information afforded by this coin we see the real value of Mohammadan numismatics. The coins of the Muslim East do not so much recall history as make it. The student is conſtantly meeting with a perfectly unknown King or even dynaſty, which fills up a gap in the annals of the Eaſt. A Mohammadan coin generally gives not only the date and place of iſſue, and the name of the ruler who cauſed it to be ſtruck, but frequently the names of his father and grandfather, his heir-apparent, his liege-lord, and other valuable genealogical data and aids to the due underſtanding of the inter-relations of different dynaſties; while the religious formulae employed will enable us to tell the ſect to which the ruler who iſſued the coin belonged, at leaſt ſo far as the broad diſtinctions of Iſlam are concerned. If the complete ſeries of coins iſſued by every Muſlim ſtate were preſerved, we ſhould be able to tabulate with the utmoſt nicety the entire line of Kings and their principal vaſſals that have ruled in every part of the Mohammadan Empire ſince the eighth century, and to draw with tolerable accuracy the boundaries of their territories at every period. Minting was ever one of the moſt cheriſhed rights of ſovereignty: the privileges of "Khutbeh and Sikkeh," that is, of being prayed for in the Friday prayers in the Moſque and of inſcribing his name upon the currency, were the firſt things the new King thought about on aſcending the throne. We may be confident that the right was exerciſed at the earlieſt poſſible opportunity, and that a prince who occupied the kingly office for but a few weeks was ſure to celebrate his royalty on a coin. Shejer ed-Durr is a caſe in point, for the coin above deſcribed muſt have been ſtruck in her brief reign of two months.

Value of Numismatic Evidence.

It is this monetary vanity of Eastern princes that makes their coinage so valuable to the historian, and indeed compels him to regard numismatic evidence as the surest testimony he can obtain. Of course it may be urged that the facts thus derived from a study of coins are not worth having; they may be absolutely true, but they relate to persons and countries concerning which nobody feels any possible interest, and even of these they tell only such meagre items as dates and chief towns, the very things we are now carefully expunging from our school-books! It is easy to reply that, like every currency, that of the Mohammadan East really supplies important evidence concerning the economic state of the country by its quality and rate of exchange. But we join issue on the main question, and venture to assert that no scrap of positive historical fact is really useless, or may not at some time be turned to important ends. The Mohammadan coinage, more than any other, abounds in historical data, and when the as yet unwritten history of the East during the Middle Ages comes to be told, the author will find no surer check upon the native annalists than the coins.

If the history of the Mohammadan East were comprised in the annals of a few great dynasties, the value of the coins would not be so considerable, for we should only learn perhaps some fresh dates or confirmation of dates already known, and the mints would only be the capitals and large towns of well-known provinces. But Mohammadan hiſtory is made up of the ſtruggles for ſupremacy of hundreds of petty houſes, and thouſands of petty dynaſts, of whoſe very exiſtence we should often be wholly ignorant but for their coins. Theſe petty dynaſts ſtruck their money at towns of which next to nothing is often known, and thus the coinage is frequently our only means of eſtabliſhing the poſition of the ſmaller towns of the mediaeval Eaſt. Sometimes theſe ſmall towns preſerve the names of cities famous in antiquity, but whoſe ſite, ſave for this numiſmatic evidence,

GOLD COIN OF 'ABD-EL-MELIK, KHALIF OF DAMASCUS, A.D. 696.

was uncertain. Thus geographically as well as hiſtorically Mohammadan coins have a high value.

Origin of the Coinage.

It took the Arabs half a century to diſcover the need of a ſeparate coinage of their own. At firſt they were content to borrow their gold and copper currency from the Byzantine Empire, which they had driven out of Syria, and their ſilver coins from the Saſſanian Kings of Perſia, whom they had overthrown at the battles of Kadiſia and Nehavend. The Byzantine gold ſerved them till the ſeventy-ſixth year of the Flight, when a new, but theologically unſound and conſequently evaneſcent, type was invented, bearing the effigy of the reigning Khalif inſtead of that of Heraclius, and Arabic inſtead of

Greek inscriptions. So, too, the Sassanian silver pieces were left unaltered, save for the addition of a governor's name in Pehlvi letters. The Khalif 'Aly or one of his lieutenants seems to have attempted to inaugurate a purely Muslim coinage, exactly resembling that which was afterwards adopted; but only one example of this issue is known to exist, in the Paris collection, together with three other silver coins struck at Damascus and Merv between A.H. 60 and 70, of a precisely similar type. These four coins are clearly early and ephemeral attempts at the intro-

REFORMED GOLD COIN OF 'ABD-EL-MELIK, A.D. 696.

duction of a distinctive Mohammadan coinage, and their recent discovery in no way upsets the received Muslim tradition that it was the Khalif 'Abd-El-Melik who, in the year of the Flight 76 (or, on the evidence of the coins themselves, 77), inaugurated the regular Muslim coinage, which was thenceforward issued from all the mints of the empire so long as the dynasty endured, and which gave its general character to the whole currency of the kingdoms of Islam. The copper coinage founded on the Byzantine passed through more and earlier phases than the gold and silver, but it always held so insignificant a place in the Muslim

'Abd-El Melik.

currency that we can afford to diſregard it in the preſent brief outline.

Religious Inſcriptions.

Specimens of 'Abd-El-Melik's reformed coinage are here engraved. The gold and ſilver both bear the ſame formulae of faith: on the obverſe, in the area, "There is no god but God alone, He hath no partner;" around which is arranged a marginal inſcription, "Mohammad is the apoſtle of God, who ſent him with the guidance and religion of truth, that he might

SILVER COIN OF THE KHALIFATE.
Struck in Andalusia, A.D. 734.

make it triumph over all other religions in ſpite of the idolaters," the gold stopping at "other religions." This inſcription occurs on the reverſe of the ſilver inſtead of the obverſe, while the date inſcription which is found on the reverſe of the gold, appears on the obverſe of the ſilver. The reverſe area declares that "God is One, God is the Eternal: He begetteth not, nor is begotten;" here the gold ends, but the ſilver continues, "and there is none like unto Him." The margin of the gold runs, "In the name of God: this Dînâr was ſtruck in the year ſeven and ſeventy;" the ſilver ſubſtituting "Dirhem" for Dînâr, and inſerting the place of iſſue immediately after the word Dirhem, *e.g.*, "El-Andalus [*i.e.* Andalufia] in the year 116." The mint is not given on the early gold coins, probably because they were uniformly ftruck at the Khalif's capital, Damafcus. The contemporary copper coinage generally offers portions of the fame formulae, with often the addition of the name of the governor of the province in which the coin was iffued.

These original dînârs (a name formed from the Roman denarius) and dirhems (drachma) of the Khalifs of Damafcus formed the model of all Muflim coinages for many centuries; and their refpective weights—65 and 43 grains—ferved as the ftandard of all fubfequent iffues up to comparatively recent times. The finenefs was about ·979 gold in the dînârs, and ·960 to ·970 filver in the dirhems. The Mohammadan coinage was generally very pure. The 'Abbâfy dînârs retained the finenefs of ·979 for many centuries, and the fame proportion of gold was obferved in the iffues of the Fâtimy Khalifs, the Almohades, and fometimes of the Almoravides, but the laft usually employed a lower *titre*. At firft ten dirhems went to the dînâr, but the relation varied from age to age. **Weight and Fineness.**

The dynafty of Umawy or "Ommiade" Khalifs, to which 'Abd-El-Melik belonged, continued to iffue their dînârs and dirhems without any change until their overthrow at the hands of the 'Abbâfis in the year of the Flight 132, and even then one of the family fled to Spain, and there continued both the Umawy line and coinage in the Khalifate **Coinage of the Khalifate.**

of Cordova, which lasted three centuries. The 'Abbâsy Khalifs, on succeeding to the eastern dominions of the Umawis, retained in all essential respects the coinage of their predecessors, substituting, however, for the formula of the reverse area, the words, "Mohammad is the apostle of God," thus repeating the beginning of the marginal inscription. They also inserted the name of the mint-city on the gold, as well as on the silver. Soon, moreover, the strict puritanism of the early Khalifs, which did not permit them to place their own names on the currency, gave way to the natural vanity of the ruler, and the names and titles of the 'Abbâsy Khalifs were regularly inserted beneath the reverse area inscription, often accompanied by the names of their heir-apparent and grand-vizir. Thus, for some 250 years the universal coinage of the Muslim Empire was of one simple and uniform type.

Dynastic Coinage.

But with the sudden and general upspringing of small independent, or only nominally dependent, dynasties in the fourth century of the Hijreh, the tenth of our era, Muslim coins acquire their highest value. The history of the Khalifs has been carefully recorded, and their coins, though they confirm and sometimes give additional precision to the statements of the historians, do not greatly enlarge our knowledge. But when the Sâmânis in Transoxiana and Khorasan, the Saffâris in Seistan, the Buweyhis in various provinces of Persia, the Hamdânis in Syria (all adopting a predominantly silver coinage), and the Beny Tûlûn and Ikhshîdis in Egypt (who coined almost exclusively gold), and the Idrîsis (silver) and Beny-l-Aghlab (chiefly gold) in North Africa, began to strike coins after the model of those of the Khalifate, but abounding in names of local dynasts, the historical value of the coinage rises. These dynastic coins always retain the name of the reigning Khalif in the place of honour, and this conjunction of names of Khalif and dynast will often supply the required chronological data, in the absence or the obliteration of a definite year.

With the advent of the Seljuk Turks, who subdued the greater part of Persia, Syria, and Asia Minor, in the fifth century of the Hijreh, the coins acquire a special importance in deciding the difficult question of the territorial divisions of the various Seljuk lines; and the numerous dynasties of Atâbegs or generals of the Seljuk armies, which sprang up as soon as the central power grew weak, possess a numismatic interest in their general adoption of Byzantine types on their large copper pieces. On coins of the Urtukis, for example, a petty dynasty of some crusading fame that ruled a few fortresses in Mesopotamia, we meet with not only the figures of Byzantine Emperors, but those of Christ and the Virgin, with mangled inscriptions of Christian import. Figures of a similar character also appear on the coinage of the Ayyûbis (Saladin's Kurdish house), and that of the Beny Zengy of Môsil and Syria, together with the earliest known representation of the two-headed eagle, which has since ob-

Christian Figures.

tained high favour in Europe. But this divergence from the eſtabliſhed theory of Iſlam was only a temporary and exceptional phaſe, due to the irruption of foreign barbarians. The contemporary dynaſties of Africa—the Fâtimy Khalifs of Egypt,

"MARAVEDI:" GOLD COIN OF ALMORAVIDES.
Struck at Cordova, A.D. 1103.

"MILLARES:" SILVER COIN OF ALMOHADES, MOROCCO.
Thirteenth and fourteenth centuries.

and the Almoravides and other Berber dynaſties of North Africa and Spain—adhered ſtrictly to the orthodox tradition which forbade the repreſentation of living things, and this was all the more noteworthy inaſmuch as moſt of theſe African dynaſties belonged to heretical ſects. Specimens of theſe Weſtern coinages are ſhown in the engravings, in which the "maravedi" and "millares" of mediaeval chronicles may be recogniſed. The ſquare ſhape is peculiar to North-Weſt Africa and Spain.

Maravedi and Millares.

Mongol Coinage.

In the ſeventh century of the Flight—our thirteenth—the Muſlim world was almoſt wholly in the possession of foreigners. The Mongols had overrun the Eastern provinces, which had not yet recovered from the inroad of the Turks, and henceforward the monotonous (chiefly silver) currency, and irregular standards, of the various Mongol houses, such as the Ilkhâns of Persia, the Jagatay family in Bokhâra, the different branches of the

SILVER COIN OF HOSEYN, SHAH OF PERSIA.
Struck at Isfahân, A.D. 1709.

House of Timur (Tamerlane), the Khâns of Kipchak, of the Krim, etc., weary the student; till the fine issues of the Shahs of Persia and the Kings and Emperors of Dehli restore something like order and beauty to the chaos that, numismatically as well as hiſtorically—the two generally go together—ſucceeded the terrible ſwoop of Chinguiz Khan. Even here, however, there are points of intereſt; and the long ſeries of coins of the Khanates of the Caſpian throw a valuable light upon the early hiſtory of the Ruſsian States under the Mohammadan ſupremacy.

Mamlûks of Egypt.

Meanwhile the Mamlûks, in their two lines—Turkiſh and Circaſſian—held ſway over the provinces of Egypt and Syria, and left many a noble monument of art and culture behind them. Their (predominantly gold) coinage, however, in ſpite of the repreſentation of Beybar's lion, and ſome forms of ornament which are intereſting to compare with the contemporary architecture, is poor and debaſed.

Berber Dynasties.

Several Berber dynaſties had eſtabliſhed themſelves ſince the eleventh century in the Barbary States, and continued for half a millennium to iſſue their large gold pieces, reſembling the coin engraved opposite. One of theſe, the line of Sherîfs of Morocco, endures to the preſent day, but the Ottoman Turks extinguiſhed the others in the ſixteenth century. This clan of Turks roſe into power about the ſame time as the Mongols and Mamlûks. From one of ten petty dynaſties that fattened upon the decay of the Seljuk kingdom of Anatolia, they became by the end of the fourteenth century rulers of all Aſia Minor and a ſlice of Europe, and the middle of the ſixteenth ſaw them poſſeſſed of an empire that ſtretched from Hungary to the Caſpian, and from Baghdad to Algiers. The Ottoman currency at firſt consisted of small silver and copper pieces, bearing no very obvious relation, either in weight or style, to the old Seljuk or the older Khalif's coinage, and for a long time they were content to use foreign gold. Mohammad II., the conqueror of Constantinople, was the first to strike gold coins, upon the model of the Venetian sequins, but of course with Arabic inscriptions. Various gold sequins or "altuns," small silver "akchehs," and copper "manghirs" constituted the Turkish currency up to the beginning of our seventeenth century. A double standard of sequins and a perfectly new

Ottoman Turks.

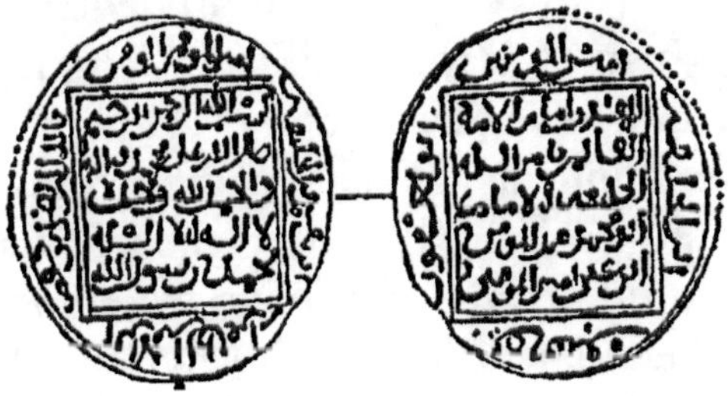

GOLD COIN OF ALMOHADES, MOROCCO. Fourteenth Century.

silver coinage, based upon the Dutch dollar, with numerous subdivisions and multiples, was then introduced, and was ever after the subject of countless modifications and degradations, until, after an unsuccessful attempt at reform by the great Mahmûd II., the modern Turkish series, approximating the monetary systems of Europe, was inaugurated by Sultan 'Abd-El-Mejîd, and is hence known as the Mejîdîyeh. A similar series, bearing the Sultan's but not the Viceroy's names, was and is in use in Egypt, and a third series, on a different basis, in Tunis. The Turkish coinage as a whole is important in its relations with the Mediterranean currencies, and it has a certain bearing upon the hiſtory of trade in the Middle Ages. It has alſo a value in determining the limits of the Turkiſh Empire at different periods, as the number of mints is very conſiderable.

The true value of Mohammadan coins lies, as has been ſaid, in their hiſtorical data. What is really wanted is a *Corpus* of Mohammadan Numiſmatics, which ſhould preſent, in well-arranged tables and indexes, the reſults of the coin-evidence of all the collections of Europe, and ſhould place them at the ſervice of hiſtorical ſtudents without compelling them to learn a difficult language and a ſtill more difficult palaeography. There is little that is intereſting in Mohammadan coins apart from their aid to hiſtory, and if their actual contributions to hiſtorical knowledge were once ſummarized and tabulated, few but inveterate collectors would want to ſtudy them. I write after finiſhing the eighth volume of my *Catalogue of Oriental Coins in the Britiſh Muſeum*, which has been going on for the laſt ten years, and deſcribes over ſix thouſand coins iſſued by a hundred ſeparate dynaſties, ſome of which conſiſt of thirty or forty Kings; and I have no heſitation in ſaying that Oriental numiſmatics is a ſcience which is intereſting mainly in its reſults. Thoſe reſults, however, are of the very firſt importance to the hiſtorian, and in this reſpect Mohammadan coins may challenge compariſon with any other ſeries without fear of being found wanting.

CHAPTER VIII.

COINS OF INDIA.

THE firſt ſection of this chapter deals with the coinage of India from its commencement to the Mohammadan Conqueſt; the ſecond ſection treats of the coins of the foreign dynaſties of Iſlam who ruled in Northern India.

The earlieſt coinage of India is, like the earlieſt works of Indian art which have come down to us, purely Greek. To trace the gradual abſorption of Greek language and art by thoſe of the older inhabitants is a poſſible and very intereſting employment. One of the moſt important and intereſting of all numiſmatic ſeries is that of the coins iſſued on the borders of the Oxus and the Indus in the ages ſucceeding the revolt of the Eaſtern provinces of the Syro-Greek Empire in the reign of Antiochus II., about B.C. 250. The earlieſt rulers of the revolted regions were Diodotus and Euthydemus, followed in the ſecond century by Antimachus, Eucratides, Menander, and a bewilder-

Greek Kings.

ing crowd of kings with Greek names, whoſe coins have reached us to teſtify, in the abſence of all hiſtorical record, to their wealth and ſplendour, their Greek language and religion, their ſkill in art and the wide extenſion of their conqueſts. The number of theſe rulers is ſo great that we muſt give up the hypotheſis that they ſucceeded one another in a ſingle royal line; rather would it appear that they belonged to a number of different, probably rival, dynaſties, who reigned in different

ANTIMACHUS, INDIAN KING. About B.C. 150.

parts of Afghaniſtan, the Panjâb, and the Indus valley. Of all theſe powerful monarchs there is ſcarcely a trace in hiſtory; their cities, their palaces, their civilization, have entirely periſhed; their coins alone ſurvive. Hence, while in the caſe of Greece and Rome coins are aids to hiſtory, in India they contain all the hiſtory we can hope to recover. And by degrees, as the number of our coins increaſes, ſo that we can form wide generalizations, and as the ſpots where the pieces of different ſorts are found are more ſcrupulouſly recorded, we may hope to be able to form an idea of the hiſtory of Greek India. At preſent we are far from being in ſo fortunate a condition; all that I ſhall now attempt is to gather from the coins a few general indications.

The coins prove that Greek rule in India went on ſpreading eaſt and ſouth during the ſecond century. Greek Kings ruled even at the mouth of the Indus, and as far as the Ganges. And their civilization, or at leaſt that of their courts and armies, was thoroughly Greek; the legends of their coins are at firſt purely Hellenic; and well-executed figures of Zeus, Pallas, Poſeidon, Herakles, the Dioſcuri, and other Greek deities prove that they brought with them the religion of their anceſtors. Probably there was a conſtantly ſetting ſtream of Greek mercenaries towards theſe remote lands, who formed military colonies in them, and peopled dominant cities which occupied in India the ſame poſition which the Greek cities of Ptolemais and Alexandria held in Egypt, and the Greek cities of Seleucia, Ragae, etc., in Parthia.

In the beginning of the ſecond century the Parthian Empire was driven like a wedge between Greek-ſpeaking countries and the Graecized cities of the Cabul valley, cutting off intercourse between the two; and the Indo-Greek cities began at once to languiſh, and their inhabitants to become more and more barbarized. We can trace the whole proceſs on coins. Eucratides and his ſucceſſor Heliocles introduce the cuſtom of adding on the reverſe of the coin a tranſlation in Indian of the Greek legend of the obverſe. And under ſome of the Kings we find traces of the barbarization of Greek divinities, as when on a coin of Telephus we find ſtrange outlandiſh figures of Helios and Selene, when on a coin of Hippoſtratus

HIPPOSTRATUS.

we find a barbarous imitation of the Greek Genius of a city, or when on coins of Amyntas we find a divinity wearing a Phrygian cap from which flames or rays iſſue.

Scythic Kings. Hermaeus, who may have reigned late in the firſt century B.C., was the laſt of the Greek Kings of Cabul. During his life came the deluge: hoſts of Sacae, Yu-chi, and other nomad tribes from the borders of China ſwarmed down upon the devoted Greek kingdoms of the Eaſt and completely overwhelmed them. But theſe barbarians adopted,

HERAUS, KING OF THE SACAE.

like the Parthians, ſomething of the civilization of thoſe they conquered. The coins of Maues, Azes, and others of their Kings bear Greek inſcriptions, and the figures of Greek divinities, and conform in moſt reſpects to Greek uſage, ſo that but for the barbarous character of the names of theſe Kings we might have ſuppoſed them to be of Greek deſcent.

The powerful and wealthy Scythian Kings who ruled in North-weſtern India in the ſecond century of our era—Kadphiſes, Kanerkes, and Ooerkes—have left us a wonderful abundance of remarkable coins, which are ſometimes found in India together with the aurei of contemporary Roman Emperors in the ſtupas or mounds which they erected over the relics of Kings or Buddhiſt ſaints. Theſe Kings did not uſe iſſues of ſilver, like their Greek and Scythian predeceſſors, but of gold. On one ſide of their coins is an effigy of the reigning monarch, and an inſcription in barbarized Greek, giving his name and titles. On the other ſide is the figure of ſome deity accompanied by his name in Greek letters; and the number and variety of theſe types are enormous. We have figures of the Greek Sarapis and Herakles, of the Perſian Mithras and Nanaia, of the Indian Siva and Parvati, and even of Buddha, who appears on the coins in the attitude of a preacher. The Pantheon of theſe barbarians muſt have been of the moſt eclectic character, though we know from their inſcriptions and other remains that they conſidered themſelves Buddhiſts.

As early as the firſt iſſues of the Indo-Greek Kings, or ſcarcely later, are the firſt coins of native fabric. Theſe are what are termed "punched coins." They are ſmall ſquares cut out of a thin plate of Native Kings.

ſilver, and impreſſed with devices by means, not of a die, but of a mere punch. The figures which they bear are very various, Buddhiſt emblems, archaic patterns, aſtrological devices, each probably the ſpecial mark of ſome mint, and authorizing the circulation of the piece ſo ſtamped in ſome particular diſtrict or city.

The punched coins circulated extenſively in Central India. And at the ſame time there paſſed in Weſtern India a great quantity of imitations of the coins of Greek and Scythian Kings. The coins of the dynaſty of Kanerkes, in particular, were copied through a ſeries of centuries, art and metal alike gradually deteriorating until in place of gold we have copper, and in place of the forms of kings and deities mere ſhapeleſs blotches.

The Sunga Kings of Magadha, who reigned in the ſecond century before our aera, have left us a few coins which are valuable becauſe of their early date. There were, however, in Northern India, before the time of Mahmud of Ghazny, notably three lines of native rulers who iſſued coins of creditable ſtyle, and impreſſed with legible Sanſkrit legends. Firſt of theſe we may name the

Guptas. Gupta Kings of Kanauj. Theſe wealthy and powerful monarchs, who ſeem to have been ſupreme throughout the whole of Northern India, iſſued money of almoſt pure Indian ſtyle, which bears types ſometimes taken from Indian religious cult, as when Parvati is depicted ſeated on a peacock; or alluſion is made to the Aſvamedha, the Indian horse-sacrifice. The gold pieces of the Gupta Kings may be ranged beside those of the powerful Scythic Kings, as illustrative of the conflict of two civilizations, the native and the foreign.

In the district of Saurastran, or Gujarat, there began, about the first century of our aera, the issue of silver coins by the Sah dynasty. These pieces are copied from those of Menander and other Greek Kings, but yet have something distinctively Hindu about them. The heads which they bear on their obverse are portraits of a succession of native Rajahs; on the reverse, in the midst of a rather long Sanskrit legend, is a Buddhist emblem, usually one which is interpreted as representing a sacred hill erected over some relic. Their fabric is remarkably clear and neat, and they look as if the race to whom they belonged was by no means backward in civilization and commerce. And it is notable that the land of Gujarat is that which would be the natural *entrepôt* of trade between the marts of India on the one hand, and those of Rome and Egypt on the other. The Sah Kings were succeeded by a dynasty of Guptas, who issued coins of quite similar kind.

Sah Kings.

Very well known to Indian collectors are the coins which show on one side a bull, on the other a horseman bearing a spear, and which are called "bull and horseman" coins. They are of silver, and the commonest class bear in Sanskrit letters the names of certain Rajput Kings who ruled in Cabul shortly before the invasion of India by Mahmud of Ghazny. The work of these is neither

Brahman Kings of Cabul.

purely Greek nor entirely Indian, but reminds us rather of ſome of the iſſues of Byzantium.

Theſe are, perhaps, the moſt important claſſes of native coins of early time; but there are many other groups. For inſtance, we have whole ſeries of coins iſſued by the Kings of Kaſhmir and of Ceylon; and in the miſt which hides early Indian hiſtory we can make out vaguely the forms of kings and dynaſties which faſt ſucceeded one another, or carried on war and commerce ſide by ſide. The majority of theſe rulers iſſued coin; and by ſlow degrees the few workers who have given attention to Indian numiſmatics are beginning to identify and arrange the multitudinous coins ſtruck by them, a proceſs which may in time bring us valuable evidence as to the diviſions and the hiſtory of early India. But as yet comparatively little has been aſcertained, and ſtill leſs publiſhed; and our readers would only be fatigued by a liſt of dynaſties as to which we have no information, and rulers whoſe names ſurvive only on the money which they iſſued, or in ſome bare dynaſtic liſt.

The Mohammadan coinage of India poſſeſſes the ſame merits and defects that have already been aſſigned to Mohammadan coins in general. We muſt not, as a rule, expect to ſee the triumphs of the engraver's art upon the face of the Indian currency. Inſcriptions, and nothing but inſcriptions, form the chief intereſt of the Indian coins of the Muſlim period; and to theſe inſcriptions belongs the principal value of the ſtudy of ſuch pieces. There is alſo the intereſt attaching to metrological peculiarities, which cannot be touched upon here, but of which the curious reader may obtain a thorough knowledge by an inſpection of the works of Prinſep and Thomas. But even the latter, *facile princeps* among living Indian numiſmatiſts, devoted as he is to the intricate queſtions connected with the weights and ſtandards of India, is ready to allow to the inſcriptions the chief place among the characteriſtics of the coinage. The value of the illuſtration that theſe inſcriptions afford, as applied to mediaeval Indian annals, is greatly enhanced, he ſays, "by the exaggerated importance attached by the Muſlims themſelves to that department of the conventional regal functions, involved in the right to coin. Among theſe peoples, the recitation of the public prayer in the name of the aſpirant to the throne, aſſociated with the iſſue of money bearing his ſuperſcription, was unheſitatingly received as the overt act of acceſſion. Unqueſtionably, in the ſtate of civilization here obtaining, the production and facile diſperſion of a new royal device was ſingularly well adapted to make manifeſt to the comprehenſion of all claſſes the immediate change in the ſupreme ruling power. In places where men did not print, theſe ſtamped moneys, obtruding into every bazaar, conſtituted the moſt effective manifeſtoes and proclamations human ingenuity could have deviſed: readily multiplied, they were individually the eaſieſt and moſt naturally tranſported of all official documents; the verieſt fakîr in his ſemi-nude coſtume might carry the oftensible proof of a new dynafty into regions where even the name of the kingdom itfelf was unknown. In fhort, there was but little limit to the range of thefe Eaftern heralds; the numifmatic Garter King-at-Arms was recognised wherever Afiatic nations accepted the gold, and interpreters could be found to defignate the Caefar whofe 'epigraph' figured on its furface. So alfo on the occafion of a new conqueft: the reigning Sultân's titles were oftentatioufly paraded on the local money, ordinarily in the language and alphabet of the indigenous races, to fecure the more effective announcement that they themfelves had paffed under the fway of an alien fuzerain. Equally, on the other hand, does any modification of, or departure from, the rule of a comprehenfive iffue of coin imply an imperfection relative or pofitive in the acquifition of fupreme power."[1]

Copper Currency.

The firft important fact to be noted about the Mohammadan coinage of India is that while the gold and filver were generally more or lefs adaptations, affimilated to ancient Indian ftandards, of the dînâr and dirhem which prevailed over the whole empire of Iflam, the copper currency retained as a rule its Indian character, and preferved thofe local characteriftics which it poffeffed before the invafion of the Muflims. In other words, the coins moft in requeft were left in the form which was beft underftood by the people who ufed them, while the lefs frequent gold and filver, the Court currency, received the imprefs

[1] *Chronicles of the Pathan Kings of Dehli*, p. 2.

of the ruling religion. So we find the conquering Mahmûd of Ghazny, the firſt Muſlim to ſnatch any part of India, iſſuing copper coins with Hindu characters ſuch as the people of the Panjâb would underſtand, and with the image of the Bull Nandy, ſacred to Hindus, but repugnant to Mohammadans, while his ſilver coins retain all the puritanical plainneſs that belongs to orthodox Iſlam. Mahmûd's ſucceſſors, the dynaſty of Ghaznawis or "Ghaznevides," who eſtabliſhed themſelves at Lahore, continued to mingle this native coinage with their imported formulas of faith. The ſucceeding dynaſties adopted the ſame principle, and admitted the Bull and the Chohan or Cabul horſeman to a place beſide the profeſſion of faith in one God; and we may ſtate as a general fact that the common copper, or more frequently billon, currency of India, under Mohammadan rule, remained Indian and local, and retained the old ſymbols and characters of Hinduſtan.

Muslim Dynasties.

The moſt important Mohammadan dynaſties of India were the ſo-called Patans of Dehli, with the ſubordinate but often independent line at Bengal, who reigned over most of Northern India from the end of the twelfth to the middle of the ſixteenth century of our era; and the Moguls, who were the ſucceſſors of the famous Timur or Tamerlane, and following the Patans extended their ſway over a ſtill wider area, from the middle of the ſixteenth century to the well-remembered days when England ſet an Empreſs in the place of the great Mogul. These two great houses really fill up the chronology of Mohammadan numismatics in Hindustan, but by no means exhaust the geography. The number of smaller dynasties, native or Muslim, who struck coins either in their own characters, or, more rarely, the Arabic style, is legion. Among the more important of these may be mentioned the Bahmany Kings, who ruled the greater part of the Dekhan, from Kulbarga, (which they re-christened Ahsanabad, or the "Most Beautiful City,") from the fourteenth to the sixteenth century; the Kings of Jaunpûr, Mewâr, Malwah, and Gujarat, who sprung into independence on the weakening of the central power in the fourteenth century, and generally lasted till the great annexations of the Mogul Emperors Baber and Akbar in the sixteenth.

Patans. The Patans and Moguls, however, may be selected as the Mohammadan coins of India *par excellence.* The Patans introduced a gold and silver coinage of singular purity and equal weight in either metal (about 174 grains), with often identical inscriptions, called the Tankah, which the Moguls afterwards converted into the gold mohr and silver rupee, which are so familiar to readers of Indian history. The inscriptions of the Patans are in Arabic, as a rule of slight pretensions to calligraphic excellence, but clear and solid, and presenting the usual statistics of the name of sovereign, of mint, and date, with sometimes a reference to the *fainéant* 'Abbâsy Khalifs who had been set up in Egypt by the

Mamlûks on the deſtruction of the Khalifate at Baghdad by Hulagu Khân. Beyond ſome curious poſthumous iſſues and this homage to a decrepit Khalifate, there is little that is particularly intereſting to any but metrologiſts and profeſſed numiſmatiſts in the Patan coinage. One ſovereign, however, poſſeſſed a genius for innovation, and his coinage preſents not a few features of intereſt. This was Mohammad ibn Taghlak (A.D. 1324-51), a prince whoſe character abounds in aſtoniſhing contraſts. "Generous to profuſion, an accompliſhed ſcholar, abſtinent, a firm defender of his faith, and the moſt experienced general of his day," he was yet poſſeſſed by a ferocious ſpirit that knew no mercy or regard for human life, and curſed with "a perverſion of intellect which induced him to allow deſpotiſm to run into inſane fury at any ſign of oppoſition to his will."[1] It was his fate at firſt to gather the empire together more firmly and with wider boundaries than ever; and then, by the eccentricity or madneſs of his rule, to ſow the ſeeds of that general diſintegration which barely waited for his death before it diſplayed its independence in every part of the empire. Among the ſigns of Mohammad ibn Taghlak's eccentricity is his coinage. It teſtifies to his taſte, inaſmuch as it is infinitely better engraved than any of the iſſues of his predeceſſors; and it bears witneſs to his paſſion for novelty, ſince it affords illuſtrations of ſeveral monetary reforms, all of which collapſed

Mohammad ibn Taghlak.

[1] E. Thomas: *Chronicles*, p. 202.

almoſt as ſoon as they were inſtituted. Firſt Mohammad ibn Taghlak reſolved to alter the ſtandard Tankah, which had hitherto been of the uniform weight of 174 grs. for both gold and ſilver, and to raiſe the gold to 200 grs., and lower the ſilver to 140; but he failed to make his new ſtandards acceptable to his ſubjects, and in three or four years the old Tankah had to be reſtored. His next attempt was a much bolder flight. He had apparently heard of the fiduciary paper currency which Khubilai Khân had ſucceſsfully introduced into the Celeſtial Empire, and which had been imitated, with very different reſults, in Perſia, and he reſolved to try the effects of a forced currency in his own dominions. No fraud was apparently contemplated, for the Dehli treaſury was overflowing, and when the experiment failed, the forced pieces were bought in at the mint at the nominal value, without any ſcrutiny for clipping or counterfeiting. This forced currency was of braſs and copper, and was engraved with words meant to compel their acceptance, such as "He who obeys the Sultan, verily he obeys God," and an inſcription ſtating it to be the equivalent of the ſilver Tankah; but no threats, even of ſo abſolute a deſpot as the Patan King, could commend theſe pieces to the people, and in leſs than three years they were abandoned.

Moguls of Dehli.

The Mogul coins have inſcriptions mainly in Perſian, and are alſo remarkable not only for occaſional eccentricity of ſhape, ſuch as the ornate oblongs which Akbar iſſued, but for the repreſentation of figures. The zodiacal rupees and mohrs of Jehangîr are well known, with the ſigns of the Zodiac engraved in bold relief; but the same Emperor even went ſo far as to engrave a portrait of himſelf in the act of raiſing the forbidden winecup to his lips. As a rule, however, the Mogul coinage contents itſelf with the uſual notices of names, titles, mints, and dates, and felicitous references to the monarchs' happy and

GOLD MOHR OF JEHANGÎR.

auſpicious reigns. Such was the inſcription of the Sikkeh rupee which (on a principle of frequent application at Dehli, when a king of doubtful authority ſought to ſupport himſelf upon the monetary credit of ſome predeceſſor) was retained by the Eaſt India Company till 1835, long after the Sovereign to whom it applied had gone to his Paradiſe: "Defender of the Mohammadan religion, mirror of the grace of God, the Emperor Shah Alam ſtruck this coin to be current throughout the ſeven climes. Struck at Murſhidâbâd in the year 19 of his fortunate reign." Sikkeh Rupee.

CHAPTER IX.

CHINA AND JAPAN.

THE coinages of Eaſtern Aſia are often the moſt valuable records we poſſeſs of the various nations' progreſs in wealth and civilization. Much of ancient hiſtory is gathered from them, and they are ſometimes the only clue to events for which hiſtorians would otherwiſe have to draw largely on their imaginations. In them we find hiſtorical proofs and materials—records which illuſtrate the political events in the life of great empires—data illuſtrating ſchemes for ſupplying the deficiency of metals, or avoiding the neceſſity of a more extenſive metallic currency. We ſee in China, for inſtance, the continued ſtruggle of the primitive ſyſtem of barter with the ſyſtem of fiduciary money required by the enlargement of the population and the development of exchange; and we ſee, alſo, in the application of economical principles very different from thoſe of Europe, the various attempts made by the Government to detain the people in a mediocrity of material life (not the *aurea mediocritas* of the poet), where an abſence of wants and deſires keeps them within the range of their ideal of happineſs.

Theſe conſiderations, intereſting to the economiſt and hiſtorian, are not the only elements of value in the ſtudy of the coinage, beſides the bare ſtatements of facts and dates which form the ſkeleton of hiſtory. The illuſtrations and ornamentations of the medals, charms, and tokens exemplify the ſuperſtitions, the habits and cuſtoms of the people, and make ſome amends for the chief defect of the coinage of the Far Eaſt, the lack of artiſtic excellence.

The civilized clans who bore the generic name **China.** of Bak or "flouriſhing," and travelling eaſtwards brought to China all the elements of a culture indirectly derived from the old focus of Babylonia, had not been taught in their previous home, weſt of the Hindu-kuſh, any other currency than that of weighing metals. Their earlieſt traditions do not point to any other; the development of barter and the uſe of cowries aroſe from neceſſity, and intercourſe with the indigenous tribes of their new country. The ſucceſſion of the words employed to denote the various ſubſtitutes of the as yet undiſcovered money is in itſelf ſuggeſtive of what took place in former times. The expreſſion uſed by later hiſtorians when ſpeaking of the early pſeudo-money is *pit*, a character meaning "wealth, riches." We muſt underſtand from the traditions that in the time of the Great Hot Bak-ket (Ur-

Bagash of Babylonian tradition), money was *metal*, and that afterwards, from the time of Nak Khunte (Nai Hwang-ti, ? B.C. 2250) and his Chinese successors, it became any exchangeable merchandise. For the people of Shang and of Ts'i, pieces of silk or hempen-cloth were money; later on, in the feudal states of Ts'i and that of Kiu, knives (*tao*) were used as currency. During the three dynasties of Yao, Hia, and Shang (B.C. 2100-1080), gold, silver, and copper were employed, besides cloth, tortoise-shell, and cowries.

Shell Currency. The use of shells as a medium of exchange by the ancient Chinese is a matter of peculiar interest in its antiquity, and its connection with the once widely extended cowry-shell currency. We find it mentioned at its very outset among the newly arrived Chinese, in their earliest book, the *Yh-King*, where, as an equivalent of "riches," we read "100,000 dead shell-fishes." The tortoise-shell currency is also mentioned in the same canonical book. Shell-currency began under the Hia dynasty (2000-1550 B.C.), when they had relations with the aborigines of the south and south-east of their newly conquered dominion. To what extent it was carried previously to their time we know not, but we have literary evidence that, with the superior culture which they had brought with them, they soon gave to shell-currency a development corresponding to their higher wealth and requirements.

Traces of the use of shells as a medium of exchange have remained crystallized in the written and ſpoken languages; the ideogram *pei* "ſhell" has the meaning of wealth and riches, and has been added as a ſilent determinative to many characters of the ſame claſs of meaning: goods, property, ſelling, prices, cheap, dear, ſtores, etc.; but it is worth noticing that the uſe of *pei* in this ſecondary meaning does not appear in the earlieſt characters of the language. In the wonderful *Geographical Survey* which goes by the name of Yü the Great, and might be as old as the eighteenth century B.C., the people of the iſlands along the coaſts of Yang-tcheu had to bring cowries as tribute. Yang-tcheu was the ſouth-eaſt diviſion of the Chineſe dominion, or rather of the regions upon which they eventually extended their ſuzerainty; its ſouthern borders were ill-defined, but it included the modern provinces of Tcheh-Kiang, Fuh-Kien, etc. It was from the iſlands of that part of China that the cowries exhibited at the International Fiſheries Exhibition of South Kenſington, 1883, were ſent.

Cowries were not the only ſhells uſed; that of the tortoiſe of various ſpecies and ſizes was uſed for the greater values, which would have required too many cowries; and a ſurvival of the old cuſtom has remained in the language, where the expreſſion *knei-hwo*, or tortoiſe-ſhell money, is uſed elegantly to denote a coin. Several ſorts of Cypraea were employed, one of which, the "purple ſhell," two or three inches long, was formerly found on the ſhores of the prefecture of Teng-tchen, north of the Shantung peninſula.

The celebrated claſſic of the Mountains and Seas (*Shan Haï King*), of which the firſt thirteen books have reached their bulk by an innumerable ſeries of incorporated additions ſince the time of the Shang dynaſty, twelfth century, down to the fourth century B.C., indicates the ſtreams and waters where the precious and variegated ſhells could be found; *i.e.*, mainly in the ſouth-eaſt and weſt. And the *Pen-tſao* claſſic, for which an earlier origin is claimed, ſtates that the cowries (*pei-tze* or *pei-tch'i*) live in the Eaſtern Sea; that is, ſouth-eaſt of the Shantung peninſula.

All theſe ſhells, excepting the ſmall ones, were current in pairs, and it is this practice which is alluded to in the following third ſtanza of an ode of the *Book of Poetry*, commonly attributed to the tenth century B.C.:

> "Luxuriantly grows the after-southernwood,
> In the midſt of that great height,
> We ſee our noble lord
> And he gives us a hundred pairs of Cypraea ſhells."

Mas She, the well-known editor of the *Book of Poetry* in the ſecond century B.C., commenting upon the ſhell-currency, ſpeaks of *tze-pei*, or purple Cypraea, but only as ranking after the ſea-tortoiſe-ſhell, meaſuring 1 foot 6 inches, which in his time could be obtained but in Kiu-tchin and Riao-tchi (Cochin-China and Annam), where they were uſed to make pots, baſins, and other valuable objects. We learn by this ſtatement that the uſe as currency of larger ſhells than the Cypraea moneta had not extended outſide China. But as to China proper, the great ſcholar we have juſt quoted could hardly ſpeak from perſonal experience, as the ſhell-currency no more exiſted officially in his time. Big ſhells were ſtill appreciated and ſought for as an object of luxury, and remained thus long afterwards. We find recorded in the *Han Annals*, that the Emperor Wen, in 179 B.C., having preſented the King of Southern Yueh with a hundred robes, the latter, with other preſents, returned five hundred of purple Cypraeae. The ſhell-currency was, however, fading away. It had received a great blow a long while previouſly from Hwei Wen, the Prince of Ts'ing, who in his ſecond year, *i.e.* 335 B.C., recogniſing the difficulties of finding a proper ſupply of ſhells and cowries, and the rapidly increaſing demand for a convenient currency, altogether ſuppreſſed it. The inland poſition of Ts'ing, far away from the ſources of ſupply, combined with the fact that metallic coins of various ſhapes and ſizes had begun to be recogniſed as a more practicable medium of exchange in the other ſtates of the Chineſe agglomeration, were the two main reaſons which led this anceſtor of the founder of the Chineſe Empire to aboliſh the cumbrous ſyſtem of ſhell-currency and to adopt the more perfect ſyſtem of metallic coins, already put in practice by private perſons in ſeveral of the neighbouring ſtates. He iſſued then the round copper coin, with a central ſquare hole, and the legend *pan-liang* (=$\frac{1}{2}$ ounce), indicating its value, which was afterwards imitated by the rulers of the Han dynaſty, and is, in fact, the

Earliest Metal Coinage.

direct and uninterrupted ancestor of the Chinese coins of the present day.

A time-honoured system like the shell-currency, however, could not disappear without struggling a while in out-of-the-way places, and, among a people of routine like the Chinese, could not lack supporters. It is to this conservative tendency that the country was indebted for an attempt to revive the old-fashioned currency. Wang Mang, the usurper who ruled in China (A.D. 9-23) between the two great Han dynasties, wanted, indeed, to rescind all the innovations introduced in the country by the eclipsed dynasty. Accordingly he enacted new statutes—one of which re-established a shell-currency consisting of five categories, the higher one of tortoise-shells being divided in ten classes. How far these differed from the old system we are unable to say for want of proper information; still, it is not unlikely that the discrepancies were small. But the intelligent part of the people, and the traders, objected to the revival of the antiquated system; and, in A.D. 14, Wang Mang had to cancel his former decrees. After his time we hear no more of the cowry-currency in China proper; but we trace its influence in the issue of small copper coins, shaped, indeed, as a small Cypraea, roughly imitated by their ovoidal or pear-like form, and commonly called Dragon's-head coins and Ant-coins, or Ant-nose coins. Some have been found of three different sizes, with the respective legends, *Liang* (for 1 oz.), *pan-liang* (or ½ oz.), and *Koh luh tchu*, "each ſix tchus," written in a rather out-of-the-way manner; but certainly, by the ſtyle of writing, iſſued in the laſt centuries before the Chriſtian era, in Tſu, the ſouthernmoſt ſtate of the Chineſe confederation.

The working of mines in China has rarely been left open to private enterpriſe; the authorities ſeem to have been afraid to leave the people free to acquire riches in that way; and as a rule they kept it for themſelves, and exerciſed much care and moderation in its uſe. Strict regulations have always forbidden the extraction of metals beyond limited quantities. Recourſe to the mines could take place in primitive times only in caſes of inundation or other great need. We find in the fragments of a ſtill exiſting work on government and legiſlation, by an able financier, Kwan-tze, who was a prime miniſter of the feudal state of Tai, in 685 B.C., an alluſion to the effect of ſuch floods: "When," he ſays, "from eaſt, weſt, north, and ſouth, all over a ſurface of 7,000 or 8,000 li, all intercourſe with theſe parts was cut off by the inundation, and in conſequence of the length of the way, and the difficulties of reaching them, neither boat nor cart could penetrate thither; the people therefore relied on, and employed according to their meaſures, pearls and gems as the highest commodities, then gold, and, as the third and lower claſs, knives and cloth." Mines.

Metals in lumps were conſidered, ſince the beginning of the Shang dynaſty, as a ſource of proſperity; they were called *trinon*, "ſpring or source," and the name lasted till its substitution by a quasi-homonym *tsien*, in allusion to the small copper implements of husbandry used later as currency. It is from the same time that the habit of hoarding bullion originated. We read that when the Shang dynasty was overthrown by Wu Wang, the founder of the Tchou dynasty, all the wealth accumulated by the last King, the scapegoat of the abuses and mistakes of his whole lineage, in the splendid palace called the Deer Gallery, was sacked and distributed to the people.

Tchou Dynasty. With the accession of the Tchou dynasty (1122 B.C.), a new era opened in the history of Chinese money. Regulations were established to fix the relative value of all the exchangeable commodities. The honour of this institution is attributed to the great Duke of Ts'i, who in 1103 B.C. established the rules of circulating money for the nine administrative boards of finance, which had been organized previously by another famous administrator, the Duke of Tchou. From commentaries of ancient date we understand that the gold circulated in the shape of little cubes of one square inch weighing a *kin;* the copper in round tongue-like plates was weighed by drachms (*tchu*); the silk cloth, 2 feet 2 inches wide, in rolls of 40 feet length formed a piece. The great man who had so successfully introduced order and principles in matters which seem to have been hitherto left to the caprice of individuals or to local and momentary necessity (and who, by-the-way, was not a Chinese, but a native of the aboriginal tribes of the Eaſt), retired to the Dukedom of Ts'i, where he iſſued the ſame regulations as in the Middle Kingdom. We have an inſight into the working of the new organization ſome hundred and fifty years afterwards, from a chapter of the *Shu King*. At the end of the reign of King Muh of Tchou, *i.e.* previous to 947 B.C., enactments were made for the mulcts and fines; to redeem the penalties ſuch as branding, mutilation or death, the culprit was allowed to pay 100, 200, 500 or 1,000 *hwan*. The *hwan* was a ring of copper weighing 6 oz., and this ſo far correſponds to the round ſhape enumerated in the Record of Inſtitutes of the great Duke of Ts'i.

The Duke Hwan of Ts'i (the fourteenth ſucceſſor of the former), who ruled from 685 to 644 B.C., and whoſe prime miniſter was the worthy financier Kwan-tze, of whom we have ſpoken above, in order to make known and acceſſible to the public the various weights, commiſſioned the Left Maſter of the Horſes to caſt ſome metal from the mines of the Tchwang mountain. The Duke Hwan was the leader of the feudal princes of the Chineſe agglomeration, and he ſwayed the empire under the nominal ſuzerainty of King Hwey of Tchou, and his regulations were therefore of a more momentous character than thoſe of any other prince in his dominion. Of the ſame Duke tradition ſays that from the bullion caſt at his own command he ordered the Inner Great Officer Wang yh to carry 2,000 *tſien* to the ſtate of Tſu, in order to purchafe a living ftag. What was the unit reprefented here by the expreffion *tfien*, is not ftated. Should we truft the word itfelf, it meant a fmall implement of hufbandry in metal, which, being frequently ufed for its weight and intrinfic value, became the current expreffion for money.

Adze Currency.

Indeed, the only obligation of weighing the metal for currency had not prevented the ufe of any object or implement for the purpofe of exchange according to their verified weights; the choice of the tools of conftant and daily ufe among a people exclufively occupied in agricultural purfuits naturally commended itfelf. Small adzes and billhooks above all were prominent by their large number and eafy handling. We can readily conceive how at firft the exchange of fuch tools would be accepted with facility by the people in their tranfactions; they could be either employed for their primeval object if wanted, or exchanged with readinefs in cafe of need. However, there was no limit to the felection of any particular form, while the employ of metal in bare lumps was never difufed. All forts of objects were made ufe of for exchange in early times, and their endlefs variety may be gathered from the following enumeration of ftrangely fhaped moneys of old: "Thofe like a bridge croffwife were commonly mufical-ftone money; thofe fhaped as a comb were commonly padlock money; thofe fhaped as a half-moon were the half-moon money;" the author goes on to mention the fiſh-ſcale money and the ſhell-money. Specimens of theſe rare ſhapes rarely appear in numiſmatic collections, and only in caſts, which are always open to ſome kind of ſuſpicion as to the genuineneſs of the original uſed for moulding. We do not know how far the regulations of the great Duke Wang, and thoſe of his later ſucceſſor, Duke Hwan, limited the variety of ſhapes; but ſmall implements of huſbandry were thoſe which were almoſt excluſively uſed for a long period, eſpecially ſmall adzes, chiſels, ſpades, or planes. They are an intereſting ſurvival of a peculiar tool of the ſtone age, hitherto found nowhere elſe than in South-Eaſtern Aſia. While all the hitherto found implements of this rude ſtage of induſtry are limited to a few types which preſent only ſlight variations in whatever country they are excavated, the type we are ſpeaking of is an exception. Its name, "ſhouldered-headed celt," is pretty well deſcriptive of its ſhape, which is cloſely imitated in the bronze implements of China uſed for currency. The only characteriſtic of the ſtone antecedent, which has diſappeared becauſe of the thinneſs of the metal, conſiſts "in the edge being ground down on *one* ſide like a chiſel, inſtead of on both ſides like an axe, as is uſually the caſe." The ſhouldered-headed celts are generally found in the Malayan peninſula, in the lower part of Burmah, within the provinces of Pegu and Tenaſſerim; they have been found at Chutiâ Nâgpûr, in Central India; and quite lately at Semrang Sen (ſouth-weſt of Lake Tanli-Sap), in Cambodia.

Weights and Implements.

Thus we can trace, up to the adminiſtration of Kwan-tze, a twofold development in the hiſtory of Chineſe moneys. Beſides the weights properly ſo-called, whatever may have been the occaſional employ made of them, aroſe the cuſtom of caſting ſmall implements, which for convenience were uſed in exchange, of a regular ſhape and approximate weight; and gradually, as a natural ſequence of that ſyſtem, came the practice of having them inſcribed with the name of the place or city where they were caſt and put in circulation.

Ring Weights.

The ſyſtem of ring-weights, which may, perhaps, be traced to an Egyptian ſource, was continued down to the foundation of the Chineſe Empire, when it was ſlightly modified into the pattern ſtill in uſe in the preſent day. When King Hwei Wan of Ts'in, the future conqueror of the whole of China, wanted to throw over the ſtill ſurviving uſe of cowry currency, in 338 B.C., he ordered ring-weights to be caſt, of which ſpecimens are found. Thoſe hitherto known bear the inſcription of their weight, "weighing 1 oz. 12 drs.," or "1 oz. 14 drs.," or only "12 drs.," differences which are ſuggeſtive of a larger number of varieties at preſent unknown.

Relics of the other ſhapes of metallic currency are ſtill in exiſtence, though not in large numbers, in the European collections. Of the *tch'ang*, or adze or ſpade-pattern, we know by actual ſpecimens that ſome were caſt ſpecially for the purpoſe of currency; for they are too light to have been intended for practical work Some do not bear any inſcription whatever, but uſually they are inſcribed with the name of the town where they were caſt; this cuſtom was of courſe of later introduction, when ſome tool-ſhaped objects were caſt in large numbers, without a view to their uſe as implements, or in ſmaller ſize than was required for induſtrial purpoſes. Theſe pſeudo-coins were inſcribed with the name of the place or city, and they were commonly called ſlip-weights, or leaf-weights, or helping-weights, ſlips or leaves. They were not iſſued by the governments, but by private individuals. Specimens, with the indication of 2 Kins, 1 Kin, $^1/_2$ Kin, and of proportionated ſizes bear the names of the cities of An-yü, Yü, Shan-yang, Liang, etc. Though a private buſineſs, the central government ſeveral times attempted to modify it. Thus King Tchwang of Tſu, who ruled in his principality from 612 to 589 B.C., vainly endeavoured to create a nominal currency by reducing to the value of units the larger pieces actually worth ſeveral units; and a ſimilar failure attended in 523 B.C. the iſſue by King, the ruler of Tchou, of large pieces (hitherto unidentified), intended to ſuperſede altogether the ſmall ones in circulation, which the King fancied were too light.

Leaf Weights.

During the ages following, which are known as the Period of the Contending States, money was multiplied at a great rate in the Chineſe agglomeration. The confederation of the various ſtates, after having laſted ſeveral centuries, had ceaſed to exiſt, and each of the principalities was fighting for ſupremacy over the others; and

Period of the Contending States.

in ſome of the ſtates the fight was in fact a ſtruggle for life. After ſome two centuries of inceſſant wars, ſeven ſtronger ſtates ſurvived, only to be finally ſubdued and abſorbed by the moſt powerful of them, the weſtern ſtate of Ts'in, the ruler of which eſtabliſhed the Chineſe Empire in the middle of the third century, and proclaimed himſelf firſt Emperor in 221 B.C.

Knife Money of Ts'i.

For numiſmatics, the ſtate of Ts'i during this period of contention is far the moſt important. The moſt widely known currency of Ts'i at that time is the *knife-money*, which conſiſted in a ſort of billhooks, ſome ſeven inches long, curved, and the handle terminating in a ring. The ſhape was that of an implement of huſbandry in bronze, of which a rude ſpecimen is exhibited in the Chineſe Gallery of the South Kenſington Muſeum. The ſtate of Ts'i was one of the moſt powerful of the Chineſe ſtates: it roſe in 1122 B.C., and was one of the laſt which reſiſted the ever-growing ſtate of Ts'in, as it was not ſubdued before 224 B.C. It covered what is now a large part of Northern Shantung and Southern Tchih-li, and always exerciſed an important influence in the empire. We remember that the financial Inſtitutes of the Tchön dynaſty were eſtabliſhed by the firſt Duke of Ts'i. The population of this region has been conſpicuous for its intelligence and boldneſs; and in the *She-King* the praiſes of female beauties are all ſung for ladies of Ts'i. The merchants of Ts'i, with their enterpriſing tendencies and the incitement of the ſea-trade, always diſplayed a daring which proved moſt uſeful to the progreſs of their countrymen. This intereſting feature is revealed to us by their knife-coinage, which gives proof of the extent of their commercial relations. The legends of the knife-coins bear poſitive teſtimony to the aſſociations which exiſted between ſeveral towns of the Ts'i ſtate, among themſelves, as alſo with towns of other ſtates. We do not know by whom theſe iſſues were really made, whether they were caſt by order either of the communities in partnerſhip or otherwiſe, or of aſſociations of

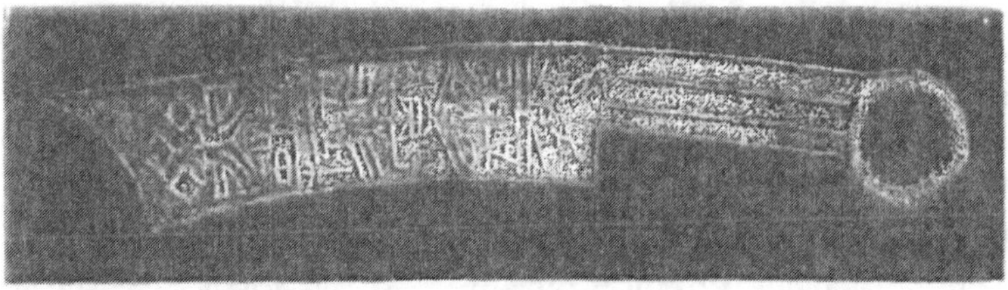

KNIFE MONEY.

traders independent of the communal adminiſtration.

The knife-currency did not outlive the ſubmiſſion of the ſtates of Ts'i and Wei and their abſorption by that of Ts'in, which ſtarted a new currency. It ceaſed to be recogniſed as the ordinary money, and took refuge in out-of-the-way places outſide the borders of China. Though we have no intermediary proof of its continued exiſtence, for lack of information we cannot help connecting with it and conſidering as a ſurvival of the old practice, ſtill exiſting in the preſent century among the Khamti and Sing-Pho tribes on the ſouth-weſt borders of China, of uſing ſmall ſquare iron *dhas* or knives as currency. The very name of theſe *dhas* is obviouſly connected with the Chineſe *tao* or knife-money, and ſpeaks for itſelf.

Leaf Money.

A ſort of deſcendant of the older weights, known as ſlips for weight, or leaf-money, received a greater development than the knife-money. The latter were too large to be the common and popular medium of exchange in a country where the exigencies of life were ſo ſmall and ſo cheap that every man needed 1,000 pieces of money or a little more a year; the equivalent of which in our money of the preſent day ſhould be about eight ſhillings, which was a ſufficient income for a man in China in the third century B.C. In the ſecond half of the fourth century, the King of Tchao (a ſtate to the ſouth of the modern Tchih-li and Shan-ſi provinces) granted to Tchang-y the uſe of ſaddle-money: another name for leaf-money. All the leaf-money of that period may be claſſed in two diviſions, one with ſquare, and the other with pointed feet. They bear on the obverſe the name of the place where they were iſſued, and generally on the reverſe a ſerial figure. The twenty and odd towns whoſe names occur were ſcattered all over the various ſtates, but were moſtly ſituated in the ſtates of Ts'i and Wei. Theſe two ſtates fought to the laſt againſt their abſorption by the powerful ſtate of Ts'in; it is clear that the multiplication of their money during that period of warfare was for the purpoſe of helping and maintaining their ſtruggle. Their rude workmanſhip, and the ſimplifications of characters drawn by ignorant hands, exclude any poſſibility of their being the produce of a ſtate coinage. The ſigns of the legends are abbreviated ſo looſely, in defiance of all principles of orthography, and they offer ſo many variants, that we may be ſure that they are the work of private individuals among the people.

The leaf-money did not die out altogether with the foundation of the Chineſe Empire; it lingered in obſcure corners, and was not extinguiſhed by the ſtate currency iſſued by the Ts'in dynaſty. **Gold Currency.**

Of the early gold currency we have very little to ſay. It could not be in frequent uſe in a country where life was ſo cheap, and it was reſtricted to the purchaſe of jewels or preſents from the princes and wealthy people. Except in the financial arrangements of the Tchöu dynaſty as eſtabliſhed by the great Duke of Ts'i, we hear only of one hiſtorical inſtance of the uſe of the 1 inch cube of gold, or *kin*, weighing one pound, which had been made the ſtandard.

In the fourth century B.C. we read of an *yh* of gold, but we know nothing more of it. It was probably a weight of precious metal in the lump. Under the Ts'in dynaſty, the *yh* was the unit for gold, and it was then equal to 20 *liang* in weight. When the Han dynaſty aroſe, the Ts'in inſtitutions were revoked, and the old cubic inch of gold or *kin* was again the unit as under the Tchöu dynaſty. A ſpecimen of this curious money exiſts in the Cabinet des Médailles, at Paris, and a great ſcholar, Ed. Biot, has tried (but in our opinion unſucceſsfully) to aſcertain by its weight the ſtandard of the ancient Chineſe.

STATE COINAGE. With the Ts'in dynaſty appears the firſt ſtate mintage of the central government, the lineal antecedent of the preſent coinage. Of the gold currency we have already ſaid the little that can be recorded. Ts'in Dynasty. The copper money was round, with a ſquare hole in the centre: "round as the ſky, ſquare as the earth." The pieces were ſubſtantially the ſame as thoſe of the Tchöu dynaſty as far as their regular weight is concerned, and their multiples were in correct proportion to the unit; their weight agreed with that inſcribed upon them. They were marked *Pan-liang*, or half-*liang*, equivalent to the eighth part of a *kin*-weight. All that were formerly uſed as mediums of exchange—gems, pearls, tortoiſe-ſhell, cowries, ſilver, tin, etc., etc.—were no longer recogniſed as equivalent for currency in the official tranſactions. The purpoſe of the founder of the empire, Ts'in Shi Hoang-ti, was to effect a thorough aſſimilation of the various and rather heterogeneous parts of his dominion. His great achievements in this reſpect were, firſt, the ſubſtitution, for the varieties in the writing which had gradually ariſen with the independence of the ſtates, of a uniform ſtyle of writing, a ſort of ideographical tranſcription which could be underſtood everywhere, deſpite the differences of the vernacular dialects; and, ſecond, his attempts at eſtabliſhing a State money. The burning of the books, which, indeed, has deprived the world of many ancient records which nowadays would be invaluable treasures, and must therefore be deeply regretted, was nevertheless an act of political wisdom, in order to clear away the impediments by which the ultra-conservatives tried to check his steps. The new Emperor wished to withdraw, out of the reach of the literati and of the people at large, all the accumulated historical traditions, which by the numerous examples there recorded as patterns of conduct, offered too much ground for protesting against the spirit of innovation and progress which characterised his government.

The dynasty founded by this great ruler in 221 B.C. for "ten thousand years," finished in troubles and rebellions against an atrocious and tyrannical policy after only fifteen years, and was soon succeeded by the great *Han* dynasty, which during four centuries, with a slight eclipse of sixteen years, ruled the empire (204 B.C. to 190 A.D.).

Han Dynasty.

The *Hans* considered the money of the Ts'in too heavy and inconvenient, and they authorized the people to cast some *leaf-money;* while the gold coins were again of the weight of a pound, as under the Tchou dynasty. But the small copper pieces became gradually so thin, that indeed they deserved their nickname of elm-leaf money; and they were multiplied to such an extent that they lost their former value, and prices rose enormously. In order to mitigate this evil, the Empress Kao (185 B.C.) issued pieces of 8 *tchus*, equal in value to the half-ounce pieces (*pan-liang*) of the preceding dynasty; but it was found impossible to withdraw the elm-leaf money from circulation. Eleven years afterwards, the Emperor Wen-Ti, in the fifth year of his reign, tried to meet the difficulty by the issue of pieces having the same legend of *pan-liang* as before, but weighing only 4 *tchus;* and with the intention of rooting out false coining, he let the people cast their own money. The remedy, however, was insufficient, and some uneasiness was felt by the Emperor as to the influence of two feudal and almost independent states which issued their own money at a higher standard than that of the Chinese Empire.

Counterfeiting. The Emperor, in face of the failure of free mintage to check the counterfeiters, was obliged to forbid the people to cast their own money. Ring-Ti (156-140), the successor of Wen-Ti, was accused of having issued false gold coins; so that the people eagerly used the money introduced by the feudal state of Teng. False coiners practised their profession, and severe sentences could not stop the ever-growing evil. Wu-Ti, whose reign of fifty-four years was the most glorious of his dynasty, and whose generals carried the Chinese arms into the heart of Asia, issued, as a palliative measure, a money of real value, bearing the design of 3 *tchus;* but five years later it had to be suppressed again, because it was counterfeited and clipped, and pieces of 5 *tchus*, the standard of the dynasty, were then cast like those introduced by the Empress Kao. But all this was of no avail againſt the counterfeiters, who iſſued ſuch quantities of debaſed coin, that the genuine money nearly diſappeared in ſome parts of the Empire, where pieces of cloth had to be uſed again as a medium of exchange. To face ſuch an emergency it was decided to aboliſh all the then exiſting pieces which had a nominal value of half an ounce, but which in reality contained only 4 *tchus*, and to make new pieces of a weight of 5 *tchus*, furniſhed all around with a raiſed edge, in order to prevent the coins from being filed.

The third currency iſſued by order of the Emperor Wu-Ti conſiſted of three ſorts of pieces of different ſize and form, made of tin and ſilver melted together, and of a nominal value far beyond the intrinſic. The firſt was round, with the deſign of a dragon, emblem of the Imperial dignity, weighing 8 *liang*, and its value was fixed at 3,000 pieces of money. The ſecond was ſquare, with the deſign of a horſe, weighing 6 *liang*, and worth 500 pieces. The third was oblong, with the deſign of a tortoiſe, weighing 4 *liang*, and worth 300 pieces. The reſult of theſe fiduciary iſſues was very unſatisfactory; and their end was ſad indeed. The very year of their iſſue they could no longer circulate, having been counterfeited on a great ſcale, not only by the people, but alſo by the ſtate officials. No ſpecimens of this fanciful mintage ſeem to be ſtill in exiſtence; and the repreſentations of it which appear in ſome native books of numiſmatics were drawn from the written deſcription, and the falſe ſpecimens which appear ſometimes in collections were made from the drawings, for ſale to collectors.

The Shang-lin Mint.

After twenty-three years ſpent in theſe unſucceſsful eſſays, the Emperor Wu-Ti was at laſt convinced that the evil was more deeply rooted than had been hitherto ſuppoſed, and that ſome more adequate meaſures had become neceſſary. Accordingly, with theſe wiſe views, great changes were made in the monetary management of the empire. Every diſtrict and province was not allowed, as formerly, to caſt its own money; and a ſtate mint was eſtabliſhed in the capital of the empire, under the direction of three members of the Shang-lin, or Academy, which had been created by the ſame Emperor in 138 B.C. All the metallic currency formerly in uſe was withdrawn and brought to the Shang-lin mint to be melted and recaſt; and all money not iſſued by that mint was conſidered illegal. The moſt ſkilled of the falſe coiners were engaged as workmen at the mint. The money iſſued was that of *5-tchu* pieces, which, being very well made, remained the ſtandard, excepting temporary mintages, during ſeven centuries, or until the iſſue of the *Kai yuen tung pao*, the ſtandard coin of the T'ang dynaſty, in 622 A.D. Theſe (*5-tchu*) pieces were of the now uſual pattern—round, with a ſquare hole in the centre, ſize 6 of Mionnet's ſcale, with a ſmall raiſed edge all around. In conſequence of the draſtic meaſures taken by Wu-Ti, the counterfeiters had little chance during the latter part of his reign; and we do not hear of them during the ſhort rule of his ſucceſſor Tchao-Ti (86-73 B.C.). However, in the long run, they proved to be ſtronger than the law of the land. Under the Emperor Suan-Ti (73-48 B.C.), in the years 71 and 60 B.C., it was neceſſary to make ſome official variations in the diſpoſition of the deſign by the addition of a raiſed edge on both ſides of the ſquare central hole. But in the reign of the Emperor Yuen-Ti (48-32 B.C.) the counterfeiting had again reached a dangerous level; the forgers were more than 100,000 in number, and propoſals were ſeriouſly diſcuſſed by the councillors of the Crown to aboliſh the metallic currency, and ſubſtitute in its ſtead grain, ſilk, cloth, and tortoiſeſhell as a medium of exchange; but it was difficult to make a ſudden change in money which had been for a long time in circulation. The only means of checking the counterfeiters then was to iſſue from time to time new alterations, in the ſhape of additional lines or dots on the 5-*tchu* pieces. We hear no more of changes in the mintage until the uſurper Wang Mang, half a century later. From 217 B.C., when the Shang-lin mint began to caſt money, till the beginning of the reign of the Emperor Ping-Ti (1 A.D.), the amount of pieces iſſued was 280,000,000,000. In the time of the Emperor Yuen-Ti (48-32 B.C.) the treaſury of the Imperial palace amounted to 4,000,000,000, and the privy purſe contained 1,800,000,000 pieces of money.

The moſt eventful period in the hiſtory of Chineſe money is that of the eighteen years during **Wang Mang.**

which Wang Mang the usurper ruled the country, first as Regent, and after as Emperor. He began to cancel the various decrees enacted by the Han dynasty, and reverted again to the money of the Tchou dynasty, the multiple and unit pieces, or, as the Chinese say, the mother and child, weighed in proportion to each other. He also made again what he supposed to have been the pieces of Ring *King* of the Tchou dynasty, and he reintroduced the knife-shaped money. It is easy to judge how far these revived shapes were different from the originals when we compare the knife-shaped money of his issues to actual specimens of the older currency. The so-called knives of Wang Mang have but the name in common with their originals; they are half as long and much thicker, while the ring at the end of the handle is replaced by the shape of a thick piece of money with rim and central square hole.

Revival of Knife Money.

When the usurper took actual possession of the Imperial throne (9 A.D.), he was afraid of all that would remind the people of the eclipsed dynasty. As the name of *Lin*, the founder of the dynasty, contained the characters *kin* ("metal"), and *tao* ("knife"), Wang Mang feared that his own knife-money would record the name of its founder (an apprehension which later on proved to be well grounded), and he decreed the abolition of the two sorts of knives and of the 5-*tchu* pieces. He substituted new sorts of currency of gold, silver, tortoise-shell, cowries, and copper. Of the tortoise-shell and cowries thus revived we have already spoken. The gold piece was, of course, in imitation of the ancient rule of the Tchou dynasty, and was called *kin* (pound), with a value of 10,000 copper pieces. In silver there were two pieces of different values based on a unit called *liu* (=8 *liang*); their difference consisted only in the quality of the silver, and their value was 1,580 and 1,000 *cash*. As to the shape of this gold and silver money, we know nothing, and no specimen is known to exist.

The copper money received the name of *pu* by a revival of the oldest name used in the state of Ts'i previously to the financial Institutes of the Tchou dynasty, when *pu* (or cloth) was the principal medium of exchange in this region.

Revived Han Dynasty

In A.D. 23, the usurper Wang Mang was murdered, and the second Han dynasty began to rule. The currency of the country was in frightful disorder; the last issues of Wang Mang were no longer accepted, because they existed only in counterfeit, and the old 5-*tchu* pieces were in such small numbers that cloth, silk, metals, and rice were all used as currency, every individual making the most of them. However, Kwang Wu-Ti, the new Emperor, was not able, through the difficulties of the situation, to cast money before 40 A.D., and the pattern then used was that of the 5-*tchu* pieces, the standard currency of the Han. The only modification subsequently made was the addition on the reverse of four straight strokes from the corners of the central hole to the outside rim. Some iron 5-*tchu* pieces had been cast during the troubles at the end of the laſt reign, two being equivalent to one of copper.

Division of the Empire.

No other currency than the copper *5-tchu* pieces was iſſued till the end of the Han dynaſty (220 A.D.), and the enſuing diviſion for over fifty years of the empire into three kingdoms, Shuh, Wei, and Wu,—except ſmall copper pieces iſſued in 190 A.D. by the laſt Emperor, Hien-Ti, to ſupply the *5-tchu* pieces; for which, as the neceſſary quantity of copper was not available, he ſeized many copper objects and ſtatues, eſpecially thoſe of Fei-lien or Fóng-pöh, the God of the Winds, who had incurred his curſe.

Wei.

Four hundred years of monetary troubles and diſorders had not convinced the rulers of the neceſſity of a ſound currency. The King of Wei, in the north, thought that the beſt means of avoiding all theſe difficulties was to ſuppreſs the metallic currency altogether. Accordingly he aboliſhed the *5-tchu* pieces, and ordered the people to uſe as currency only grain and ſilk. It was only opening another door to the counterfeiters, who, inſtead of caſting bad metal, put moiſt grain in the bags, and wove thin and fleecy ſilk, so that after forty years it was neceſſary to return to the metal currency, and pieces of the time-honoured *5-tchu* pattern were caſt again and put in circulation.

Wu.

In the ſtate of Wu, the eaſternmoſt ſtate of the three, matters were ſtill worſe. In 236 A.D. were iſſued large pieces (8 of Mionnet's ſcale), with the legend *Ta tſinen wu pöh* ("Great money

500"), and two years afterwards larger ones (9$^{1}/_{2}$), *Ta tſinen tang tſien* ("Great money worth 1000"), which were ſoon counterfeited on a ſmaller ſcale, ſo that it was deemed adviſable to diſcontinue their mintage, and to melt them for implements. In 256 A.D. was iſſued another mintage, the pieces whereof in the ordinary pattern were worth 100 *tſien*, as indicated by their legend, *Tai-ping peh tſien* ("100 *tſien* [or *caſh*] of [the period] Tai Ping"), which were of courſe ſoon imitated in a ſmaller ſize. This is the firſt example of the uſe of the name of the reign or *nien-hao* in the denomination of the money. The caſe is worth noticing, though only ſporadic examples are ſtill found during the following centuries. Gradually the cuſtom became more general, and later on, from the T'ang dynaſty up to the preſent day, the iſſues are diſtinguiſhed by the names of the years during which they were caſt. Since the Ming dynaſty the *nien-hao*, which were generally changed ſeveral times during one reign, have been made uniform for the full length of a reign, and to a certain extent have become identified with the ruler's own name, which is too ſacred to be pronounced during his lifetime.

Later Ts'in Dynasty.

Though the ſhape of the currency was pretty well ſettled, we ſtill find ſome eccentricities in the iſſues, partly due to the abſence of the neceſſary quantity of metal. The Ts'in dynaſty (265-317 A.D.), who re-united the empire under one ſway, iſſued diminutive 5-*tchu* pieces (ſize 2 of Mionnet's ſcale), and two large iron pieces (ſizes 9 and 15), worth 100 and 1,000, and so marked from top to bottom *Yh peh* and *Yh tsien* respectively, with *Yung ngan* ("Eternal peace") from right to left, denoting the name of the year (304 A.D.), when they were cast.

The Two Empires.

During a period of one hundred and fifty years, the empire was nominally divided between two Emperors, though in fact it was for a while partitioned into nine different states, in seven of which the rulers had not assumed the Imperial title. Of course, money too was in great disorder, but it is worth noticing that the Tartars, who ruled in the northern part of the Yang-tse Kiang, while the lawful heir of the ancient Chinese had removed to the south, had much more sound views on financial economy than the Chinese themselves, with all their painful and costly experience.

Southern Empire.

In the Southern Empire, under the Sung dynasty (420-477 A.D.), the Emperor Wen-Ti issued, in the year 430, copper pieces with a raised edge, and the design 4 *tchus*, which were equal in value to the old 5-*tchu* pieces; these pieces were hard to counterfeit, but very soon the old frauds began again. Hia Wu Ti's 4-*tchu* coins, with double legends (454-456), and his later 2-*tchu* pieces, were largely imitated, till they received derisive nicknames from the people, who called the thin ones "weed-leaves," and the small ones "goose-eye money."

At the beginning of the Liang dynasty (502-556 A.D.), in consequence of the closing of the state mints in sheer despair, money was so scarce that it was employed only in the capital, Nanking, and its vicinity. In order to put an end to the fraudulent dealings of the money-changers, it was decided to fuperfede the copper money by iron money, and pieces bearing the legends *Ta Kih wu tchu*, *Ta Fuh wu tchu*, *Ta t'ung wu tchu*, in iron were put in circulation. *Ta t'ung* only is a name of year, being that of the years 527, 528. But this was the folution of a difficulty by the creation of a new one. Iron could be got much more eafily than copper, and as the Government itfelf could not refift the temptation of making large profits, in ten years the iron money fell to one-third of its intended value. **Iron Money.**

When the Tch'en dynafty (557-587 A.D.) arofe, among the confufions caufed by the fall of the Liang, all the iron money was difcarded, and the new princes reverted to the old 5-*tchu* pieces, which, in refpect to the ftill circulating "goofe-eye money," had a relative value of 10 to 1.

Northern Empire. While all thefe monetary troubles and wild experiments were going on in the Southern Empire, more fober views and found economical principles had guided the Tartar rulers in the north. Indeed, their people, many of whom had fettled in China, were not accuftomed to metallic currency, and continued bartering as formerly, while the Chinefe themfelves ufed the former currency. It is only the feventh ruler of the Topa or Wei dynafty (386-532 A.D.), Hiao Wu-Ti, who directed in 477 A.D. that the falaries of all the ftate officers fhould be reckoned by money to be used henceforth in the empire, at the rate of 200 pieces of copper money, being equal to a piece of silk. The new money was inscribed *Tai Ho wu tchu*, or "5-*tchu* of (the period) Tai-ho." Fifty years afterwards false coining had impaired considerably this money, and new ones had to be cast with the legend *Yung ngan wu tchu*, or "5-*tchu* of (the period) Yung ngan" ("Eternal peace").

Sui Dynasty. Under the Sui dynasty (581-618 A.D.), who ruled again over the whole empire, attempts were made to revive the old standard pieces of 5 *tchus*, and new ones were cast with the new distinctive feature of a broader ring. But the innumerable issues of money which had been made in the preceding centuries in the various states, and which were locally still more or less in circulation, had caused the most hopeless confusion. The old standard was no longer trusted by the people, who were obliged in the North-Western provinces, west of the Hoang-ho river, to use money from the foreign countries of the West with which they had commercial intercourse.

MODERN COINAGE.

Tang Dynasty. With the great T'ang dynasty rises a great change for the better in the metallic currency of China. As we have seen at the end of the last period, the 5-*tchu* pieces, which had been the standard money for more than eight centuries, had fallen into such discredit that it was impossible even to retain the name. An entirely new money was established, bearing the legend *Kai yuen t'ung pao* (or "Current money of the newest beginning "), weighing half as much again as the old 5-*tchu* pieces (*i.e.*, $7^1/_2$-*tchu*), with a ſize of 7 on Mionnet's ſcale. On the reverſe was a nail-mark, which ſince then has ſpread all over the Eaſt, in Japan as in Corea and Annam. The origin of this curious mark is attributed to this incident: when the Under-Secretary of the Cenſors, Ngeu-yang-ſiun, who had himſelf written the characters of the legend, ſhowed a model in wax of the new money, the Empreſs Wen-teh in touching it left on the wax the impreſſion of her nail.

Limited Issue.

The new money was so good that it ſoon ſpread all over the empire, and has never been ſurpaſſed. The only reproach was that it was not iſſued in sufficient quantities to meet the requirements of the traders. This inſufficiency led to ſeveral abuſes. The pieces were counterfeited in a mixture of iron and tin by ſkilful forgers, againſt whoſe cunning the officials were powerleſs. The Emperor tried to aboliſh the new money leſs than forty years after its firſt iſſue, and cauſed the ſtate-money to be provided with a new legend (*Hien K'ing t'ung pao*); but it was ſoon found impoſſible to go on with the new meaſure, which therefore was withdrawn. The only practicable means was to make terms with the counterfeited money, and to accept it in payment. In 666 A.D. a new money with the legend *K'ien fung* (the year-name) *tung pao*, was iſſued, to be accepted at the rate of one new for ten old pieces; but it ſoon became neceſſary to caſt again the *Kai yuen* pattern. The current money always circulated by ſtrings of 1,000, and thus the falſe pieces eaſily eſcaped detection. Under the reign of the Empreſs Wu (684-704 A.D.), therefore, it was forbidden to make payment in pieces ſtrung together; they were to circulate looſe, that the copper, tin, and iron pieces might be diſtinguiſhed at once.

Dearth of Metal. All the efforts of the Government were of no avail. The iſſue in 758 A.D. of larger money directed to be the equivalent of 50 and of 10 of the old pieces, was received with contempt by the people, becauſe they had no intrinſic value. The metallic currency was ſo poor that ſtones for grinding rice were received as money of an intrinſic value at the rate of 1 to 10 *caſh.* The great difficulty to overcome, for the Government, was the ſcanty ſupply of copper. Though it had been forbidden to any individual to ſtore up more than a fixed quantity of the precious metal, the amount in circulation had gradually diminiſhed by the melting of the good copper pieces to make vaſes, implements, and Buddhiſt figures. In 809 A.D. private perſons tried to circulate ſilver money by working the ſilver mines of the Wuling Mountains (ſouth of Hunan province), but this was ſoon prohibited by the Government.

Confiscation of Buddhist Treasures. At laſt it was found neceſſary to regulate the uſe of the various metals. In 829 A.D. it was ordered that the Buddhiſt figures and ornaments, inſtead of being made of copper, ſhould be made of lead, tin, clay, or wood, and the girdle either of gold, ſilver, Perſian braſs, or ſteel blued and polished; only for mirrors, gongs, nails, rings, and buttons, copper might be used. This restrictive measure was only the prelude of another of a more sweeping character. By the natural reaction from the extraordinary favour bestowed upon Buddhism during the previous reigns, this religion, from its excessive development and the immoderate pretensions of its devotees, came under the displeasure of the Emperor Wu Tsung, who, in 845 A.D., decreed its suppression. 4,600 monasteries and 40,000 smaller temples were destroyed; 260,500 monks and nuns were compelled to return to lay life; more than 15,000,000 acres of land were seized, and 150,000 female slaves were freed. All the copper statues, mallet-bells, gongs, and clapper-bells were confiscated to the profit of the Government, and melted to cast money of the *Kai-yuen* pattern in about twenty-five mints, of which the name was marked on the reverse of the pieces. This new supply of money was received with great favour, because of the quantity of gold supposed by the people to have been mixed with the copper in the temples.

The continuation of the numismatic records of China is a tedious repetition of all that we have seen thus far. Insufficiency in the supply of copper, and struggles against the counterfeiters, with the additional complications of a double standard caused by the temporary casting of iron money under the Sung dynasty and of the development of the paper money, which, from small beginnings in 806 A.D., attained a paramount importance under

Yuen and Ming Dynasties. the Yuen or Mongol dynaſty, which caſt very ſmall quantities of copper-money. The Ming dynaſty had alſo a poor mintage. It is only the preſent dynaſty, the *Ta Ts'ing* Mandchu, who iſſued a regular and efficient mintage. From the time of the Ming dynaſty the year-names have been reduced to one for each reign, ſo that the legend was henceforth the ſame for the whole mintage of a ruler.

Mandchu Dynasty. Regularity, however, is fairly ſecured in the iſſues from the mint of the Board of Finance in the capital, which are the pattern for the provincial mints; but the ſhrinking of the cool metal, when frequently repeated by the caſting from moulds made from pieces and not from the pattern, produces ſometimes a ſenſible difference, which is certainly not diſadvantageous to ſome of the mint-maſters. The authorized proportion of the alloys was, till 1722, copper 50, zinc $41^{1}/_{2}$, lead $6^{1}/_{2}$, tin 2; after that time the compoſition conſiſted of equal parts of copper and zinc. The obverſe bears the name of the reign, read from top to bottom, and the words *tung pao*, or "current-money," from right to left. On the reverſe the name of the mint in Chineſe, or in Mandchu and Chineſe, or in Mandchu only. There has been only one dark period in the preſent mintage, which for a time ſunk to the loweſt level during the great Taï-ping rebellion. The ſupply of the copper mines was ſtopped, and it was neceſſary to caſt iron money, the worſt of its kind that was ever made.

Silver circulates generally caſt in ingots, in ſhape rudely reſembling ſhoes, and for that reaſon called "ſhoe-ſilver." With the exception of two unſucceſsful (becauſe counterfeited) attempts in 1835 and 1856 to caſt ſilver dollars, the Government has never iſſued ſilver money. In Fuhkien province and Formoſa iſland, in 1835, a large iſſue of native dollars was made to pay the troops on that iſland; the legend was, "Pure ſilver for current uſe from the Tchang tchöu commiſſariat, (weight) 7 *mace* 2 *candareens.*" At Shanghai, in 1856, the *taels*, or dollars, were of the ſame weight and purity (417·4 grs. troy); and beſides the inſcription in Chineſe and in Mandchu, they had an effigy of the god of longevity on the head, and a tripod on the tail, to authenticate the official origin. Gold, caſt into ingots, alſo circulates by weight.

Private individuals have ſometimes cauſed ſilver to be caſt as money; but they are generally ſatisfied to make, with European appliances, imitations of the Mexican and old Spaniſh dollars which are in currency; theſe, as they paſs from hand to hand, are punched with the ſeal or ſtamp of the owner by way of endorſement; and when the marks are ſo numerous that there is no room left on the coin for more, they are melted.

The Japaneſe records tell us nothing about the means by which barter was carried on previous to the uſe of metals, which do not appear in the Empire of the Riſing Sun before the fifth century A.D. Theſe records claim to go back uninter- JAPAN.

ruptedly to 660 B.C., ſo that, even admitting that this far-reached date has to be ſhorn of ſeveral centuries, there is ſtill a long lapſe of time during which regular means of exchange might have been recorded.

Earliest issues.

In the *Ko-ji-ki*, or "Records of Ancient Matters," lately tranſlated with great learning and induſtry by Mr. Baſil Hall Chamberlain, the firſt appointment of a treaſurer is recorded during the reign of the Emperor Tza-ho Wạke, or Ri-chin, who ruled from 400 to 405 A.D., according to the "accepted chronology;" and ſeveral, but not all, native numiſmatiſts of high ſtanding attribute to his immediate ſucceſſor, Midzu-ha Wake, or Han-zei, in 408 A.D., the iſſue of rough ſilver coins, flat and irregular diſks, with a ſmall round central hole bearing ſeveral marks of rude ſtars of ſix lines, and ſometimes undiſtinguiſhable ſtrokes, ſize 9 of Mionnet's ſcale. *Mu-mon-do-ſen*, *i.e.* coins bearing no characters, are more often claſſified among the *Kitte-ſen*, *i.e.* coins iſſued proviſionally in times of diſturbances and warfare, and therefore very coarſely made, being generally cut out of a plate of metal inſtead of caſt.

The genuineneſs of the next coins in date, *i.e.*, copper coins iſſued in 683 and 690 A.D., has remained comparatively unchallenged. They conſiſt in flat and irregular diſks of copper, with a ſmall round central hole; ſize, 6 of Mionnet's ſcale; marks, 4 croſſes, each in a circle.

The working of metallic mines in Japan began very late—674 for ſilver, 708 for copper, 749 for gold; and previous to theſe dates the ſupply of metal by foreign importations was very limited, and if wanted, it was always eaſy to get the copper *caſh* from China. It is only in 708 A.D., after the diſcovery of copper mines, that the Japaneſe began to caſt regularly copper coins, of the ſame ſhape as had then been common in China for many centuries; viz., round, with a ſquare hole in the centre. The Chineſe ſyſtem of the year-names, in Japaneſe *Nengo*, which had been adopted ſince 645 A.D., was followed in the legends of the coins. The diſcovery and working of copper mines was conſidered ſo important an event for the country, that the actual *Nengo* was changed into *Wa-do*, *i.e.*, Japaneſe copper; and the legend of the coins was *Wa-do-kai-tchin*, which may be rendered "New precious article of the *Wa-do* or Japaneſe copper period." The Japaneſe recogniſe the various iſſues of their coins by differences in the ſhape of a character, or of a ſtroke of a character, and ſo claſſify three iſſues of the *Wa-do* coin, all rather roughly caſt, and a fourth iſſue of a ſuperior workmanſhip, imitated from the celebrated Chineſe *Kai-yuen* coin, to which it is like in form, ſhape of characters, and general appearance. Fifty-two years afterwards, in A.D. 760, there were ſo many forged *Wa-do-kai-tchin* in circulation, that the Government decided to iſſue a new coin, which was caſt, with the legend *Man-nen-tſu-ho*, or "Current money of ten thouſand years," in four iſſues. A ſilver coin, worth ten of the copper ones, was put in circulation the

Imitation of Chinese Money.

ſame year, with the legend *Dai-bei-gen-ho*, "Fundamental money of the great tranquillity."

Ten other copper coins were ſucceſſively iſſued in A.D. 765, 796, 818, 835, 848, 859, 870, 890, 907, and 958; gradually decreaſing in ſize and workmanſhip till 870, and in material afterwards. The legends are often undecipherable, and in the laſt coins the metal is largely alloyed with lead; in ſome caſes they are made entirely of the latter metal. The execution was careleſs, and the reſult was a rather disreputable money. Theſe twelve coins conſtitute the antique coins of the country, or, as the Japaneſe call them,[1] *Jū-ni-hin* ("The twelve kinds"). After the coinage of the latter coin, in conſequence of political troubles, no copper coins whatever were iſſued by the Central Government for over 600 years. Mintage in lead had begun as a ſecondary currency with the iſſue of 835 A.D., and down to 1302 the twelve antique coin patterns circulated in lead or in tin.

Lead Currency.

Chinese Coins in Japan.

During this long interruption in the iſſue of copper coins, the Chineſe *caſh* ſupplied the deficiency. Coins of various dynaſties of China formed the currency of Japan, eſpecially coins of the Northern Sung, and the Ta-tchung, Hung-Wu, and Yung-loh coins of the Ming; theſe were largely imitated. We cannot be aſtoniſhed to ſee them imitated to a ſomewhat large extent. For inſtance, the Chineſe Sung coins of Siang-fu (1008 A.D.), Tien-Sheng (1023), Kia-yu (1056),

[1] W. Bramſen, *The Coins of Japan*, p. 7.

Ming-yuen (1032), Tcheping (1064), Hi-ming (1068), Yuen-fung (1078), Yüen-yu (1086), Shaosheng (1094), Yuen-fu (1098), were moulded, and specimens cast and issued in quantities at Mito in the province of Fitatsu. In some cases new patterns were made, such as for the *Yuen-fung* coin with five varieties, two being moulded from the Chinese, and three made anew, which exhibits a finish and excellence of workmanship and bronze casting far superior to its Chinese original. All these issues were made by the private Daïmios in their own estates, and not by the Central Government; the metal was bronze, from the finest quality downwards, and sometimes a very poor alloy, and indeed lead. The *Yung-loh* (A.D. 1403) coin of the Ming was imported in not inconsiderable quantities, and largely imitated, not only from moulds of the coin itself, but also with new patterns. The device was used for gold, silver, white alloy, lead as well as for bronze, of which metal a larger coin was also issued.

With the period *Ten-sho* (1573-1591) commences a new era for Japan generally, as well as for its coins. Gold, silver, and copper coins began from thence to be regularly issued. In 1587 the "Current money of Ten-sho," *i.e.* the coin inscribed with the legend *Ten-sho-tsu-ho*, was first issued. As might be expected after the art of coining had been so neglected for centuries at the capital, this coin is not well made; there seems to have been a very limited number of copper coins cast, while silver coins of the same Ten-sho Coinage.

deſign were iſſued in larger quantity, the conſequence being that the former are at preſent much rarer than the latter. While in the twelve antique coins the characters of the legends were read $\begin{smallmatrix} & 1 & \\ 4 & & 2 \\ & 3 & \end{smallmatrix}$, the order was changed into $\begin{smallmatrix} & 1 & \\ 4 & & 3 \\ & 2 & \end{smallmatrix}$ in this new iſſue and the after ones.

The *Bun-roku-tſu-ho*, in copper and in ſilver, were iſſued in 1592, and followed in 1606 by the *Kei-tcho-tſu-ho* (four varieties and two ſizes), in 1615 by the *Gen-na-tſu-ho*, with a ſerial of 1 to 30 on the reverſe. The *Kwan-ei-tſu-ho*, firſt iſſued in 1636, preſents an almoſt endleſs variety of iſſues, due to the fact that the coinage was continued for over 225 years, during which the device of the copper and iron coins of the Government remained unchanged, with the exception of a few coins of a higher denomination. All the copper coins iſſued from *Wa-do* up to the period of *Kwan-ei*, and all the copper and iron coins *Kwan-ei-tſu-ho*, excepting the large-ſized iſſue with wave-like lines on the reverſe, are of the value of 1 *mon*. The various iſſues of different ſizes, caſt of copper or iron, with or without inſcription on the reverſe, are claſſified to the extent of more than 1,000 by the native numiſmatiſts.

In 1768 coins of the *Kwan-ei-tſu-ho* pattern were iſſued in braſs and afterwards iron, the reverſe being covered with twenty-one wave-like lines; they were to be worth 4 of the ordinary *mon*. The number of the wave-like lines was afterwards reduced to eleven. The laſt coins of this pattern were caſt ſo late as 1860, in iron, of two ſizes, a larger and a ſmaller one. In 1835 a large, oval, bronze coin, having on the obverſe *Tem-po* above and *tſu-ho* below the ſquare hole, was put in circulation; on the reverſe, above the hole, are the two characters *To-hiaku*, "worth 100," indicating that the value of the coin was 100 *mon*, and under the hole the mark of the mint. There are two varieties, diverſified by the reſpective ſizes of the rim and of the ſquare hole.

Finally, in 1863, was iſſued the laſt regular copper coin, with the legend *Bun-Kiu-ei-ho*, "Everlaſting money of Bun-Kiu (period)," with eleven wave-like lines on the reverſe; worth 4 *mon*, three varieties; alſo caſt in iron. Beſides the iron coins caſt by the central Government and current throughout the country, others were at various times iſſued by the feudal lords (Daïmios) for the excluſive uſe of their own dominions, or by certain chief towns. The moſt peculiar of this claſs, frequently met with in the collections, is ſquare, with rounded corners, inſcribed *Sen-dai tſu-ho*, *Sen-dai* being the name of the dominion where this pattern was caſt in ſeveral iſſues, of which the firſt took place about 1782. Space, however, fails us to ſpeak of the various peculiarities of theſe feudal iſſues; or the iron coins caſt in moulds of Chineſe caſt of a thouſand years earlier; or the token-like pieces iſſued at Mito in 1866-68, with the couplet:

Iron Coinage.

> May your wealth be as vaſt as the Eaſtern Ocean,
> And your age as great as the Southern Mountains.

Bean Coinage.

We can only refer to the ſilver-copper, or billon coinage, of which the moſt curious examples are the ſilver-bean coins, ſhaped, as their name ſuggeſts, in various ſizes, from a ſmall pea to a large bean. Beginning in 1601 down to 1859, they are variouſly ſtamped; but the marks, which are made rather at random, are generally undecipherable. In 1711, etc., they were marked with the figure of Dai-Koku, the god of wealth, ſitting on two rice bales, and holding his lucky hammer in the right hand, while the left graſps a ſack of money flung over one ſhoulder. Each time Dai-Koku gives a blow with his hammer, the wallet he has by him becomes filled with money, rice, and other things, according to what may be deſired.

Silver Coinage.

In our rapid ſurvey of the minor currency we have mentioned ſeveral of the regular iſſues of ſilver coins, caſt on the ſame patterns as thoſe in lower metals. By far the largeſt quantity of ſilver-money circulated under other ſhapes, viz., flat, ſquare, oblong, plates, and lumps. Thoſe of the firſt model were iſſued only during the laſt and the preſent centuries. The well-known ſmall oblong coins in ſilver are quite modern, except the *T-ſhu* and *Ni-ſhu* pieces, iſſued ſince 1772. The *Itſi-bu* and *Ni-bu* pieces were iſſued till 1868; the former ſince 1846, and the latter ſince 1818. The *Ni-bu*, of golden appearance, preſents an intereſting peculiarity, while the other named coins were of ſilver of the uſual fineneſs; the *Ni-bus* were of ſilver, with a percentage of gold added, which was brought out on the ſurface of the piece after the coin was made, by treatment with acids.

Silver in lumps by weight was moſt likely in uſe a long while before the evidence of the native collections and numiſmatic records begin. The oldeſt, four inches in length, ſtamped with creſts, ſtars, etc., is aſcribed to the period 1570-80. In the official records we hear of an iſſue of the ſame kind in 1601. Thoſe of 1695 bear all around fragmentary ſtamps of Dai-Koku, the god of wealth. In 1706, 1710, 1711, 1714, 1736, 1820, 1859, large ſilver lumps of various ſizes were in circulation, and bear marks which traditions underſtand to have been ſtamped at thoſe dates; the evidence is of a moſt ſhadowy character, and reſts on the mere aſſertion of the native writers.

Large plates of ſilver of various ſizes, and ſmaller ones like the gold *Obo-bang* and *Ko-bang*, were alſo iſſued between 1570 and 1580, but the practice ſeems to have been discontinued. In ſome provinces ſilver was alſo uſed in lumps, from which bits of the required value were cut and weighed.

Previous to the adoption of the European ſyſtem in 1870, round gold coins had been very rare indeed. A gold coin of the ordinary ſhape, pattern, and ſquare hole in the centre, was iſſued in 760, with the four Chineſe characters *Rai-ſhing-ki-pao* as legend. One of the endleſs ſeries of the *Kwan-ei-tſu-ho* legend, and another in imitation of the Chineſe *yung-loh*, conſtitute the whole ſeries Gold Coinage.

of the inſcribed coins. Another well-known round coin is that iſſued in 1599 by Hide-yoſi, better known under his poſthumous name of Tai-kan-ſama, the powerful general who inſtituted the high poſt of *taikun*. This rather ſmall coin bears on one ſide ſix ſtamps, one central of the *Kiri-mon*, and on the other ſide five ſtamps of the ſame, with the minter mark in the centre. The *Kiri-mon*, or creſt of the Mikado, is compoſed of three leaves pointed down with three flowers (one of ſeven and two of five petals) above, of the *Paulownia Imperialis*; it differs of the *Kiku-mon*, or Imperial badge of Japan, which conſiſts of a conventional pattern of the chryſanthemum with ſixteen petals, and muſt be diſtinguiſhed from the badge of the Takugawa family, to whom belonged the later *Shôguns*, and which conſiſted in three mallow leaves within a circle, their points meeting in the centre. In 1727 diviſionary pieces, or *itſi-bu*, *ni-ſhu*, and *iſ-ſhu* pieces ſo-called, were iſſued round, bearing on the obverſe the *Kiri-mon* on the upper left ſide, with the examiner's ſtamp, and underneath, on the right hand ſide, the mark of the value; on the reverſe are the mint ſtamp and the name of the year. The *ni-ſhu* and *iſ-ſhu* pieces have on the reverſe the name of the particular kind of gold of which it is coined. By far the commoneſt ſhape of the gold coins iſſued ſince the ſixteenth century to twenty years ago was that of oblong boards, with rounded angles, excepting for the ſmall pieces. Their denominations were the following: *Oho-ban*, "large plate," of

10 ryo; *Goryo-ban*, "5 ryo board;" *Ko-ban*, "ſmall plate," of 1 ryo; *Ni-bu*, "two parts," of 1/2 ryo; *Itſi-bu*, "one part," of 1/4 ryo; *Ni-ſhu*, "two ſhu," of 1/8 ryo; *Iſ-ſhu*, "one ſhu," of 1/16 ryo. The largeſt were more than 6 1/2 inches in length, and the ſmalleſt 3/8 of an inch. They were ſtamped with the *Kiri-mon* in round, fan-ſhaped, or pentagon compartments, ſeverally repeated, the value, the ſtamp of the mint; and on the ſmall ones is ſometimes the date of iſſue. Beſides theſe ſtamps, the large coins often bear ſeveral punches of the mint-examiner, teſtifying to their genuineneſs. Fees uſed to be charged by the duly appointed officers of the Imperial mint or treaſury for certifying the value of the large ones, or *Oho-ban;* and, in order to have theſe fees paid often, they had recourſe to the ingenious device of marking them ſo that the marks could eaſily be obliterated, and the plan of writing the requiſite ſigns in Indian ink was adopted; in conſequence, the pieces were always wrapped up ſingly in ſilk wadding and paper, and the greateſt care taken in handling them to prevent the writing being defaced.

CHAPTER X.

MEDALS.

THE science of Numismatics has to deal not only with those metallic objects which have actually passed current as money, but also with the numerous specimens in the precious or other metals which are designated medals—specimens, that is to say, issued to commemorate some personage or event, but not employed as media of exchange. The application of the word "medal" to this class, in contradistinction to coins, is a recent one: Italian and French writers of the fifteenth and sixteenth centuries use *medaglie* and *médailles* to signify coins which, being no longer in circulation, are preserved in the cabinets of collectors as curiosities. Even in the last century our own word medal was so employed. The "medals" of the Roman Emperors, to which Gibbon often alludes in his notes to the *Decline and Fall*, are, of course, what we now know as coins; and Addison's *Dialogue upon the Usefulness of Medals* is, for the most part,

The word "Medal."

a treatiſe on Roman Imperial coins. The Shilling of Elizabeth, which is made to relate its adventures in the *Spectator*, obſerves that at the Reſtoration it came to be "rather looked upon as a medal than an ordinary coin." In the preſent chapter we ſhall of courſe employ the word "medal" in the ſenſe which it has now generally acquired.

An inquiry into the hiſtory of the medal need not lead us far back into antiquity. The Greeks had abſolutely no diſtinct claſs of objects correſponding to our medals, while even their coin-types were only in rare cases of a commemorative character. The coin-types of the Romans, indeed, are often directly alluſive to hiſtorical events, and the Romans iſſued a ſpecial ſeries of metallic objects not intended for circulation as currency; but even theſe latter pieces (known to modern numiſmatiſts as the "Roman medallions") can hardly be conſidered as the actual prototypes of the modern medal. Between the lateſt Roman medallions, which are of the time of Honorius, and the firſt productions of the famous Italian medalliſts of the fifteenth century, there is a great chaſm, and the medals of the new Italy are in no ſenſe the deſcendants of the old. The firſt Italian medals muſt, indeed, be reckoned as a new artiſtic product of their time: the proceſſes by which they are made are not thoſe of the older coin or medallion engravers, and they are, at firſt, entirely unofficial in character. It is only by degrees that the medal becomes more or leſs official, and is employed to comme-

Italian Medals.

morate important public events. The earlier ſpecimens of Italian workmanſhip were not intended to commemorate events or even to do honour to illuſtrious men after their deceaſe; they were deſtined rather to ſerve the purpoſe of the painted portrait or of the modern photograph. The noble families of the time welcomed with a natural eagerneſs this new art, which not only portrayed their features with all the power of painting, but which rendered them in a material which itſelf was *aes perenne*, and which was readily available for tranſmiſſion from friend to friend.

Firſt of theſe great creators of the medal, in time no leſs than in merit, ſtands Vittore Piſano of Verona, whoſe artiſtic activity in this direction Pisano. belongs to the ten years 1439-1449. Piſano is known alſo as a painter (his medals often bear the ſignature "Opus Piſani pictoris"), and it is, no doubt, a circumſtance having an important influence upon the beginnings of modern medallic art that he and moſt of his fellow-workers were not by profeſſion engravers of coin-dies, but followers of the arts of painting and ſculpture. The art of coin-engraving, which had attained to ſuch perfection in the hands of Greek and even of Roman artiſts, had during the Middle Ages ſuffered a terrible eclipſe. Artiſtic portraiture was dead, and even the taſk of producing mere likeneſs was eſſayed no longer: the bold relief of Greek coin and Roman medallion was emulated no more, and although in the fourteenth century an ornate and not unpleaſing ſtyle had begun to manifest itself on coin-reverses, it never passed the limits of decorative skill.

It was open, of course, to Pisano and his followers to take the processes of die-engraving as they found them—to accomplish what they could within such limitations—to give likeness and life to the conventional heads of the obverse, and employ their taste and invention in improving the designs of the reverse. Trained, however, in the liberal school of painting and sculpture, they hesitated to pour their new wine into the old bottles. These medallists of the fifteenth century are distinguished above all other medallists by the largeness and freedom of their style; they required a yielding substance to work upon, and a broad space wherein to carry out their conceptions. For producing medals of great size and in high relief, the mechanical processes of die-engraving were at that time quite inadequate; and hence it is that all the early medals, and many of those produced in the sixteenth century, are not struck from dies, but cast from moulds. The first Italian medallists made their models from the life in wax—working, in fact, as did the sculptor of bronze who modelled in clay—and from these wax-models they prepared, by a careful and elaborate process, a mould into which the metal was finally poured. To Pisano himself about thirty extant medals have been attributed. They are distinguished (as indeed are all the works of the great medallists of Italy) by their splendid portraiture—portraiture of the highest kind, which

New Process of Casting Medals.

not only reproduces faithfully the features of man or woman, but which also reveals character, and which delights especially to show character only in its nobler traits.

The medallic art of Pisano (and in an equal or less degree that of his contemporaries) is further distinguished by the excellence of its reverse designs—designs remarkable for originality, and for strength combined with grace, and which are never chosen at hazard, but selected for their peculiar fitness to adorn the circular field of a medal. As characteristic specimens of Pisano's work, let us mention the two famous medals, "Venator intrepidus" and "Liberalitas augusta," each bearing the head of Alfonso the Magnanimous—"Divus Alphonsus rex triumphator et pacificus"—and having as their reverse types admirable representations of animals: the one a boar-hunt, the other an eagle surrounded by a vulture and other inferior birds of prey. In the representation of animals Pisano took especial delight, and we often find them introduced in the reverses of his medals. As a rule, he does not attempt elaborate allegorical subjects; but his reverses often show some comparatively simple design, taken from ordinary life: thus a medal of his of Sigismondo Pandolfo di Malatesta, which has, as usual, a portrait of the prince for the obverse, shows Malatesta also on its reverse, this time as a full-length figure in armour.

This artist's turn for realism does not, however, preclude the production of several works inspired by pure poetic fancy. A conspicuous instance of this may be found in the medal which he made for Leonello, Marquess of Este, on the occasion of his marriage in 1444. Just as the poet Spenser, when he wrote the *Prothalamion* of the noble Ladies Somerset—"against their bridal day which

ITALIAN. PORTRAIT OF MALATESTA NOVELLO, BY PISANO.

was not long"—imaged, by a charming yet stately fancy, the subjects of his verse as swans, so the artist Pisano, playing on the name Leonello, portrayed his bridegroom as a lion. A little Cupid or winged genius of marriage stands holding out to the lion an unrolled scroll, whereon in musical characters is displayed the lion's marriage-song.

This design, which to a reader unacquainted with the original might seem too fanciful, is redeemed from being a mere *concetto* by the noble figure of the lion and the graceful grouping. Another of Pisano's reverse designs, which shows the same qualities of stately grace and fancy, is that on the medal of Cecilia Gonzaga—"Cicilia virgo filia Johannis Francisci primi marchionis Mantue"—a lady who afterwards became a nun. Cecilia is represented sitting amidst a rocky landscape, with her hand resting on the head of the unicorn who reclines beside her, while above them hangs the crescent moon. But to dwell at length upon the reverses of Pisano's medals, or upon his medallic portraits of "many nobles and personages renowned in arms or distinguished for learning," we should need an entire chapter.

Followers of Pisano.

Matteo Pasti, who worked from 1446, was the first distinguished medallist who followed in the train of Pisano. He, too, was a native of Verona, and probably a pupil of his great fellow-citizen, whose influence on his style is traceable. Sperandio, who worked at the end of the fifteenth century, is also of the school of Vittore. He made numerous medals of the Estes, and of members of the Bentivoglio family, of Pope Julius II., and others. To the same century belong Giovanni Boldu, Guacciolotti, Enzola, and Melioli, as well as Lixignolo, Pollajuolo, and others, who have left behind them productions of great merit. After the first impulse had been given, the art had, indeed, soon spread to the northern cities of Italy

—to Mantua, Padua, Milan, Brefcia, etc.—and, fomewhat later, to the cities fouth of the Apennines.

The Italian medallifts of the fixteenth century worthily carry on the work begun by their forerunners of the fifteenth. Though with them fomething of the large treatment of the earlier mafters is loft, we find, on the other hand, the greateft variety in the defigning of reverfes, remarkable fkill and delicacy in the execution of details, as well as abundant examples of excellent portraiture. A difference of a technical kind diftinguifhes the new medallifts from the old; for with the beginning of the fixteenth century there came in the art of ftriking medals from engraved dies, and though all the medals of larger module continued to be caft till the end of the century, the fmaller fpecimens, which then began to multiply, were ftruck by the new procefs. We obferve, indeed, that moft of the medallifts of the fixteenth century were alfo goldfmiths or gem-engravers, and were thus led naturally to the engraving of dies. To fay even a few words of each of the many remarkable medallifts of this century would be impoffible here, but the very names of Pomedello and Spinelli, Cellini and Francia, Romano and Caradoffo, Valerio Belli, Lione Lioni, Paftorino of Siena, and the reft, are full of charm to every lover of Italian medals. Of thefe names, we can only felect but one or two, referring the reader for more detailed notices to the works of Friedlaender, Armand, Heifs

Sixteenth Century Medallists

and others, and to the Britiſh Muſeum *Guide to the Italian Medals*, by Mr. C. F. Keary.

Francia. Francia, who is conſpicuous as one of the earlieſt of this band of medalliſts, began life, as is well known, as a goldſmith, and acted for ſome time as director of the mint of Bologna. Vaſari has a very intereſting paſſage on his work as a medalliſt:—“ That in which Francia delighted above all elſe, and in which he was indeed excellent, was in cutting dies for medals; in this he was highly diſtinguiſhed, and his works are moſt admirable, as may be judged from ſome on which is the head of Pope Julius II.—ſo lifelike that theſe medals will bear compariſon with thoſe of Caradoſso. He alſo ſtruck medals of Signor Giovanni Bentivoglio, which ſeem to be alive, and of a vaſt number of princes who, paſſing through Bologna, made a certain delay when he took their portraits in wax: afterwards, having finiſhed the matrices of the dies, he deſpatched them to their deſtination, whereby he obtained not only the immortality of fame, but likewiſe very handſome preſents.” Medals by Francia of Julius and Bentivoglio may ſtill be ſeen in the Britiſh Muſeum. The medals of another renowned goldſmith, Benvenuto Cellini, are not very numerous. He was Maſter of the Mint to Pope Clement VII., for whom he made two portrait-medals.

Benvenuto Cellini.

In connection with portraiture, the name of Paſtorino, who died about 1591, is of eſpecial intereſt, as he devoted himſelf with ardour almoſt entirely to this branch of art, and attained in it

Pastorino.

wonderful ſucceſs. The number of his medals is conſiderable, for (as Vaſari ſays of him) "he has copied all the world, and perſons of all kinds, great nobles, diſtinguiſhed artiſts, and perſons of unknown or of low degree." His delicate and beautiful ſtyle makes him eſpecially happy in his portraits of women and children. To the reverſe-deſigns of the medals of this century we cannot refer in detail; but we muſt dwell for a moment upon the reverſe of a medal in the Britiſh Muſeum by Annibale Fontana (1540-1587)—a work of **Fontana.** ſingular charm and beauty, though contraſting ſtrongly in its picture-like character with the reverſes of the early medalliſts. It repreſents Hercules in the Garden of the Heſperides. The hero is ſtanding in calm dignity beſide the Tree, his right hand outſtretched to pluck its golden apples: its dragon guard he has already ſlain, and is trampling the carcaſe beneath his feet. In the diſtance are ſeen the towers and cities of men in the light of the ſetting ſun.

It muſt be added that very few medals in the Italian ſeries commemorate *events:* their chief ſtrength lies in portraiture, and their intereſt may **Portraits.** be reckoned rather artiſtic than hiſtorical, although, as has been truly ſaid, "in this aſtoniſhing ſeries of portraits the chief actors in the tragedies and comedies of thoſe times paſs before us, their characters written in their faces." After the cloſe of the ſixteenth century the medals of Italy ceaſe to be of high artiſtic merit. But we ought not to forget to mention that a continuous ſeries of contemporary Papal portraits, from Nicolas V. onwards, is to be found on the medals. Probably the moſt intereſting piece in this claſs, from an hiſtorical point of view, is the famous medal ſtruck by Gregory XIII. to commemorate the Maſſacre of St. Bartholomew in 1572. Three ſpecimens of this medal are exhibited in the Britiſh Muſeum; the firſt in ſilver, by Federigo Bonzagna, ſhows as its obverſe type the buſt of the Pope himſelf, and on the reverſe—*tantum religio potuit*—is repreſented the Deſtroying Angel holding ſword and croſs, while around are men and women wounded, or dead, or flying before her. The legend is "Ugonottorum Strages," and the date 1572. A ſecond example is in bronze, gilt; a third, in bronze and ſlightly varied, is thought to be of more recent date.

Massacre of St. Bartholomew.

German Medals.

The Italian Renaiſſance did not fail to make its influence felt in the medallic art of other European countries, and it was from Italy that Germany derived the practice of caſting medals, through Peter Fiſcher, who had ſtudied art beyond the Alps. But although a foreign importation, the German medal ſoon acquired a diſtinct and national character. The minute and patient induſtry which diſtinguiſhed German workers in other branches of art diſplayed itſelf likewiſe in their medal-work. Their productions are alſo thoroughly German in their tendency to avoid idealizing any repreſentation; but if they lack the nobility of the Italian maſters, they derive true force and artiſtic value from their naïve and vigorous realiſm. Among German medalliſts two names are eſpecially conſpicuous—one, Heinrich Reitz, the goldſmith of Leipzig, who worked for the Electors of Saxony, and in whoſe productions has been traced the influence of Lucas Cranach—the other, Friedrich Hagenauer of Augſburg, whoſe ſtyle is of greater ſimplicity than that of Reitz. The medals executed by the goldſmiths of Nuremburg and Augſburg

GERMAN. PORTRAIT OF J. RINGELBERG.

are extremely numerous; moſt of them are unſigned, and it is even difficult to ſeparate the productions of the two great centres, though Nuremburg has a diſtinct ſuperiority, due to the influence of Albert Dürer Many of the earlier German medals are ſtruck, for the Germans had made conſiderable improvements in the appliances for ſtriking money: thoſe ſpecimens which are caſt have been delicately chaſed after the caſting.

The ſixteenth century is the period during which the production of German medals attained its higheſt degree of excellence. As an original art, it may be ſaid to have periſhed in the commotions of the Thirty Years' War. Comparatively little attention has been paid to the German ſeries by numiſmatiſts and collectors, but it deſerves much more than it has yet received.

French Medals.

The medallic art in France had a longer leaſe of life than in Germany, and its hiſtory is of conſiderable intereſt. In ſpite of a few early native efforts, this art may be ſaid to have come into exiſtence under the auſpices of Italy. Thus we find that the firſt medal with a French effigy, that of Louis XI., was executed at Aix by an Italian, Franceſco Laurana. Another early medal, repreſenting Charles VIII. and Anne of Brittany, caſt at Lyons in 1494, was the work of a French goldſmith, Louis le Père, who had been inſtructed in the medalliſt's art by Nicolo Spinelli, of Florence. Yet it muſt be obſerved that this medal is French rather than Italian in character, and the medals made by native artiſts under Louis XII., for inſtance thoſe of Louis and Anne of Brittany (1500), and of Philibert le Beau and Margaret of Auſtria (1502), are evidence to prove that a purely French ſchool might have maintained itſelf with very little Italian aſſiſtance. Under François I., however, very diſtinct encouragement is given to Italian artiſts; and Benvenuto Cellini made for this ſovereign a medal with the regal effigy. Another Italian artiſt of merit,

Giacomo Primavera, alſo worked for France, and has left medals of Catherine de Medicis, the Duke of Alençon, the poet Ronſard, and others.

The medals of the latter half of the ſixteenth century, partly ſtruck and partly caſt, are generally unſigned: the ſeries of large medallions repreſenting Henry II., Catherine de Medicis, Charles IX., and Henry III., has been attributed to Germain Pilon, a medalliſt who worked for Charles IX. With the acceſſion of Henry IV. begins the fine ſuite of medals by Guillaume Dupré, an artiſt whoſe productions well continued the traditions of the large caſt medals of Italy. He worked both under Henry IV. and Louis XIII., and, like the Italian maſters of the fifteenth century, undertook, and accompliſhed with great ſucceſs, the caſting of his own medals. All the more important perſonages among his contemporaries were eager for the privilege of being portrayed by Dupré; and in his medallions, as a French writer has remarked, though with a *ſoupçon* of exaggeration, he has left poſterity "une galerie iconographique de ſon temps, dont la beauté et l'interêt égalent ceux des oeuvres analogues de la Renaiſſance italienne. Perſonne n'a donné au portrait numiſmatique un accent plus vivant et plus vrai; perſonne n'y a mieux rendu la phyſionomie d'une époque." After Dupré, fine medals ſtill continued to be produced by the two chief French medalliſts of the ſeventeenth century—Claude Warin, engraver to the mint at Lyons, who died in 1654, and Jean Warin, the Engraver-General of Coins, whoſe death

Dupré.

The Warins.

took place in 1672. The long ſeries of medals of Louis XIV. is hiſtorically intereſting, though it too faithfully reflects the pompous and conventional art of his time.

The firſt medals of Napoleon, ſtruck between 1796 and 1802, are of indifferent execution and Napoleonic Medals. deſign. Under the direction of Denon they gradually improved, and at length attained to ſome degree of artiſtic merit; the heads of Napoleon by Andrieu and Droz, from the buſt by Chaudet, are intereſting portraits touched with ideal beauty, and ſome of the reverſes of the Paris mint medals are not inelegant compoſitions. Perhaps the moſt hiſtorically important medals of the Napoleon ſeries are thoſe connected with the propoſed invaſion of England. In May, 1804, Napoleon took the title of Emperor, and in July of the ſame year he left Paris to viſit the camp of Boulogne and the "Army of England." About this time there was ſtruck a medal which is ſtill extant and not uncommon. Its obverſe ſhows the head of Napoleon, and the reverſe a male figure ſqueezing a leopard between his legs while he throttles it with a cord. The legend relates to the flotilla of *prames*, or flat-bottomed boats and gunboats, which was to tranſport the invading army acroſs the Channel:—"En l'an XII. 2,000 Barques ſont conſtruites." The invaſion being certain to ſucceed, nothing ſurther was needed but a commemorative medal. There is reaſon for believing that in this year a die was actually prepared for a medal recording the ſucceſs of the invaſion to be ſtruck in London when the army arrived there. No ſpecimens ſtruck from this die are now known to be extant, but the Britiſh Muſeum poſſeſſes an electrotype which is believed to reproduce the reverſe of the original die. Its type and inſcriptions have reference to the victorious "Deſcente en Angleterre." A powerful naked figure has in his graſp a human being whoſe body ends in a fiſh's tail. It is the Hercules Napoleon deſtroying the ſea-monſter England. In the exergue may be read the modeſt legend, "Frappée à Londres en 1804." A French medal with a ſimilar type was really iſſued two years later, but the "Deſcente" and "Frappée" legends have diſappeared thereon in favour of the conſolatory Virgilian quotation: "Toto diviſos orbe Britannos." **Frappée à Londres.**

We have yet to ſpeak of the medals of Holland and of thoſe of our own country. Both the Dutch and Engliſh ſeries, which in the ſeventeenth century run much into one another, are attractive rather because of their hiſtorical intereſt than by reaſon of their artiſtic merit. By hiſtorical intereſt we do not, however, mean to imply that the medals furniſh us with any very large amount of information not derivable from the documentary ſources, but that they have the property of making hiſtorical events more vivid and more eaſily realized. Though medals can be regarded only as a ſlight and imperfect index to the hiſtory of any notable epoch, yet ſomething, at any rate, they do ſhow of its very form and preſſure. They are the mirrors which the men of the paſt delighted to hold up to **Dutch Medals.**

every momentous event—or to every event which ſeemed to them momentous; and they are mirrors, moreover, which have the magic power of ſtill retaining the images which they originally reflected.

The Dutch medals of the ſixteenth century, though not without occaſional picturesqueneſs, are certainly not the fineſt of their time; they have, however, much hiſtorical intereſt—a feature which they ſhare with thoſe of the ſucceeding

DUTCH PORTRAITS OF C. AND J. DE WITT.

century. In point of art the ſeventeenth-century pieces are poor, and they convey their political alluſions by means of elaborate allegory Many of the portraits on Dutch medals are noteworthy, eſpecially thoſe of William the Silent, Prince Maurice, the De Witts, Van Tromp, and De Ruyter. In the reign of our William the Third, the Dutch ſeries fills up gaps in the Engliſh; indeed, ſeveral Dutch medalliſts worked at different periods for Engliſh monarchs.

The medallic ſeries of England opens in the reign of Henry VIII., and the pieces at firſt are commemorative chiefly of perſons, and not of events. Of Henry himſelf there exiſts a buſt executed after a portrait of Holbein. Another of Henry's medals proclaims his ſupremacy over the Church:—"Henricus octavus fidei defenſor et in terra Eccleſiae Angliae et Hiberniae ſub Chriſto caput ſupremum." The King's ſupremacy was confirmed by Parliament in 1534, though this English Medals.

ENGLISH. PORTRAITS OF PHILIP AND MARY, BY TREZZO.

medal was not made until 1545. The moſt intereſting portrait medals of this time are thoſe of Anne Boleyn, Thomas Cromwell, and Sir Thomas More. More's medal bears the date 1535—the year of his death—and its reverſe typifies him as a cypreſs-tree which has fallen beneath the ſtroke of an axe, and derives therefrom a more fragrant odour, "Suavius olet." Theſe early ſpecimens, as well as the portrait medals of Edward VI., are caſt and highly chaſed. Of Mary and her huſband we have, beſides other repreſentations, admirable half-length figures on a medal produced at Madrid by the Italian artist Trezzo, while in the service of Philip. This medal is the first signed one in the English series; and the fact that it is executed by a foreign artist is (unfortunately for the artistic credit of England) not to be noted as exceptional, but as the rule; for the history of our English medallists is, as we shall see, to a great extent the history of the medallists of other nations.

Elizabeth. The reign of Elizabeth, especially, has to show some excellent portraits by foreign artists. Chief amongst these in beauty and in interest is the medal of Mary Queen of Scots, made and signed by the Italian Primavera, who worked chiefly in the Netherlands, and, as was noted before, in France. Its date is uncertain, but it was probably produced about the same time as the Morton portrait, which was painted in 1566-67, during Mary's imprisonment in Lochleven Castle. Modern casts of this medal have a reverse added to them, but the original is merely a copper plaque. Stephen of Holland, who lived for a short time in England, executed, chiefly in the year 1562, a number of meritorious portrait-medals (cast and chased), principally, however, of private persons. Personal medals of the more celebrated men of the Elizabethan era are unhappily not very numerous. The less important public medals of this reign may well be passed over in favour of those which commemorate the defeat of the Armada. Several of these pieces, somewhat varied in their details, are still in existence, and as they are of oval form, and

Armada Medals.

furniſhed with ring and chain for ſuſpenſion, it is probable that they were diſtributed at the time as decorations. It is intereſting to note that the moſt important do not bear the ſignature of any foreign medalliſt, but are, as it would ſeem, the work of native artiſts. Foremoſt of all the Armada medals muſt ſtand the large gold piece with the full-face buſt of Elizabeth, encircled by the legend, "Ditior in toto non alter circulus orbe." The obverſe of this extraordinary medal, with its high relief, its brilliant colour, its almoſt barbaric profuſion of dreſs and ornament heaped upon the crowned and ſceptred Queen, ſeems to ſpeak the very euphuiſm of medallic language, and is wonderfully characteriſtic of its age. The reverſe is conceived in a ſoberer manner. It repreſents a bay-tree ſtanding upright and alone upon an iſland; its leaf alſo is not withered, nor has the lightning power to ſcathe it; for, ſays the legend, "Non ipſa pericula tangunt." The alluſion is, perhaps, not merely to the defeat of the Spaniards, but alſo to the calm which had followed the political complications of the time—"the Queen of Scots was dead; James of Scotland had been conciliated; France and the Vatican were baffled." Upon another medal of this period, England is repreſented as an ark floating, "ſaevas tranquilla per undas."

Two other medals of Dutch workmanſhip, but alſo referring to the great victory over Spain, have ſtill to be noticed. One of theſe, which was probably ſtruck by the direction of Prince Maurice, reprefents the Church ftanding firm on a rock amid ftormy waves; the other has a quaintly expreffed allufion to the confederation formed againft Elizabeth by the Pope, the King of Spain, the Emperor, and others. Upon one fide are feen the Kings of the earth and the Rulers taking counfel together, but "Blind"—as the Latin fuperfcription warns them—"Blind are the minds of men, yea, and their hearts are blind;" the floor of their council-chamber is covered with fpikes, for "Durum eft contra ftimulos calcitrare." On the other fide, the Spanifh fleet is driven on the rocks, and around are the words of the Pfalmift, quoted from the Vulgate: "Thou, O Lord, art great, and doeft wondrous things; Thou art God alone!"

James I. The medals of James I. are principally Dutch, and for the moft part commemorative of individuals. It fhould be noticed that feveral of them are ftruck from dies, and not caft, for at this period the invention of the fcrew for ftriking coins and medals was coming into general ufe. Mechanical improvements of this kind, though very important to the mint-mafter, who naturally wifhes to turn out his coinage with all poffible rapidity and neatnefs, will be found both in England and other countries to exercife a baneful influence upon the art of medals. The hard and machine-made look of the later ftruck medals too often contrafts unfavourably with the older fpecimens produced by cafting and chafing. To this reign belong the engraved, or, as they fhould rather be called, the ftamped medals of

Simon Paſſe, the clearneſs and neatneſs of whoſe ſtyle is very pleaſing. Simon, who was the ſon of Criſpin Paſſe, the artiſt of Utrecht, reſided for about ten years in England, and executed a large number of prints and portraits. His medals are chiefly of James and the royal family. Amongſt the few public events commemorated in this reign are the peace with Spain, concluded in 1604; and the alliance of England, France, and the United Provinces againſt Spain. Curiouſly enough, the Gunpowder Plot, which made ſo deep an impreſſion on the popular mind, is alluded to only on a ſingle medal, and that a Dutch one. This medal ſhows a ſnake gliding amongſt lilies and roſes, and has the legend, "Detectus qui latuit."

Charles I.

The moſt noteworthy medals of the early part of the reign of Charles I. are thoſe by Nicholas Briot, who, after being chief engraver to the Paris mint, came to England and executed a number of dies and moulds for medals as well as dies for the Engliſh coinage. With the outbreak of the Civil Wars there begins in England a period of exceptional medallic intereſt. During the lifetime of the King, and under the Protector and Commonwealth, medals continued to be made in extraordinary numbers. Some of theſe record the ſucceſſes of the contending parties, but moſt of them are what are called "badges"—medals, that is to ſay, of oval form, furniſhed with a ring for ſuſpenſion, ſo that they could be worn by partiſans of either ſide. When we reflect that theſe pieces were once worn by the actors in that memorable drama, they can hardly fail to awaken a peculiarly pathetic intereſt; and this intereſt is much enhanced by their frequently preſenting the portraits of the remarkable men of the time. Among the portraits appearing on badges, or on other medals, are thoſe of Eſſex, Fairfax, Waller, Laud, Strafford, and many others. A portrait of Hampden exiſts on a ſmall engraved plate, but it is probably of eighteenth-century

Common-wealth.

work. Of Cromwell and his family there are a conſiderable number of medals, as well as of men conſpicuous among the opponents of the King, ſuch as Ireton, Lilburne, Lambert, and Thurloe. The battle of Dunbar is commemorated by a medal ſhowing on its obverſe a buſt of Cromwell in armour, and, in the diſtance, the battle itſelf, with the inſcription, "*The Lord of Hoſts*—[watch-]word at Dunbar, Septem. y. 3, 1650." The reverſe diſplays the Parliament aſſembled in one Houſe with the Speaker. To the time of the Commonwealth alſo belong ſeveral "Naval Rewards" (1650-1653), eſpecially the fine medals ſtruck by

Blake Medals.

the Parliament in commemoration of Blake's victories over the Dutch, and diſtributed to various officers. A ſpecial medal records the ſaving of the *Triumph*, Blake's flag-ſhip: "For eminent ſervice in ſaving y. Triumph, fiered in fight wh. y. Duch in July, 1658." Another medal of this time has engraved upon it an Engliſh legend which has a quaint Latin ring about it: "Robt. Blake. *Born* 1598. *Died* 1657. *He fought at once with Ships and Caſtles. He dared the Fury of all the Elements, and left an Example to Poſterity which is incredible; to be imitated.*"

The continuous and eager demand for medallic badges and memorials at the epoch of the Civil Wars was fortunately well reſponded to by three artiſts of merit. Two of theſe, the brothers Thomas and Abraham Simon, who employed their talents on the Parliamentary ſide, have produced ſome of the moſt praiſeworthy works in the Engliſh ſeries: their place of birth is uncertain, but they may, perhaps, be claimed as Engliſhmen. Thomas is eſpecially well known, from his connection with the Engliſh mint. He it was who made the ſplendid coins with the effigy of the Protector, and the famous "Petition Crown" for Charles II. The two brothers produced medals ſingly or together: in the caſe of a joint work, it ſeems that Abraham Simon made the model, while Thomas, a more ſkilful engraver, did the after-chaſing. The Simons appear to have firſt made their models in wax, and then to have caſt the medals from moulds in ſand. Moſt of the medals of Charles I. and the Commonwealth are caſt and chaſed. Thomas Rawlins, the medalliſt who worked for the King, and who, after the death of Charles, prepared ſeveral commemorative medals for the adherents to the royal cauſe, cannot be ſpoken of ſo favourably as the Simons. "His work was above the average, but it failed to attain the ſharpneſs and high finiſh which characterize that of his two rivals." Theſe three artiſts continued to work after the Reſtoration; but the chief medalliſt under Charles II. was John Roettier, the ſon of a native of Antwerp. His medals,

The Simons.

Rawlins.

which are always ſtruck, are ſharply cut, and ſhow good portraits as well as ſome picturesque reverſe deſigns. Another medalliſt who worked in Roettier's ſtyle, though with inferior ſkill, was George Bower, or Bowers. Both Roettier and Bower continued to produce medals under James II. and, for a time, under William III.

An abundance of loyal medals heralds and inaugurates the Reſtoration. Charles is the ſun juſt riſing from the ſea—the leafleſs branch ſoon to recover greenneſs—the Jupiter deſtroying the proſtrate giants. Many royaliſt badges, with the effigies of the King and his father, probably belong to this time: one intereſting medal was doubtleſs beſtowed upon ſome faithful follower of Charles, for it bears the royal head, and is inſcribed with the words, "Propter ſtrenuitatem et fidelitatem rebus in adverſis." The important engagements between the naval powers of England and Holland receive due illuſtration from medals —Engliſh, Dutch, and French. The Popiſh Plot, and eſpecially one incident—the murder of Sir Edmund Berry Godfrey—have left curious medallic evidences of themſelves. The medals relating to Godfrey all contain ſome ſatire upon the Jeſuits. On one remarkable ſpecimen in pewter, two monks, ſtyled "Juſtice-killers to his Holineſs," may be ſeen ſtrangling Godfrey, overlooked by the Pope, who is himſelf prompted by the devil. This is "Rome's revenge, or S^r. Edmvndberry Godfrey mvrthered in the pope's ſlaughter-hovs." One other medal of this reign—that ſtruck by Bower

Charles II.

Popish Plot.

to celebrate the acquittal of Shaftesbury on the charge of high treason—ought not to be here omitted. Its obverse has a portrait of the Earl, and the reverse is a view of London, with the sun appearing from behind a cloud; the legend being "Laetamur: 24 Nov., 1681." This is the piece alluded to with so much bitterness in Dryden's satire called *The Medal:*

> "Five days he sate for every cast and look,
> Four more than God to finish Adam took;
> But who can tell what essence angels are,
> Or how long Heaven was making Lucifer."

The reign of James II., though brief, has left its traces on a considerable number of medals. Many of these are Dutch, but they are perhaps more full of interest than the official English medals. The Rebellion of Monmouth is recorded on several specimens. One, by the Dutch artist Jan Smeltzing, bearing on the obverse the head of the Duke ("Jacobus infelix Dux Monumethensis"), has a reverse of unusual power—the ghastly decapitated head of the ill-fated leader lying upon the ground, and spouting blood—"Hunc sanguinem libo Deo Liberatori." The attempt of James to restore Catholicism by the repeal of the Test Act, and the Trial of the Seven Bishops, receive full illustration, especially the latter event. One well-known medal gives portraits of Archbishop Sancroft and the Bishops; another, showing seven stars in the midst of the starry heavens, likens the seven prelates to the "sweet influences" of the Pleiades—"Quis restringet Pleiadum

James II.

delicias." On yet another ſpecimen, alſo bearing medallions of the Biſhops, a Jeſuit and monk are ſeen vainly endeavouring to undermine the Church, a viſible edifice built on a rock, and ſupported by a hand from Heaven—"The Gates of Hell ſhall not prevaile!" The other medals of this reign refer chiefly to the flight and abdication of the King, and to the birth of the young prince James. Some of the Dutch medals make very broad hints as to the legitimacy of the youthful heir. On one curious ſpecimen Truth is ſeen throwing open the door of a cabinet, within which ſtands a Jeſuit, thruſting through a trap a child with pyx and crown. The name of this ſuppoſititious child whom Father Petre or ſome other papiſt is thus introducing to the world is inſcribed on the cabinet door—"Jacobus Francis Edwardus."

Pretender Medals.

The Flight of James to France conducts us naturally to the medals of the Stuart family, of whoſe members there are ſeveral memorials of this kind: many of them, no doubt, were ſtruck for preſentation to the faithful adherents who viſited the princes in exile, or were iſſued to awaken intereſt in the Jacobite cauſe. One very pleaſing medal of this ſeries repreſents the youthful Charles Edward and his brother Henry; before Prince Charles is ſeen a ſtar, with the motto "Micat inter omnes." Another medal—clearly, however, not iſſued by the Stuarts—ridicules the two attempts of the Elder Pretender to recover the Engliſh throne in 1708 and 1716; a map of

Great Britain and Ireland, with ſhips at ſea, is diſplayed, with the dates of the expeditions, and the legend "Bis venit, vidit, non vicit, flenſque receſſit." A very intereſting evidence of the ſtill unſurrendered "right divine" is to be found in the *touch-pieces* of the Stuart family. Previous to the reign of Charles II., the Engliſh ſovereigns who touched for the cure of the ſcrofula or "King's evil," diſtributed to their patients the current gold coin, called the *angel*. Under Charles II., who exerted his healing powers for an enormous number of perſons, and under James II., a medalet having types ſomewhat ſimilar to thoſe of the *angel* was ſubſtituted, and hung round the neck of each afflicted perſon by a white ribbon. The Elder Pretender claimed the power as well as his two ſons Charles and Henry, and of all three, touch-pieces are ſtill extant, Henry's bearing the ſtyle of Henry IX. The practice of touching was repudiated by William III., and finally abandoned by George I. Between theſe reigns, however, Anne had been willing to diſpenſe the royal gift of healing, and one child whom ſhe touched (unhappily without reſult) was Samuel Johnſon, whoſe golden touch-piece, pierced with a hole for ſuſpenſion, may ſtill be ſeen in the Britiſh Muſeum. Boſwell records that when, on one occaſion, Dr. Johnſon was aſked if he could remember Queen Anne, he anſwered that he had "a confuſed, but ſomehow a ſolemn, recollection of a lady in diamonds and a long black hood."

Touch-pieces.

The medallic ſeries of William III. and Anne

William and Mary. Anne. is due to the efforts of Dutch artifts, the moft active of whom were the Smeltzings, Luder, Hautfch, Bofkam, and Croker, a German. Their medals are in many refpects fimilar to thofe of John Roettier, but in lower relief; the reverfes are generally pictorial and full of minute detail, which is not always ineffective, though their art on the whole is decidedly poor and conventional. The medals of William and Anne form the completeft fuite in the Englifh feries; any attempt, indeed, to give a detailed reference to the events which they commemorate would amount to a repetition of nearly all the beft-known events in Englifh hiftory, from the Battle of the Boyne to the Peace of Utrecht. This continuous record is far lefs fatisfactorily kept on the acceffion of George I. At that time there were few medallifts in England, and the Dutch no longer worked for us. The medals of his fucceffor are, however, commemorative of feveral important events, efpecially of thofe connected with the War of the Auftrian Succeffion, the Jacobite Rebellion of '45, and the Conqueft George III. of Canada. The long reign of George III. is very fertile in medals, of which a good typical felection, down to the Battle of Waterloo, may be feen in the public exhibition galleries of the Britifh Mufeum. The greater portion of the medals of this period which are there exhibited relate to "the ftruggles of England with her American colonifts, and to the fubfequent wars with France, Spain, and Holland by fea and land. Following thefe are feveral pieces commemorating fome of the battles of the Peninſular War, and bearing portraits of the principal generals, and a few perſonal medals of ſtateſmen and others."

Some remarks muſt be made on the intereſting claſs of Engliſh *Military and Naval* medals. The Armada medals already mentioned may be regarded as the earlieſt of the claſs, though it is not known that they were iſſued by authority. In 1643 Charles I. granted medals to ſoldiers who diſtinguiſhed themſelves in Forlorn Hopes, and many of the Royaliſt and Parliamentary "badges" were doubtleſs intended as military rewards. Under the Commonwealth were diſtributed the Dunbar medal, and thoſe for Blake's victories over the Dutch, to which we have already alluded. After the Reſtoration, military awards were occaſionally iſſued, though the firſt decorative medal, ſubſequent to the Commonwealth, having a ring for ſuſpenſion, ſeems to be that for the battle of Culloden.

Military and Naval Medals.

"Again a long period elapſes during which no decorative medals appear; and the victories of the Nile and Trafalgar would have remained unrewarded, but for the munificence and patriotiſm of two Engliſhmen, Alexander Daviſon and Matthew Boulton. In 1784 the Eaſt India Company acknowledged the ſervices of its troops by awarding a medal for the campaign in the Weſt of India, an example which originated a cuſtom; and from that time, as long as India remained under the control of the Company, medals were awarded for all ſubſequent wars. The firſt medal

Indian Medals.

issued by authority in England in this century, is that given for the Battle of Waterloo. It was conferred, by order of the Prince Regent, upon every officer and private present at that battle; but no acknowledgment was made of all the brilliant engagements in the Peninsular War till 1847, when a medal was issued for military services between the years 1793-1814. At the same time a corresponding medal for naval services was ordered to be struck for all naval engagements during the same period. Since the accession of her Majesty, medals have been awarded for every campaign, as well as others for 'meritorious service,' 'long service,' etc. Besides the medals issued by the authority of the Crown and those of the East India Company, there are a number of Regimental medals. These were struck at the expense of the officers of the regiments, for distribution among those who served under them; but this custom ceased when a public acknowledgment was made of the services of the army."[1]

Waterloo.

Present Condition of Medallic Art.

The unsatisfactory condition of the medallic art in England—and, indeed, in other European countries—during the present century has been justly lamented; and its productions must too often seem to those acquainted with the best efforts of Greek engravers and Italian medallists to be almost beneath contempt, and beyond the power of criticism to amend. To entertain a very sanguine expectation as to the future of this interesting branch of art would, perhaps, be some-

[1] H. A. Grueber, *Brit. Mus. Guide to Eng. Med.*, p. xv.

what rash; but there is certainly no real ground for denying the possibility of reinstating it in something of its pristine glory. If England cannot at once produce a school of medallists worthy to rank with the Italians of the fifteenth and the sixteenth centuries, her artists may at least begin by shaking themselves free from the trammels in which they have moved so long and so painfully. And, first, there is certainly needed a reform in the present rapid but deadly mechanical processes of producing medals: the old Italian casting and modelling in wax—the old Greek method of striking with the hammer on "blanks" not uniformly flat, must reassert their superiority—especially in the case of medallic portraiture. To create original artists—to breathe a new spirit into medal designs—particularly the reverse designs—is, indeed, a far more difficult task; yet at least it is possible to abandon in part, if not entirely, that classicism, or rather pseudo-classicism, which so long has reigned supreme. To press the inhabitants of Olympus into the service of modern art—to employ the symbolism of that Pagan creed outworn to commemorate a Methodist Conference or a Medical Congress, is in itself a confession of weakness; and though a few artists, such as the Wyons, may in a few instances claim to have imparted congruity and gracefulness to their classical designs, yet in the majority of modern medals these two essential qualities are suggested only by their absence. Modern students of art, and even the ordinary English public, have begun to display an

Classical Designs.

The Wyons.

increasing desire to know and enjoy the remains of classic Art, but it is to the fountain-head that they rightly turn—to Hellas, and not to Rome. It is useless, therefore, at this time of day, for a medallist to hope to conjure with mythological puppets of Hercules and Mars, and well-nigh impossible for him to awaken by classic emblem and divinity the sympathies of an audience for whom the wings of Victory have long lost all their swiftness, and the steeds of Neptune all their animation. Yet it must be observed that already there are signs of better things. Among the medals exhibited to the public at the British Museum will be noticed

Legros. a series by Professor Legros of large portrait medallions of several eminent Englishmen—Carlyle, Tennyson, Gladstone, and others—which have been in the first instance modelled in wax, and then transferred to metal by casting. This new departure in medallic portraiture is very interesting, and the boldness of style in the medals in question is worthy of praise; but it must be remarked that the heads are treated sketchily, and seem to have little or no affinity to the material in which they are wrought. The Italian artists, on the contrary, even when working in their boldest and largest style, were never sketchy, but paid attention to finish, especially in the details of the hair and eyes, and even in such a minor matter as the lettering of the legend. Professor Legros has not at present essayed what is, perhaps, the still more arduous task of producing original designs suitable for the *reverses* of medals. In the reverſe of the Aſhantee War medal, deſigned by Mr. Poynter, we muſt admire the originality which makes itſelf independent of the conventional claſſic reverſes—here, at laſt, we have real negroes, and real Engliſh ſoldiers in their helmets, introduced in a ſcene which is in itſelf a genuine artiſtic expreſſion of the event intended to be commemorated by the medal. Yet even here it muſt be objected that the artiſt ſhows the want of a familiar and practical acquaintance with the material in which his ideas are expreſſed; and his deſign, though it would probably expand into an excellent painting, is far too confuſedly picturesque for the limits of a ſmall medal, and as a reverſe-deſign cannot therefore be pronounced ſucceſsful.

Poynter.

INDEX.

Published by

Facsimile Publisher
Ashok Vihar, Delhi-110052 (India)
Website: www.facsimilepublisher.com

Distributed by

Gyan Books Pvt. Ltd.
5, Ansari Road, Daryaganj, New Delhi-110002 (India)
E-mail: books@gyanbooks.com, Website: www.gyanbooks.com